Longman Exam Guides

FRENCH

John Carter

LONGMAN
London and New York

Longman Group UK Limited
Longman House, Burnt Mill, Harlow
Essex CM20 2JE, England
and Associated Companies throughout the world

*Published in the United States of America
by Longman Inc., New York*

First published 1988

British Library Cataloguing in Publication Data

Carter, John
   French.—(Longman exam guides)
   1. French language—Problems, exercises,
etc.
   I. Title
   448   PC2112

ISBN 0-582-29717-6

Library of Congress Cataloging-in-Publication Data

Carter, John, 1938–
   French.
   (Longman exam guides)
   Includes index.
   I. French language—Examinations, questions, etc.
I. Title.   II. Series.
PC2119.C37   1987   448'.007'6   86–21319
ISBN 0-582-29717-6

Set in Linotron Times

Produced by Longman Singapore Publishers (Pte) Ltd.
Printed in Singapore

Contents

Editors' Preface

Much has been said in recent years about declining standards and disappointing examination results. Whilst this may be somewhat exaggerated, examiners are well aware that the performance of many candidates falls well short of their potential. Longman Exam Guides are written by experienced examiners and teachers, and aim to give you the best possible foundation for examination success. There is no attempt to cut corners. The books encourage thorough study and a full understanding of the concepts involved and should be seen as course companions and study guides to be used throughout the year. Examiners are in no doubt that a structured approach in preparing for and taking examinations can, together with hard work and diligent application, substantially improve performance.

The largely self-contained nature of each chapter gives the book a useful degree of flexibility. After starting with Chapters 1 and 2, all other chapters can be read selectively, in any order appropriate to the stage you have reached in your course. We believe that this book, and the series as a whole, will help you establish a solid platform of basic knowledge and examination technique on which to build.

We would like to thank Graham Clarke, Head of Modern Languages, Longsands Community College, St. Neot's, for much helpful advice.

Stuart Wall and David Weigall

Acknowledgements

We are grateful to the following for permission to reproduce copyright material:

Casterman SA Editeurs for an extract from *Le Revers De La Médaille* by Pierrette Sartin © Casterman; the editor for an adapted extract from pp v–ix *Contemporary French Civilization* Vol VIII Nos 1 & 2; Librairie Artheme Fayard for an extract from pp 3–4 *Histoire D'Angleterre* by André Maurois; Editions Fleuve Noir for an extract from pp 66–67 *Coplan Traque Le Renard* by Paul Kenny; Editions Gallimard for an adapted extract from *La Traversée De Paris* by Marcel Ayme © Editions Gallimard; Editions Bernard Grasset for an extract from *La Tête Contre Les Mures* by Hervé Bazin; Editions Julliard for extracts from *La Parade* by Jean-Louis Curtis and *De La Dictature* by Maurice Duverger; the editor for the extracts from two articles entitled 'Nos robots sous les mers' and 'La ruée vers l'or de l'espace' by Martine Castello in *Le Figaro* 24/10/ 85 & 18/8/86 Copyright Le Figaro 1987; the editor for extracts from the articles 'Mille petites republiques paisibles' by M C Betbeder in *Le Monde* 10/8/80, 'Mon village en querre et en paix' by G Pessis Pasternak in *Le Monde* 3/9/84 and 'La coopération industrielle: un impératif pour l'Europe' by J M Quatrepoint in *Le Monde* 2/8/83; Mail Newspapers plc for an extract from an article in the *London Standard* (1981); the author's agents on behalf of The Royal Literary Fund and Doubleday & Co Inc for an extract from a short story by Somerset Maugham in *Somerset Maugham: Collected Short Stories*; Editions Albin Michel for an extract from *Le Chateau Des Brouillards* by Roland Dorgeles; Editions du Seuil for an adapted extract from *Grand-Bretagne* by Jean Bailhache

and the following examination boards for questions from past examination papers:
The Associated Examining Board; Joint Matriculation Board; Oxford and Cambridge Schools Examination Board; Scottish Examination Board; University of Cambridge Local Examinations Syndicate; University of London School Examinations Board; University of Oxford Delegacy of Local Examinations; Welsh Joint Education Committee.

Chapter 1   Examination requirements

The first step which you should take when you begin preparing for an advanced level examination in French is to read the syllabus carefully. You will need the information which it contains in order to plan your study programme. Make sure that the syllabus relates to the examination that you are going to take. Set texts and topics change periodically and recent revisions of A-level syllabuses plus the introduction of the A/S-level (Advanced/Supplementary) syllabus have resulted in a number of changes affecting the format and content of the examinations. Normally, your tutor or teacher will provide you with all the information that you need but it is always helpful to double check. If you do not have access to a syllabus write to the Examination Board concerned. The address of each Board is included in Table 1.1

Tables 1.1 and 1.2 give a profile of each of the main advanced level French syllabuses on offer in the United Kingdom (Note that when these syllabuses are available to candidates taking the examination at an overseas centre they may differ slightly from the 'home' syllabus). You should check with the actual syllabus for information concerning prescribed texts and topics and for further details of the papers that you will be required to take.

Table 1.1 Requirements and formats for French Advanced Examinations

Abbreviation	Board and address	Papers	Length	Marks	Description of papers and questions
		A-level			
AEB	Associated Examining Board Wellington House Aldershot Hampshire GU 11 BQ	Paper 1	¾ hour	20%	Listening comprehension. Questions and answers in English on 3–4 extracts. Sources include talks, news items, interviews, dialogues.
		Paper 2	2 hours	20%	1. A passage of about 300 words for translation into English. 2. A passage of 750–800 words with questions to be answered in English.
		Paper 3	2½ hours	20%	1. Questions answered in French on a passage in English. Questions involve translation and summary. 2. A 250 word composition in French in response to stimulus material.
		Paper 4	2½ hours	20%	Civilisation, literature and culture. One essay of about 350 words in French on each of two topics relating to France.
		Oral	15 mins	20%	1. Discussion on material provided by Board. 2. Discussion on topic prepared by the candidate. 3. General questions.
		A/S-level			
		Paper 1	1 hour	35%	Listening comprehension. 1. 6–7 short items (news, short extracts, etc.) 2. Interview or discussion. Questions and answers in English.
		Paper 2	1¼ hours	35%	Reading comprehension. 1. 6–7 passages in French of 60–300 words. Questions and answers in English. 2. Prose passage in French of 1,000–1,200 words. Questions and answers in English.
		Paper 3 Oral	15 mins	30%	1. Discussion on material provided by the Board. 2. Discussion on topic chosen from list of 20. 3. General conversation.
		A-level			
Cambridge	University of Cambridge Local Examination Syndicate Syndicate Buildings 17 Harvey Road Cambridge CB1 2EU	Paper 1	2½ hours	27%	1. Prose translation. 2. Essay in French.
		Paper 2	2 hours	27%	1. Translation into English. 2. Reading comprehension, Questions and answers in English.
		Paper 3	3 hours	27%	Literature. Prescribed texts.
		Paper 4	2/3 hour	8½%	Listening comprehension. Questions and answers in English.
		Oral	15–20 mins	10½ %	1. Reading. 2. Conversation and prepared topic.

Table 1.1 Requirements and formats for French Advanced Examinations (*contd.*)

Abbreviation	Board and address	Papers	Length	Marks	Description of papers and questions
		A/S-level			
Cossec	Cambridge, Oxford and Southern School Examinations Council Syndicate Buildings 1 Hills Road Cambridge CB1 2EU	Paper 1	1 hour	20%	Listening comprehension. News, broadcasts, dialogues. Questions and answers in English.
		Paper 2	2½ hours	40%	Responsive reading. 1. Questions and answers in English on 500-word passage in French. Some translation into English. Letter in French. 2. Comprehension and/or summary based on 500-word passage in French.
		Oral	30 mins	40%	1. Role-play. 2. Discussion. 48 hours preparation time. 3. Discussion on candidate's chosen reading.
		A-level			
JMB	Joint Matriculation Board Manchester M15 6EU from 1988	Paper 1	3 hours	25%	Internally assessed course-work based on works of fiction and non-fiction. Essays in French *or* Prescribed texts. Section A to be answered in French, Section B in French or English.
		Paper 2	3 hours	35%	Questions on two texts in French. Translation into English, translation into French, free composition in French, reading comprehension.
		Paper 3	1½ hours	20%	Listening comprehension tested by questions and answers in English and summarising. Test based on tape-recordings made by native speakers.
		Oral	15 mins	20%	1. Role-playing. 2. Reporting. 3. Conversation. External examiner.
		A/S-level			
		Paper 1	1 hour 20 mins	30%	Listening comprehension. Questions and answers in English or multiple choice.
		Paper 2	2 hours	30%	Reading comprehension. A number of short passages in French. Questions and answers in English. *or* Internal assessment of course-work. 2 extended essays in English (total of 2,000 words for the 2 essays).
		Oral	15 mins	40%	1. Role-play. 2. Presentation based on visual material. 3. Conversation.

Table 1.1 Requirements and formats for French Advanced Examinations (*contd.*)

Abbreviation	Board and address	Papers	Length	Marks	Description of papers and questions
		A-level			
		Syllabus A			
London	University of London School Examinations Council Stewart House	Paper 1	3 hours	33⅓%	Literature. Prescribed texts. 4 texts. At least one from each of Section A and Section B.
	32 Russell Square	Paper 2	1½ hours	16⅔%	Essay in French of 350 words.
	London WC1B 5DN	Paper 3	1½ hours	16⅔%	Translation into French of passage of 240 words.
		Paper 4	2 hours	16⅔%	1. Translation from French (50 marks) 2. Reading comprehension (50 marks) Questions and answers in English on passage of 500–600 words.
		Paper 5	1/2 hour	7½%	Listening comprehension. Questions and answers in English on a recorded passage of about 400 words. *or* Dictation. A passage of French of about 170 words.
		Oral	20 mins	10½%	1. Reading (25 marks) 2. Conversation (75 marks)
		Syllabus A – Revised Syllabus June 1989 onwards			
		Paper 1	3/4 hour	15%	Listening comprehension. Questions and answers in English.
		Either Paper 2	2½ hours	25%	Literature. Prescribed texts. 3 answers.
		Or Paper 3	2½ hours	25%	Prescribed topics. 2 answers in French
		Paper 4	2½ hours	20%	Guided writing and essay (250 words) in French.
		Paper 5	2 hours	20%	Translation into English. Passage of 200 words. Reading comprehension. Questions and answers in English, Passage of 500–600 words.
		Paper 6 Oral	20 mins	20%	1. Reading. 2. Study Extract discussion. (20 mins preparation time) 3. Conversation.

Table 1.1 Requirements and formats for French Advanced Examinations (*contd.*)

Abbreviation	Board and address	Papers	Length	Marks	Description of papers and questions
		Syllabus B			
London		Paper 1	2 hours	20%	Essay. 500 words in French in answer to a question on a prepared topic.
		Paper 2	1½ hours	15%	Guided composition. 250 word essay based on stimulus material.
		Paper 3	1½ hours	15%	Translation into French. Prose passage of about 240 words.
		Paper 4	2 hours	20%	1. Translation from French (10%) 2. Reading comprehension (10%) Questions and answers in English on a passage of about 500–600 words.
		Paper 5	½ hour	10%	Listening comprehension. Questions and answers in English on a recorded passage of about 400 words.
		Oral	20 mins	20%	Discussion of material provided; some reading aloud; general conversation.
		A/S-level			
		Paper 1	1 hour	25%	Reading comprehension. 1. Passage in French of 250–300 words. Questions and answers in English. 2. Answer in French 10 questions or write report or letter of 250–300 words in French.
		Paper 2	40 mins	25%	Listening comprehension. 1. 3/4 short items in French. 2. 2 longer items in French. (Total of 600–700 words.) Questions and answers in English.
		Paper 3	1 hour	15%	Writing in French. A non-specialised, formal letter, report or leaflet of 200–250 words.
		Paper 4 Oral	20 mins	35%	1. Giving information in French. Candidates prepare stimulus material in English. 2. Eliciting information in French on basis of data given in English. 3. Discussion of dossier-based prepared topic-project.

Table 1.1 Requirements and formats for French Advanced Examinations (*contd.*)

Abbreviation	Board and address	Papers	Length	Marks	Description of papers and questions
		A-level			
		Syllabus 9820			
Oxford	Oxford Local Examinations Ewert Place Summertown Oxford OX2 7BZ	Paper 1	1 hour	11%	Listening comprehension. Questions and answers in English on a recorded passage of about 500 words.
		Paper 2	2 hours	23%	1. Translation into English. 2. Reading comprehension. Questions and answers in English.
		Paper 3	3 hours	28%	Literary and Background studies. Paper in 4 sections, A,B,C,D. Candidates answer 4 questions. May answer all from D (Background) but not more than 3 from Section A or three from Section B or 2 from Section C.
		Paper 4	1½ hours	11%	Essay in French of 250–300 words.
		Paper 5	1¼ hours	17%	Translation into French.
		Oral	about 15 mins	11%	1. Reading. 2. Conversation based on written stimulus. 3. General conversation. External examiner.
		Alternative syllabus 9821			
		Paper 1	1 hour	12½%	Listening comprehension. Questions and answers in English on a recorded passage of about 500 words.
		Paper 2	2 hours	22½%	1. Translation into English. 2. Reading comprehension. Questions and answers in English.
		Paper 3	2 hours	15½%	Use of French. A series of linguistic tests (e.g. Cloze, re-phrasing, substitutions)
		Paper 4	3 hours	25%	1. Summary in French. 2. Essay in French of 250–300 words.
		Oral	35 mins	25%	1. Reading. 2. Conversation based on extract from prepared book. 3. General conversation on at least 2 further books. 4. General conversation.

Table 1.1 Requirements and formats for French Advanced Examinations (*contd.*)

Abbreviation	Board and address	Papers	Length	Marks	Description of papers and questions
		A/S-level			
Oxford		Paper 1	1 hour	35%	Listening comprehension. 1. Short items. Questions and answers in English. 2. A longer time. Questions and answers in English.
		Paper 2	2 hours	35%	Reading comprehension. 1. A number of passages in French, varying in length. 2. A longer passage, 1 chosen from 3. Tested in various ways: answers in English/summary/translation into English.
		Paper 3 Oral	20 mins	30%	1. Discussion based on written or taped stimulus. 2. Discussion of 1/2 topics chosen from prescribed list.
		A-level			
O and C	Oxford and Cambridge Schools Examination Board 10 Trumpington Street Cambridge	Paper 1	1¼ hours	25½%	1. Translation into English. 2. Reading comprehension. Questions and answers in English.
		Papers 2 and 3	2¼ hours	25½%	1. Translation into French. 2. Essay in French.
		Paper 4	3 hours	25½%	Literature and civilisation. Prescribed texts.
		Paper 5	½ hour	5%	Dictation.
		Paper 6	½ hour	5%	Listening comprehension. Questions and answers in English.
		Oral		13%	1. Reading. 2. Conversation.
		A-level *Syllabus A*			
SUJB	Southern Universities Joint Board for School Examinations Cotham Road BS6 6DD	Paper 1	2 hours	19%	Translation into English. 2 passages.
		Paper 2	2½ hours	32%	1. Translation into French. 2. Essay in French of 300 words.
		Paper 3	3 hours	27%	Set books and historical and literary background. 4 questions on Part 1 or 3 questions on Part 1 and 1 question on Part 2.
		Paper 4		9%	Listening comprehension. Questions and answers in English on a recorded passage.
		Oral		13%	1. Reading. 2. Conversation and discussion.

Table 1.1 Requirements and formats for French Advanced Examinations (*contd.*)

Abbreviation	Board and address	Papers	Length	Marks	Description of papers and questions
		Syllabus B			
		Paper 1	2½ hours	20%	Translation into English. Two passages of different styles.
		Paper 2	3 hours	25%	1. Essay in French 2. Guided composition. An exercise requiring one extended answer or 2 shorter answers in the form of a reply or counter argument to a passage or passages given in French.
		Paper 3	1¼ hours	20%	1. Listening comprehension. A recording (10–15 mins) including several voices. Candidates write a summary. 2. Dictation.
		Oral	¼ hour	15%	1. Reading. 2. General conversation.
		Project		20%	A detailed essay of about 3000 words written in English or French.
		A-level			
WJEC	Welsh Joint Education Committee 245 Western Avenue Cardiff CF5 2YX	Paper 1	3 hours	27%	1. Translation into French. 2. Essay in French.
		Paper 2	1¼ hours	17%	1. Translation into English. 2. Reading comprehension. Questions and answers in English/Welsh.
		Paper 3	2/3 hours	13%	Listening comprehension. Questions and answers in English/Welsh.
		Oral	¼ hour	18%	
	Either	Paper 5	3 hours	25%	Literature. Prescribed texts.
	or	Paper 6	2½ hours	25%	Extended language option.
		A-level			
NISEC	Northern Ireland Schools GCE Examination Council Beech Hill House 42 Beech Hill Road Belfast BT8 4RS	Paper 1	3 hours	30%	1. Translation into French. Either 1 or 2 passages. 2. Essay in French of 250 words.
		Paper 2	1½ hours	20%	1. Translation into English. 2. Translation into English but from 1988 Reading comprehension.
		Paper 3	3 hours	25%	Literature. Prescribed texts.
		Oral		25%	1. Dictation. 2. Reading. 3. Conversation. 4. Listening comprehension. Questions and answers in English.

Table 1.1 Requirements and formats for French Advanced Examinations (*contd.*)

Abbreviation	Board and address	Papers	Length	Marks	Description of papers and questions
		Grade II			
IOL	The Institute of Linguists Educational Trust Mangold House 24a Highbury Grove London N5 2 EA	Part 1	20 mins	20% 30% 30% 20%	1. Prepared talk. 2. Conversation. 3. Sight translation into English. 4. Sight translation into French.
		Part 2	30 mins	100%	1. Listening comprehension and written summary. English summary of a spoken passage of about 100 words.
		Part 3	1½ hours	50% 50%	1. Translation into English. 2. Translation into French.
		Part 4	2½ hours	100%	Background knowledge of France. 3 answers in French of about 200 words each. The Paper will consist of 3 sections. Not more than two questions may be answered from any one section.
		Intermediate Diploma			
		Part 1	25 mins	20% 30% 25% 25%	1. Prepared talk. 2. Conversation. 3. Oral summary in English of a passage of French of about 250 words. 4. Ad hoc interpreting.
		Part 2	3 hours		1. Summary in English of a passage of 600–800 words. 2. Translation into English. A passage of French of about 300 words on a semi-specialised topic. 3. Translation into French. A passage of 250 words on a non-specialised subject.
		Part 3	3 hours		Background knowledge of France. 3 essays in French of about 350 words each.
		Final Diploma			
		Part 1	25 mins	30% 30% 40%	1. Prepared talk. 2. Interpreting. 3. Conversation.
		Part 2	3 hours	100%	Either essay in French of 750–1000 words or Précis in French of a passage in English of 1200–1500 words.
		Part 3	3 hours	25% 25% 25%	1. Translation into English. A passage of about 250 words. 2. Translation into French. A passage of about 250 words. 3. Translation into French.
		Part 4	3 hours		Background knowledge of France. 3 answers of about 500 words in French.
		Part 5	3 hours	25%	Special subject. One of three options: Long essay, 1500 words in 3 hours; Technical translation, 2 passages of about 500 words in 3 hours; General interpreting.

Table 1.1 Requirements and formats for French Advanced Examinations (*contd.*)

Abbreviation	Board and address	Papers	Length	Description of papers and questions
RSA	Royal Society of Arts Examination Board Murray Road Orpington Kent BR5 3 RB	**Certificate for Secretarial Linguists**		
		Part 1	20 mins	3 short answerphone messages in French to be written in English.
		Part 2 (The exercises must be typed)	2 hrs 55 mins	1. Letter in French in reply to a letter in French. 2. Summary in English of a text in French of about 1000 words. (Summary involves selection of specific information). 3. The writing of a memo in French on the basis of instructions given in English. 4. Translation of a letter from French to English.
		Part 3 Oral	20 mins	1. The candidate conveys in French a message given in English and asks a question. 2. Social/business situation face to face. 3. A continuation of the conversation into a more general topic area.
		Diploma for Bilingual Secretaries Part 1 (Tasks must all be keyboarded)		Tasks based on video recording of meeting. 1. The writing of a report of the meeting in English. 2. Letter in French in reply to letter in French. 3. The writing of a memo in French on the basis of a memo in English.
		Part 2	3 hours	1. Translation from French into English of about 200–250 words. 2. Summary into English of a document in French of 1200–1500 words, requiring selection of specific information. 3. A reply in French to a request for information in French, drawing on information in English.
		Part 3 Oral	25 mins	1. Candidate initiates telephone conversation to gain information. 2. Discussion of candidate's explanation of a 200 word newspaper article in English concerning France, leading into general conversation. 3. Candidate interprets between an executive of an English company and a French-speaking visitor.

Table 1.2 *The table below indicates which skills and areas of knowledge are tested in the examination set by the Examining Boards.* (*Contd. overleaf.*)

Topic	AEB A-level	A/S-level	Cambridge A-level	A/S-level, Cossec	JMB A-level	A/S-level	London Syllabus A A-level	A/S-level	London Syllabus B A-level	Oxford Syllabus 9820 A-level	A/S-level
Grammatical accuracy	•	•	•	•	•	•	•	•	•	•	•
Vocabulary	•	•	•	•	•	•	•	•	•	•	•
Essay in French	•		•		•		•		•	•	
Narrative essay	•		•		•		•			•	
Discussion essay	•		•		•		•		•	•	
Translation into French	•		•		•		•		•	•	
Reading comprehension	•	•	•	•	•	•	•	•	•	•	•
Summary	•			•	•						
Listening comprehension	•	•	•	•	•	•	•	•	•	•	•
Translation into English	•		•		•		•		•	•	
Literature	•		•		•		•		•	•	
Oral	•	•	•	•	•	•	•	•	•	•	•

NB The table does not represent an exhaustive list of the elements in each examination. Check with current syllabus.

Table 1.2 (*contd.*)

Oxford Syllabus 9821 A-level	O&C A-level	SUJB Syllabus A A-level	SUJB Syllabus B A-level	WJEC A-level	NISEC A-level	IOL Grade II	IOL Intermediate Diploma	IOL Final Diploma	RSA Cert. for Sec. Linguists	RSA Diploma for Bilingual Secretaries
•	•	•	•	•	•	•	•	•	•	•
•	•	•	•	•	•	•	•	•	•	•
•	•	•	•	•	•	•	•	•		
•	•	•	•	•	•					
•	•	•	•	•	•	•	•	•	•	•
	•	•		•	•	•	•	•	•	
•				•	•					
•			•			•	•	•	•	•
•	•	•	•	•	•	•			•	•
•	•	•	•	•	•	•	•	•	•	•
	•	•		•	•					
•	•	•	•	•	•	•	•	•	•	•

Chapter 2

Examination techniques

EXAM PREPARATION

As you will realise when you run through the list of chapter headings of this book, the A-level or post A-level French examination tests both different types of *knowledge* and a variety of language *skills*. The A-level candidate may be required to take as many as five written papers and an oral examination which test on the one hand knowledge and understanding of "content" (literature or background studies) and on the other hand skills such as essay-writing in French, translation into French or English, aural comprehension, reading comprehension and competence in spoken French. It is therefore essential at the outset to make yourself fully aware of exactly what is required by the particular Examination Board whose papers you are going to take, since the Boards vary somewhat in their requirements and in the options that they offer. You can do this by checking the examination syllabus and by asking your course tutor. There is a full listing of the addresses of the Examination Boards on p. 2–10.

You should also find out from the syllabus the percentage mark carried by each of the papers that you are preparing for. You will not find it necessary to allocate your time in exactly the same way but you should, for example, guard against devoting too little time to preparing for a paper which carries a very significant proportion of the marks.

It will then be helpful, once you have identified the type of "content" paper that you are going to take, and the different skills that are to be tested, if you study the corresponding chapters of this book. They will help you avoid false assumptions concerning various parts of the examination, such as the notion held by many candidates that translation into English, one's own language, requires less attention than other tests. They will also help you to be aware of the work that you will need to get through in order to reach A-level or post A-level standard, and to form an understanding of what the examiner will be looking for and of how examinations are marked. Take note of this information and make certain that you know from the beginning of your course exactly what you are aiming at and the ground that you personally will need to cover.

Once you have established these *longer-term* objectives, it is important that you organise more *immediate* tasks according to a weekly and daily timetable. Keep to it but make it realistic and divide your study time into periods of manageable length. Make good use of your time and remember that there are many useful language-learning activities that fit comfortably into the odd half an hour, such as reading a few pages of French to build vocabulary or listening to a comprehension tape or a news bulletin. With language work in particular, keep a record of what you have covered – grammatical structures, vocabulary areas, etc. This will serve to indicate what you have achieved and to check that you are in fact acquiring a sufficient grammatical competence and vocabulary to cope with the essay in French, prose translation and indeed all other language exercises.

The key to success in any examination is *adequate preparation* and the language student, perhaps more than the student of any other subject, must lose no time in getting the preparation under way. It needs to be understood that the learning of new material or revision cannot be left to a late stage and certainly not to the last minute. What is learnt hurriedly will not be properly digested. Learning a language is not unlike learning to play a musical instrument: in addition to understanding the rules or theory it is necessary to be able to perform a skill. Successful performance requires practice and that practice should be constant and spread over a period of time. The structures and vocabulary of the language must be used and reused until the rules have been internalised, so that they are followed spontaneously. It is only in this way that you will be able to produce written or spoken French effortlessly and accurately enough to achieve the highest level in the examination. And it is the highest level that you should constantly aim at.

From the beginning and throughout the course make the most of classes. Try to participate *actively* in discussions of set texts or background topics and take every opportunity to use and practise your French. It will help if you think ahead and come to your class prepared. If you attend a literature or language class having prepared the ground and having tried to anticipate the content of the discussion or the lesson, you will have a sense of purpose which will make your learning more interesting and efficient. Prepare some questions you might ask and take a critical interest in the subject area to be discussed. Try to take notes which do not have to be copied out neatly later (it wastes time) and be rigorously accurate when you take notes in a language class. It is clearly counter-productive to first record and then diligently learn misspelt items of vocabulary or grammatically incorrect examples.

After the lesson you should spend time *reviewing* the material. Check your notes and add to them by following up references and prescribed reading. Reviewing the material you have covered should be an active period of study. Spend time thinking about the new material you have learnt and try to relate it to the rest of your knowledge of the subject. Evaluate the new ideas or the new language structures with your longer-term examination goals in mind. Ask yourself how the ideas which have emerged from a discussion could be developed to form an examination answer or part of one. Extract from any language text that you have worked on in class those expressions and structures which you can identify as being useful for a "narrative" essay or a "discussion" essay or for your translation work. Make a conscious effort to think and write about those aspects of your set texts or background topics which have been explained and discussed in class. Also make a point of practising and reusing any new items of language.

You should, of course, complete *all* the work set by your tutors. Remember, however, that doing a piece of course-work, such as handing in a language essay or a translation, is only half of the exercise. There is equal value in looking critically at your performance and in devising means of improving it. Always go through marked work when it has been returned in order to analyse your strengths and weaknesses. This is particularly important in your language work where you must be prepared to learn from your mistakes. Tackle them without delay, classify them and keep track of them. Examination scripts show only too clearly that language errors may cover a wide range of categories and that many of these are easily neglected. Therefore *identify* your errors and make sure that you understand *why* they have occurred. Knowing what you are doing wrong and why is the first step to putting it right.

REVISION

It is unwise, particularly as far as your language work is concerned, to think solely in terms of a revision period which occupies the few weeks which precede the examination. In language learning it is necessary to carry out *continual short-term revisions* throughout the course in order to ensure that what you have learnt in the early stages can be carried forward as part of your active stock of vocabulary and structures. Remember that a weak performance at A-level in those parts of the examination which test written or spoken French, is nearly always caused by a lack of elementary knowledge. It is not too much of an exaggeration to say that A-level candidates fail because they have forgotten what they once knew well in the second or third year of the O-level course. Make sure that this does not happen to you by frequently submitting your work to a critical review.

By the time you reach the weeks before the examination, language revision should have been reduced to a minimum and should consist of a final review of troublesome points that have already been worked on, or a review of vocabulary notebooks, grammatical examples and sections of the course-book which are already familiar.

Immediately before the examination it is a good idea to read texts you know well or an undemanding novel and to listen to tapes, simply to have French going through your mind.

Revision of literature or background material should begin early so that there is still time to fill any gaps which you may discover in your knowledge. Your revision will be most effective if, instead of merely running through past notes, you *do* something with them. Reduce them to lists of main ideas and summaries that can be memorised. Organise your notes to form the basis of an examination answer and devote plenty of practice to answering and to framing answers in the time allowed. Take questions from past papers and prepare outline answers. Devise your own questions. Go through your material and imagine that you are giving a lecture on it or explaining it to a friend. If you make revision a part of active study you will be better able to remember and use your material creatively in the examination.

ESSAY-WRITING

A number of the papers included in the examination will test specialised skills such as listening comprehension, reading comprehension, or translation. You will find advice on preparing for these tests in the chapters which follow. Essay-writing occupies a rather different position. You may be required to write essays in *English* in those papers which examine set literary texts or topics related to contemporary France; you may be called upon to write an essay in *French* which is a test both of command of the language and of literary appreciation or knowledge of contemporary France; you will also be required to write an essay in *French* which is primarily a linguistic test and not a test of knowledge. (It is essential to check the syllabus to be certain of what is required.) The remarks which follow concern mainly the essay in English which features in the literature or background paper but the general principles apply to the French essay (discussed in detail in Ch. 5).

There is first of all a distinction to be made between the essays that you write as part of your course-work and those which are produced as examination answers. The course-work essay is an important part of the learning process and you can use it to establish a kind of dialogue with your tutor in order to experiment with your ideas and measure your progress. The thinking, reading and planning which it requires are an essential part of active study and a means of making the subject your own. If you make full use of this opportunity throughout the course you will master the knowledge and the writing skills which are essential in a first-rate examination answer.

When an essay is set it is preferable, even if you have a week to complete it, to begin thinking about it immediately. The first step is to *interpret* the title so that you understand exactly what you are being asked to do. Acquaint yourself (by studying past exam questions) with the terminology which examiners use. At an advanced level it is unlikely that you will be asked simply to *describe*, to *give an account of*, to *relate* or to *outline*: the key terms are more likely to be *analyse*, *compare and contrast*, *define*, *discuss*, *examine critically* or *explain*. Ensure that you understand what such terms imply and that when asked to analyse, discuss or explain, you do not simply describe.

Examination questions are carefully worded. You should therefore give attention to every word and identify every part of the question. A question such as the following on Molière's *L'Ecole des Femmes* contains a number of keywords, each of which should be responded to: "It is not difficult to sympathise with Arnolphe: he is resilient, witty on occasions and, above all, the victim of bad luck." Discuss the character of Arnolphe in the light of this opinion. The answer should discuss Arnolphe's character to decide whether he is *resilient* and *witty*; examine the situations to see whether he is a *victim of bad luck* and decide whether these elements (or any others) make it possible to *sympathise* with him. The question may be in two parts: "Contrast the characters of Burrhus and Narcisse and examine the influence which they have on Néron". Both parts must be dealt with. Remember that in considering carefully the wording and arrangement of the question you will be anticipating what the examiner will do when he draws up the mark-scheme.

When it comes to the more demanding operation of thinking out what should go into the essay, many students find it helpful to put their ideas down in diagrammatic form. The main element or idea in the question is written down and circled in the middle of the page. Then as ideas begin to flow they are jotted down around the central idea and shown as connected to, or branching off, from it. Thinking with this visual "map" in front of you may suggest further ideas which can then be plotted to show their linkage with the central idea. Such a diagram will enable you to see your essay as a whole *before* you attempt to express your argument in a discursive form and can usefully be referred to as you write up the essay.

When you begin to write avoid the mistake of adopting a plan which is a plan in name only. The least satisfactory essay is the one which has a shape only because it is possible to discern a disjointed discussion sandwiched between a pointless introduction and a false conclusion.

The poor *introduction* does little more than tell the reader that it is an introduction. Often it will introduce something general and irrelevant. You should guard against such faults. If you are writing an answer on the way in which Maupassant uses surprise endings in his short stories, the introduction should not contain generalities about the author's life and upbringing. You are not writing an introduction to a book on Maupassant; you are engaged in leading the reader directly to a specific argument. Be brief therefore. Define the terms of the question if they need to be made clear. Make your introductory paragraph strictly relevant to the points which follow and use it to arouse the interest of the reader. The often repeated advice that the introduction should be left until last is sound. You cannot focus the spotlight on the argument that you are going to develop until you are clear in your mind about what you are going to say.

Be equally careful over the *conclusion*. Avoid the rather meaningless phrases which do no more than announce that you are about to stop writing. Do not put yourself in the position of having to "tack on" a false conclusion, one which claims that the question has been answered when it clearly has not. Avoid the following approach, only too familiar to examiners. The question is: "It is the tragedy of Néron, rather than of Britannicus which is the main theme of this play". Discuss. The main body of the essay contains what is really an outline of the plot which is followed by a final paragraph which claims: "Therefore it can be seen that the tragedy of Britannicus is the main theme of the play". It is a false conclusion because it has not been demonstrated by the preceding discussion and it convinces nobody.

A conclusion should be logically related and necessary to the argument. It should not introduce any new points or afterthoughts. It serves no purpose if it simply repeats what has been discussed in the first part of the essay. A brief summary of preceding points is useful only if it genuinely concludes the argument, for example, by assembling points "for" and "against" in order to make a final, considered judgement.

In the *main body* of the essay concentrate on *making* your points, make them clearly and develop them fully. Do not leave it to the reader to extract an argument from what is simply implicit. It is here that many candidates are not thorough enough and do not do themselves justice. They identify relevant points but fail to explore them in detail or to elaborate upon them and therefore they have not responded fully to the question which has asked for discussion, analysis, evaluation or critical examination. You should use the writing of course-work essays as an opportunity to practise thinking and to develop your techniques for presenting ideas on paper. Make yourself familiar with the set text or the background topic so that you have a personal response to it, one which you can then discuss and analyse. Discuss ideas in class, ask questions, read your primary sources critically, extract from secondary sources (e.g. works of criticism) those ideas which you can make your own, and construct your "mind map" and essay plan. You will not have time to do all this when you write your *examination* answer but it is a form of training which, when the time comes, will enable you to produce a discussion of real substance and interest.

Endeavour to deal with points in *logical order* so that for the reader there is a progression which is easy to follow. Ordering an argument coherently requires practice and although your argument may seem clear in your own mind, its clarity may not be so evident to the reader. It is therefore a good idea to reread a course-work essay a day or two after writing it, trying to put yourself into the reader's position. If your idea is a valid one then spelling it out simply and completely will do it no harm. And above all, do not throw away good ideas and insights by expressing yourself inadequately.

Your argument should not only be well expressed it should be supported by appropriate *facts*, *examples* and *specific references* to the set text or other primary source. This is necessary if you are to make your discussion convincing and it is the way in which you display your knowledge and grasp of the subject. That is why it is usual for examination questions to ask specifically for examples and precise references to set texts and quotations. However when you provide these, remember that their function is to illustrate points that you are making; supplying quotations and examples is not an end in itself. You should guard against overloading an essay with quotations which are not really apt and against allowing textual references or factual examples to develop into a purely descriptive account. At A-level you are not asked to describe your knowledge but to *use* it.

The essay should be written in good, standard English. Avoid colloquial expressions and remember that the language of an essay is rather more formal than that of a classroom discussion. If you are interested in your subject and in your own ideas, you will be anxious to express them accurately. Strive for clarity and precision. Poor use of English, inaccurate spelling and an inappropriate style are self-penalising. They are faults which prevent the examiner from following the flow of your ideas, and if you fail to communicate effectively your performance can only suffer.

Before you hand in your course-work essay read it once more, asking yourself those critical questions that the examiner will ask:

- Have you answered the question/all parts of the question?
- Is the introduction useful?
- Are the points clearly made and thoroughly discussed?
- Is evidence provided to support them?
- How many good points are there?
- Could any other points be added?
- Is all of the essay relevant to the discussion?
- Is there any repetition or rambling?
- Have you used and displayed your knowledge of the subject well?
- Is the conclusion effective?

IN THE EXAMINATION

Well before the examination it is advisable to obtain a complete set of the most recent examination papers so that you are familiar with the instructions, the layout and the look of each. You will be better prepared to observe the following points when you take the examination:

1. Follow the instructions at the beginning of the paper which indicate how many questions should be answered and from which sections of the paper they may be chosen. Watch for alternative questions (either . . . or), and do not answer both.

2. If there is a choice of questions, allow yourself time to read them all and let them sink in before making your choice. Make sure (by turning each page over) that you have in fact read them all.

3. Divide the time allowed for the examination according to the number of questions to be answered. If each answer carries an equal proportion of marks, divide the time equally, allowing time for checking at the end. Remember that it is preferable, if you run short of time, to devote your last 15 minutes to starting your final answer (even in note-form) rather than add finishing touches to a previous answer. On any question marked, for example, out of 20, it is much easier to score the first marks (0–5) than the last 5 (15–20).

4. When you tackle a question:
   (a) Ensure that you have interpreted it correctly. Underline all the keywords and if you are unsure of the meaning of any of them, consider turning to another question. Pay particular attention to terms such as *discuss critically*, *explain*, *comment on*, *give reasons for*, etc.
   (b) Identify all the parts of a question and deal with all the parts in your answer. If you are asked to give *reasons for* or to discuss *ways in which*, deal with more than *one* reason or way.
   (c) Be wary of the question which is very similar to one that you have already practised. If you rush into the answer you may overlook the fact that the exam question implies a different angle or contains an additional part. Always answer the question set.

5. Spend sufficient time planning your answer. Use the methods which you have practised when writing course-work essays but adapt them to the shorter time available in examination conditions. Have in mind the check-list of questions which you have learned to ask yourself about a course-work essay before handing it in.

6. When you begin to write be purposeful and relevant from the first line. Make your introduction useful. Try to capture the examiner's attention from the start and convince him that he has picked up the script of a candidate who really has something to say.

7. Organise your time so that you have 10 minutes left at the end for reading through and checking your answers. Check for legibility, incidental errors, the names of characters in novels and plays, the accuracy of quotations in French, punctuation and the numbering of questions.

8. Finally, the examiner. Remember that at A-level examiners are likely to be experienced, practising teachers who are fully conscious of the stress which many students undergo when taking examinations. They will be understanding and only too willing to reward your work highly as long as you give them the opportunity. Keep the examiner in mind when you write. Express yourself clearly, keep your handwriting legible, present the work as neatly as possible and set out to show that you have made a conscientious effort to do what the question asks.

Chapter 3

Grammatical accuracy

GETTING STARTED

There is probably little need to stress the importance of having a sound understanding of the grammar of French and of being able to apply that knowledge accurately. Most students look on "learning grammar" as the main part of their language learning and identify it as the chief cause of difficulty when their progress in French is not very satisfactory. Examining Boards and teachers put heavy emphasis on grammatical accuracy and examiners' reports complain with such unfailing regularity about "basic grammatical incompetence" or "widespread inaccuracy" that it may seem to the struggling learner that they are obsessed with this particular problem and that they are never going to be satisfied with the candidates efforts to write and speak French. However, it is better to find a more positive lesson in what examiners have to say. Remind yourself that because of the way in which all examinations are assessed, grammatical accuracy *is* vital and that every bit of progress which you can make in this area *is* going to improve your final result.

It is inevitable, nevertheless, that you will make grammatical mistakes. It could even be argued that making some mistakes is a necessary part of learning the language but you should, of course, aim at minimising the chance of error by ensuring that your learning and practice of the structures of French are as efficient as possible from the outset. Some errors may be "useful" but others are not and prevention is always better than cure.

ESSENTIAL PRINCIPLES

WAYS OF LEARNING GRAMMAR

There is a good deal of controversy about *how* the grammar of a foreign language is most effectively learnt. In recent years there has been a move away from the idea that the learner should concentrate on learning how to manipulate the rules and a move towards the notion that the emphasis should be on practising the language as a means of communication, i.e.

on learning it through using it. Which is the best approach for the student preparing for an A-level examination? Most teachers would agree that there is a need for both approaches and that at A-level the student who is already able to handle a good deal of French which has been acquired by a process of induction based on pattern practice and on seeing language in use, will now benefit from a more formal insight into the structures of French and from a measure of grammatical description. There is a need for consciously learning the rule that pulls things together and provides short-cuts and there is a need for meaningful practice. You should therefore make sure that you have the means to learn the rule and to apply it in useful writing and speaking activities.

Course-book and grammar-book

Look critically at your *course-book* to see whether it gives you sufficient practice of the right sort. Do the grammar exercises lead you to write the kind of sentences that you would want to reproduce in your essays in French or in your prose translations? If not, then supplement your work with exercises from a more suitable course-book.

If you have not done so already, you should obtain a *grammar-book* which you can understand and learn to find your way around in so that reference becomes quick and easy. Get used to consulting it. Students sometimes complain that this is difficult because, as they have not learned basic grammatical terminology (e.g. demonstrative pronoun, possessive adjective, present participle, etc.), they are not sure what to look for. You will find however, that if the grammar-book is well indexed that you are often able to look up the French word which is causing difficulty and then find the sections where it is treated grammatically. If you start by using the grammar-book in this way you will begin to learn the basic terms and above all you will get used to looking things up.

For much of the time you will use the grammar-book for reference, to find out how to correct an error or to look for clarification of a rule, but you should also use it to revise or learn the *basic forms* of French. You should give this area of grammar priority because errors involving the forms of regular and irregular verbs, the government of verbs, the feminine or plural forms of adjectives and nouns, the form of adverbs, articles, possessive adjectives, possessive pronouns, demonstrative pronouns and personal pronouns will be considered by the examiner as elementary and will therefore rank with the more serious and more heavily penalised types of error. There are errors which are more "excusable" than others. The correct choice between the past historic tense and the imperfect, or the decision to use a subjunctive in certain contexts or even the choice between "des" and "de" often requires considerable judgement and there may be no clearly right or clearly wrong answer. Obviously, there is no difficult judgement to be made as far as grammatical forms are concerned. The plural of "cheval" is "chevaux" and the past participle of "lire" is "lu" and therefore "des chevals" or "j'ai lisé" would be considered as serious errors.

Many students find that learning grammar is not a very interesting activity. Sometimes the rules themselves do not seem to be very helpful: some of them appear to be rather illogical while others, affecting perhaps just one letter or sound, may seem irritating to the student who wants to get on with saying something worth while in French. Even worse, the rules do not always do the job you had expected them to do. They are not always watertight; they do not always explain fully the examples which you hear or read and there always seem to be numerous exceptions which also have to be learnt.

Making your own discoveries

The point to be made is that you should not treat the grammar-book as an end in itself. You will find that studying the language becomes more interesting if you use the grammar-book to help you make your *own discoveries* about the French that you come across in newspapers or that you hear on the radio and while talking to French people. Train yourself to be observant, try to find useful examples of structures and make a point of using them.

It is likely that the grammar in your course-book will be presented through texts which show structures working as they should in a context of authentic written or spoken French. The exercises which follow will be designed to give you practice in using the structure so that you can make it your own. It is important that you should realise what the teaching method of the course-book is so that you can make full use of it and continue the learning process.

- Make sure that you understand the point of the exercises.
- Ask yourself whether the exercises are going to help you to express what it is that you want to say in your essays or prose translations.
- When you have practised an important new structure ask yourself what you are going to do to keep it in circulation.
- Collect further examples from the grammar-book, the dictionary or from your own reading.

Such language study can also be carried out on passages of your own choosing, such as those that you study intensively for vocabulary-building. Try to identify useful structures for study and devise your own exercises for practising them. It is possible to do this by making up simple substitution exercises. For example, assume that you had selected the following structures:

(a) Nous sommes plusieurs à poser cette question.
   and
(b) Il a interdit à tous les élèves de revenir avant trois heures.

Instead of just underlining the sentences or writing them down in a notebook, build up further sentences on the same pattern:

(a) Nous sommes plusieurs à poser cette question.

à vouloir partir.

à étudier le français.

à suivre ce cours.

Nous sommes plusieurs à poser cette question.

Nous sommes cinq à poser cette question.

Nous sommes nombreux à poser cette question.

(b) Il a interdit à tous les élèves de revenir avant trois heures.

à tout le monde

à tous les clients

à tous les spectateurs

Some structures can be written into a mini-dialogue which can be practised with a partner. In order to use "celui-ci, celles-ci", etc. you could put together a simple dialogue:

– Est-ce que ces places sont libres?
– Non, pas celles-ci, mais prenez celles d'a côté.
– Celles d'à côté sont prises aussi.
– Ah! C'est dommage!

and then for "ces places", substitute "cette salle", "cette cabine", "ces fauteuils", etc. and make the appropriate changes to the rest of the sentence.

If you *do something* with the grammatical structures that you hope to learn, something which involves making an active contribution of your own, then you will increase your chances of making the structure "your own". Explanation alone of a grammatical point will not ensure that you will be able to reproduce it spontaneously. Remember that in order to assimilate the rule the following three elements should be present: an understanding of the rule, some form of practice and the opportunity to use the structure to express personal meaning.

Grammatical accuracy and examinations

How vital is grammatical accuracy when you write French in the examination? The answer, of course, is that it is a very important objective since grammatical inaccuracy is a major cause of failure in the prose, essay, dictation or use of French papers. However, it must be said that it is possible to make errors, even quite numerous errors, and still be awarded a pass in the examination. This is because examiners are realistic enough not to set standards of absolute accuracy as a condition of passing and because there are factors other than sheer accuracy which are taken into consideration when assessing the candidates' ability to produce French. Imagine that candidate A writes an essay which, overall, a native speaker would find agreeable to read. It is reasonably fluent, parts of it have an idiomatic flavour, the vocabulary is apt and the candidate has attempted to use a variety of structures. However, there are a dozen grammatical errors (a few wrong prepositions, some adjective agreements overlooked and occasional misuse of the partitive). Candidate B on the other hand produces an essay which has hardly any inaccuracies but it contains only a few common structural patterns which it tends to repeat and uses only a small range of vocabulary. Candidate A's essay is certain to gain the higher mark.

This should enable you to understand that you will not be assessed solely on the mistakes that you make and that it does not follow that the best strategy (at least when writing an essay) is to be over-cautious and defensive about making mistakes as this may seriously inhibit other qualities of expression.

It is also helpful to understand that there are *degrees* of error and that some errors may be considered by the examiner to be more serious than others. For example, those errors which are clearly the result of elementary misunderstanding of the rule (e.g. the structure was incorrectly learned in the first place or was not learned at all) are more serious than oversights caused perhaps by lack of attention, which may show that a candidate has learned a pattern but is inconsistent in the way he uses it. Errors involving common forms are among the more serious and the error which obscures the meaning of the whole sentence or causes ambiguity is less tolerable than the error which would cause a native speaker "irritation" without stopping his comprehension. The lesson is that it will always pay dividends to work hard to eliminate errors involving common forms, and that you should try to distinguish those errors which interfere with communication and learn to avoid them.

Teachers and examiners recognise that grammatical and other errors are inevitable as it is not within the capacity of the human mind to retain everything it has learned. Mistakes can even be seen as a necessary part of learning: getting it right is a gradual process and you learn from your mistakes. This is a useful attitude to adopt to grammatical accuracy as you work towards the examination. It may be disappointing to have a piece of written French returned to you containing many underlinings in red but it does not follow that you have achieved nothing. The errors may show that you have learned a good deal but that there is still some way to go. Adopt a positive attitude towards your mistakes.

Nature of the error	Always make sure in the first instance that you understand exactly *what* has gone wrong. What should you have written? Has your tutor understood what you were trying to express? If he or she uses a marking code is it clear to you? Why has one error been treated as more serious than another? If you ask yourself questions like these you will begin to think through your mistakes.
Cause of the error	When it is clear to you what has gone wrong and what type of mistake you have made, try to understand what *caused* it. If you can identify the cause you are more likely to be able to work out an effective strategy for dealing with the error:

- Was it a total misunderstanding, e.g. you were unaware that "vouloir que" is followed by the subjunctive?

- Was it caused by a partial misunderstanding, e.g. you were aware of the rule that a preceding direct object agrees with the past participle but were not able to distinguish direct and indirect object?
- Was it perhaps the result of a guess based on English structure, e.g. "il est arrivé <u>sur</u> le train de Paris"?
- Was it a mistaken analogy, e.g. "il est <u>mouru</u> à l'âge de 50 ans"?

Of course, it may have been a careless mistake: you were perhaps in too much of a hurry or were tired or simply not sufficiently motivated to check through your work before handing it in for marking.

Seriousness of the error

Those errors which are more serious, the ones which are going to lose you marks in the examination, should naturally be given priority. Your tutor will point out the errors which are the *serious* ones:

- Those which involve a major rather than a minor rule or an exception.
- Those which show that basic forms have not been learnt.
- Those which really stand in the way of successful communication.

However, you yourself are best placed to know whether an error is a serious one *for you*, in the sense that it is one which you make frequently.

Categories of error

You should note your errors and *classify them* so that you have an overall view of the state of your knowledge. There will be errors which occur more frequently in essays than in proses, and vice versa. If there is a type of error which you are inclined to make in both exercises it obviously needs priority treatment. Patterns of errors are often clear to see when a candidate's overall examination performance is analysed. For example, in a recent A-level examination one candidate's errors in French were distributed as follows over three written papers:

	Vocabulary	Article/ partitive	Verbs	Tenses	Prepositions	Past participle and adjective agreement
Essay in French	13	7	2	7	3	4
Prose	17	5	4	2	—	3
Dictation	—	—	—	—	—	4

Even this limited analysis produces enough evidence to show that the use of the article and partitive has not been fully understood and that adjective agreement is inconsistently observed. If the candidate had been in the habit of making his own error analysis he may well have realised what items of grammar needed most urgent attention and have avoided the loss of marks through inaccuracy. It may seem over-ambitious to hope to eliminate *all* errors from your work but it is realistic to identify and do something about *priority areas*. It could easily be the difference between a fail and success in the examination.

A STEP FURTHER

When you work on your errors try to find an activity which is going to involve you intellectually and personally. It is more helpful to use the corrected grammatical form in new sentences of your own invention rather than to copy out mechanically the corrected sentence from your prose or essay. Imagine how you would teach the point in question to somebody else or better still, work with a partner when going over corrected work. You could practise a grammar point by constructing a mini-dialogue of the type described on p. 24. It is easy to produce your own tests for grammatical points such as the distinction between des/les, des/de, etc., verb forms and tenses and the choice of prepositions. Take a passage from a newspaper or novel, blank out the prepositions or articles and after a lapse of time use the passage as a "fill-in" exercise.

It is always more effective when you are doing remedial work to find an alternative strategy and different exercises from those that you used to learn the grammar point in the first place. Rather than repeat the exercises in your course-book find something else. It is likely that your tutor will have a battery of exercises to cover troublesome points. There are also a number of self-correcting exercise books on the market which may also be of use.

FURTHER READING

Grammar-books
H. Ferrar. *A French Reference Grammar*. OUP
    or
J. E. Mansion. *A Grammar of Present-day French*, 2nd edition. Harrap
    or
L. S. R. Byrne and E. L. Churchill. *A Comprehensive French Grammar*, 3rd edition. Blackwell

French verbs
G. Brereton. *The Concise French Verb Book*. Hodder & Stoughton
    or
Le Nouveau Bescherelle – l'Art de Conjuguer. Hatier

Exercise/workbooks
B. Job. *Comment Dire. Exercises de Grammaire Auto-correctifs*. Clé International
C. Grabner et M. Hague. *Ecrire sans Fautes*. Hatier
G.D. de Salins et S. Dupré la Tour. *Nouveaux Exercices de Grammaire*. Hatier (has answers to the exercises).

Chapter 4

Vocabulary

GETTING STARTED

It may seem unnecessary to point out to the student preparing for advanced examinations in French that a fundamental requirement is the acquisition of an adequate vocabulary and that this requirement is often not met. Students are generally aware of the problems and indeed many identify vocabulary-building as the most difficult aspect of learning a new language. This is probably partly due to the fact that the task seems endless. If you read the "avant-propos" to the *Dictionnaire du français contemporain*, you will see that although it excludes much specialist vocabulary and concerns itself only with language which is in everyday use, the total number of terms recorded is in the order of 25,000. The student embarking on an A-level or similar course might well ask "How many of these terms do I need to know to succeed in the examination? Where do I begin and how do I go about it?"

AN EXAMINER'S VIEW OF VOCABULARY

It is the purpose of this chapter to suggest answers to these and other questions that the examinee may ask, but first it will be useful to consider the problem of knowledge of vocabulary from the examiner's point of view. It soon becomes clear on reading their reports on the performance of candidates that they expect a wider range of accurately used, correctly spelled vocabulary than most examinees are able to produce. The main criticisms of the examiners may be summarised as follows:

(a) When the candidate is attempting to produce French in the language essay, prose translation or oral examination, a too limited knowledge of vocabulary leads to anglicised invention (examples given are "abilité", "capabilité", "malcontent", "dépriver", "incentif", "la publique", etc.), to paraphrase and to undue repetition of terms.

(b) Candidates have insufficient knowledge of common lexical areas (examples given are school life, the home, travel and transport, politics, clothing, the weather, etc.).

(c) Too much vocabulary appears to be only half-learned with the result that nouns frequently appear with the wrong gender, terms are misspelt or are used in a way which indicates that their meaning has not been fully understood. Too often "vocabulary appears to have been dredged up from the memory in imperfect shape".

(d) When there is evidence that candidates *have* made an effort to learn vocabulary it is unfortunately often clear that terms have not been learnt in context and that learning has not been extended to include the closely associated terms and the structures which are necessary if the item in question is to be correctly used in a sentence.

(e) Many candidates do not see the need to push beyond an O-level core, with the result that they are not able to express themselves with freedom and in idiomatic French on a sufficiently wide number of topics.

These comments and the evidence in A-level scripts show that insufficient knowledge of vocabulary is the most important single factor which determines a poorer grade or failure in those papers where candidates are asked to write in, or translate from, French. There are candidates who display range and depth of knowledge but too few, it seems, have applied themselves seriously to the business of learning a reasonably rich and varied vocabulary. It may be that they have not seen the need for a systematic approach to this aspect of learning a language. They may have felt that vocabulary learning presented no great problems or have assumed that the sum of words that they are required to know are all contained between the covers of the course-book and are "just picked up as you go along". There are certainly those who neglect the question of learning vocabulary because they feel that the real difficulty in learning French lies elsewhere, in grasping the use of the subjunctive or in learning irregular verbs. It is true to say that many teachers and courses give priority to the teaching of grammatical structures. There is nothing wrong with such an emphasis provided, of course, that it does not result in neglect of vocabulary-building. You should make sure that you do not neglect it.

ESSENTIAL PRINCIPLES

The acquisition of vocabulary demands a conscious effort and a systematic approach. There are no satisfactory short-cuts. Vocabulary is not efficiently learnt through the use of hastily memorised word-lists. The evidence is that the assimilation of words to the point where they have become part of the learner's *active* vocabulary, takes place gradually and over a period of time. The conclusion to be drawn from this is evident: if you are embarking on a course of advanced

French study you must waste no time in organising this aspect of your preparation. It is not just a question of learning six new words a day for two years (although the number of new words which you should aim to learn to use by the end of a two-year course should be close to that sum); you must give yourself time to "forget" them, recognise them again in different contexts, use them and reuse them before you can be confident that they have been fully assimilated.

If you set about it in the right way the task of learning vocabulary is not a difficult or a disheartening one. It is also an area of language study where the learner can do a great deal of useful work on his own. You should therefore make sure that that personal input is taking place by getting organised and by doing it now. If you are successful in building your vocabulary it will help you to build your confidence.

THE GROUND TO BE COVERED

When you set yourself the task of learning new words systematically you will probably ask yourself how much vocabulary you will need to know in order to be certain of success in the examination. It is not a question which can be answered with any great precision. The examination syllabus will not prescribe a list of lexical items to be learnt by the candidate, and in any case this would not be a very satisfactory way of acquiring new vocabulary. You should, however, extract what information you can from the syllabus regulations. There may be an indication of the *general areas* of vocabulary or of *broad language functions* which candidates are expected to cover.

Read the descriptions given in the syllabus regulations of the various tests which make up the examination (e.g. prose, translation into English, reading comprehension, listening comprehension, etc.) to see what *type* of language you must be familiar with. Certain tests or even the whole syllabus may be based on what is described as "non-literary" language. This implies that the sources used will include works of non-fiction, newspapers, periodicals and indeed the modern media in general. The material in a "literary" syllabus, on the other hand, is more likely to be drawn from novels, plays, short stories and other works of fiction. Common sense will tell you that such information must guide your preparation and the selection of your reading material. You would not prepare yourself for writing an essay in French on, let us say road accidents, the Channel tunnel or the problems of unemployment if your language and vocabulary study were based exclusively on novels by Georges Simenon or Françoise Sagan. On the other hand, such reading would be very useful preparation for the type of prose or translation passage which are set by certain of the Examination Boards.

For further guidance (and sometimes this will be the only source of guidance available) it is important to get hold of recent examination papers. Although the lexical content is not very clearly defined in syllabus regulations, there are always *unwritten conventions* which control the choice of passages which examiners set for prose, translation into French, listening comprehension and so on. Even though the regulations state no more than "a passage of modern French or English will be set", it does not follow that there is no limit to the obscurity or specialisation of the vocabulary which the test requires the candidate to know or use. You can reassure yourself that the level of difficulty and the nature of the lexis will be controlled by the experience of the examiner and of those whose job it is (usually practising teachers) to moderate the papers.

However, knowing this will still not tell you what to learn and what to discard. You should therefore study as many recent papers as you can in order to reach as clear an idea as possible of the "style" of setting for each of the papers that you are going to take. You will be able to decide broadly on the type of texts you should begin working on for the purpose of vocabulary-building. If, for example a typical prose passage is one which asks you to translate not just terms such as "trade union", "to go on strike", "to ask for higher wages" but also terms such as "free collective bargaining", "picket" and "blackleg", then obviously you are expected to know the semi-specialised as well as the "everyday" terms which relate to aspects of modern life and institutions.

When you have found out "where you are going" in your vocabulary study, then make sure that the texts that you select for intensive reading from newspapers, magazines or novels, as well as the material in your course-book are appropriate to the lexical requirements of *all* the papers that you have to take. If, for example, your course-book is based mainly on texts dealing with contemporary socio-political issues, you will not be able to rely on it to help you prepare for a prose paper which assumes knowledge of the type of language which belongs to the narrative-descriptive passage to be found in a novel. You must allow for this when planning your reading programme.

If you follow the advice given later in this chapter on extensive reading and the close study of selected passages for vocabulary-building purposes, you will in fact be taking practical steps to cover the main vocabulary areas. However, it is also useful to be able to refer to a framework of linguistic situations to guide your reading and study. Note that the following list of topics is not a vocabulary list. It is not a question of looking the items up in a dictionary, translating them and trying to learn them. The list is intended as a guide to the type of passage that you should work on when learning vocabulary in order to cover a basic range of language situations and functions. If you aim at acquiring the vocabulary necessary for expressing yourself adequately in these areas it will help you to acquire that common core of lexis which is necessary when learning French at an advanced level.

You can also use the list to help you to analyse past papers and to organise your vocabulary notebook. You will find for example, that the situations contained in most prose translations papers correspond very closely to the topics in the list. Passages which are narrative-descriptive in nature will very frequently involve the topics listed under "People", "Daily routine", "Home and family". A good working knowledge of the vocabulary relating to those areas alone would enable the candidate to deal efficiently with many of the prose passages set by A-level boards in recent years.

Use the list as a guide to the common ground which you should cover and be prepared to supplement it in order to meet the particular requirements of the examination (or of certain papers in it) which you are going to take.

Topics	Sub-topics and examples
People	
Age	Children
	Adults
	Old people
	Ages
	Date of birth
Identity	Title
	Name
	Sex
	Address
	Place of birth
	Introductions
	Nationalities
Appearance	Size
	Colouring
	Physical difference
	Comparisons
Care of personal appearance	e.g. make-up
Postures	e.g. standing
Movement	e.g. running
The senses	
(verbs rather than nouns)	e.g. seeing
Actions	Physical, e.g. hitting
	Visual, e.g. looking
	Vocal, e.g. shouting
Display of emotions	e.g. crying
Bodily states	e.g. hungry
Disabilities	e.g. deaf
Health	e.g. ill
Common ailments	e.g. colds
Accidents	
(usually verbs)	e.g. to cut oneself
Treatment	Doctor
	Hospital
	Chemist
	Dentist
	Dressings
	Remedies

Topics	Sub-topics and examples
Character	e.g. lazy
Emotions	e.g. love
Qualities and virtues	
(usually adjectives)	e.g. kind
Vices and addictions	e.g. smoking
Mental processes	e.g. thinking
Clothing	
Everyday clothing	Male
	Female
	Indoor
	Outdoor
	Summer
	Winter
	Putting on
	Taking off
	Choosing
	Trying on
	Buying
	Making
	Care of
Special clothing	Sports gear
	Uniforms
Appearance	Colour
	Size
Material	e.g. wool
	Fashion
Accessories	e.g. handbag
Adornments	e.g. rings
Days of the week, months, seasons	
Time and date	Asking time
	Asking date
	Stating time
	Stating date
	Time at which
	Dates on which
	Approximate time
	Approximate date
	Sequence of events
	Duration
	Frequency
	Reference to present
	Reference to past
	Reference to future
	Being early
	Being late

Topics	Sub-topics and examples
Daily routine	Waking (up)
	Getting up
	Washing
	Shaving
	Brushing
	Dressing
	Undressing
	Changing
	Going out
	Setting off
	Getting to school
	Getting to work
	Meals
	Coming home
	Evening activities
	Clubs
	Organisations
	Bedtime
Leisure and weekend activities	Meeting friends
	Sports
	Hobbies
	Excursions
	TV
	Radio
	Cinema
	Disco
	Jobs
	Do it yourself
	Church
Weather	
Everyday weather conditions	
Light and darkness	
Sky	
Extremes	Heat
	Cold
	Storm
	Flood
	Drought
Forecasts	

Topics	Sub-topics and examples
Home and family	
Houses and flats	Address
	Situation
	Types
	Appearance
	Built of . . .
	Layout
	Rooms
	Furniture
	Furnishings
	Equipment
	Heat
	Light
	New houses
	Old houses
	Buying houses
	Selling houses
	Renting
	Cleaning
	Removal
Kitchen	Cooking
	Equipment
	Utensils
	Washing up
	Chores
	Washing
	Ironing
Bedroom	Bedding
	Bedclothes
	Sleeping
	Waking
	Furniture
Bathroom	Washing
	Toilet articles
	WC
Living/dining-room	Leisure
	Meals
	Laying the table
	Clearing up
Garden	Layout
	Common flowers
	Common fruits
	Common vegetables
	Equipment

Topics	Sub-topics and examples
Family and social relationships	
Family relationships	e.g. mother
Family celebrations	Birthday
	Christmas
	Wedding
Meeting, visiting, staying with, looking after family/friends	
	Visits
	Parties
	Dances
	Introductions
	Greetings
	Goodbyes
Social courtesies	Asking for
	Thanking
	Apologising
	Inviting
	Accepting
	Declining
Social correspondence	Postcards
	Informal letters
	Formal letters
Quarrels and disputes	Family
	Neighbours
School	
Buildings	Appearance
	Layout
Classrooms	Furniture
	Equipment
	Pupils' equipment
Playground	Games
Pupils and staff	
The school day	Subjects
	Timetable
	Classes
	Activities
	Outings
	Breaks
	Meals
Behaviour in school	Attitudes
	Discipline
	Praise
	Blame
Examinations	

Topics	Sub-topics and examples
Travel	
Vehicles	Land
	Sea
	Air
	Speed
	Common parts
Journeys	Planning
	Routes
	Maps
	Tickets
	Booking
	Travel agents
	Catching
	Missing
	Departure
	Stops
	Arrival
	Hitch-hiking
	Hostelling
	Stations
	Ports
	Airports
	Service stations
	Traffic noises
	Outings
	Excursions
	Picnics
	Going abroad
	Countries
	Customs
	Passports
	Exchange visits
Hazards	Accident
	Breakdown
	Delays
	Help in difficulties
Luggage	e.g. cases
Hotel, restaurant, café inn, bar	
Buildings	Appearance
	Layout

Topics	Sub-topics and examples
Staff	
Procedures	Booking
	Cancellation
	Arrival
	Departure
	Bills
	Tips
Rooms	Comforts
	Facilities
Meals, snacks	Menu
	Courses
	Dishes
	Drinks
	Ordering
	Paying for
	Serving
	Common methods of cooking, e.g. roasting
Incidents	Accidents
	Deficiencies
	Complaints

Shops and shopping

Types of shop	Common shops
Goods for sale	Food
	Drink
	Clothes
	Consumer goods, e.g. record-player
	Shop windows
Quantities	Weight
	Length
	Containers, e.g. tin of . . .
	Money
	Prices
	Counting
	Buying
	Selling
	Delivering
Markets	Street markets
	Supermarkets
	Hypermarkets
Advertising, display	Posters
	Advertisements
Banks	Obtaining cash
	Changing currency
Post office	e.g. stamps

Topics	Sub-topics and examples
Cinema, theatre, circus, fairground	
A visit to	Seating
	Tickets
	Performers
Types of film, play, concert	
Audience reactions	
Personal tastes	
Radio and television	
Use of	Sets
Channels and stations	Of own country
	Of foreigh country
Types of programme	e.g. news
Personal tastes	
Sports, amusements, hobbies	
Major sports and games	Matches
	Prizes
Places for sport	e.g. swimming pool
Children's games	
Toys	
Parlour games	Cards
	Chess
Hobbies	Photography
	Model-making
	Dancing
	Pets
	Collecting
Outdoor pursuits	e.g. camping
Personal likes and dislikes, with reasons	
Town and village life	
Urban and rural environments	Description
	Advantages and disadvantages
	Pollution
Streets and traffic	
Public buildings	
Visit to a city	
Visit to a village	
Visit to the countryside	Common birds
	Common animals
	Common flowers
	Common trees
	Common insects

Topics	Sub-topics and examples
Visit to the zoo	Common wild animals
Visit to a farm or	
vineyard	Common farm animals
	Animal noises
	Common buildings
	Common crops
	Activities, e.g. ploughing
	Equipment

Trades and professions

Manual trades	Most common (with associated verbs)
Professions	Most common (with associated verbs)
Places of work	Factory
	Workshop
	Office
Common tools	e.g. hammer
Getting a job	
Losing a job	
Unemployment	
Future career	

Holidays and festivals

Seaside	Features, e.g. beach
	Beach activities
	Ports
	Boats
	Islands
Countryside	Features, e.g. fields
Mountains	Features, e.g. summits
Going on holiday	Britain
	Abroad
Holiday correspondence	e.g. postcards
Camping and caravanning	
Festivals	e.g. Easter
National days	e.g. 14th July

Events

Faits divers	Home and abroad
War	Army, Navy, Air Force
	Spying
	Escape

Topics	*Sub-topics and examples*
Rescue operations	Disasters: flood
	earthquakes
	fire
	avalanche
	famine
	explosion
	air
	sea
	road
	rail
The law	Police
	Crimes
Personal incidents	Misunderstanding
	Disappearance
	Forgetting
	Losing and finding
	Losing one's way
	Mistaken identity
	Coincidence
	Accidents
	Amusing experiences
	Helping and being helped
Reactions	Bravery
	Fear
Mystery and adventure	Treasure
	Disguise
	Plots
Communications	
Correspondence	Materials
	Postal service
Telephone	
Telegram	
The press	e.g. newspapers
Arts	
Music	Playing common instruments
	Playing/listening to e.g. records
	Types of music
Drama	Plays
	Actors
Art	e.g. drawing
Books	Libraries
	Types of literature, e.g. novels
Exhibitions	Museum
	Art gallery

Topics	Sub-topics and examples
Fantasy and imagination	
Dreams	
Ghosts	
Magic	
Legends	
Names of natural features and products	
Common geographical features	
Very common geographical proper names	Regions
	Towns
	Mountains
	Rivers
	Seas
Points of compass	Directions
Basic products and industries	
	e.g. coal
	Common minerals, e.g. iron
	Common materials, e.g. wood
Government	
Local government services	Fire
	Police
	Ambulance
	Taxation
	Refuse collection
	Town Hall
Central government names	President, Republic
	(*Recommended Basic Requirements for Examinations in French*. Scottish Examination Board)

VOCABULARY IN CONTEXT

Even when you have established the areas of vocabulary that you will need to be familiar with (e.g. the terms required when describing people involved in daily routines, terms which occur in any exchange of information on social issues such as unemployment, the cost of living, human rights, etc.), you will still need to know *where* you are going to find this vocabulary presented in a way which will enable you to study it meaningfully and learn it. It would not be advisable to go straight to the dictionary or to attempt to learn ready-made lists of words. Words do not occur in isolation: their meaning is always partly determined by *context* and it is when words are presented in context that their function, and the way they relate to and associate with other words, is most clearly shown. The most efficient way to learn what words mean and how they work is to meet them and study them in context.

It is therefore advisable to begin by basing your vocabulary study on a *collection of texts* which include the language situations which you need to cover. A very useful selection of literary and non-literary passages for study is contained in the *Penguin French Reader* (for further suggestions see p. 49). An anthology of this type, chosen to extend your vocabulary in a planned fashion, should be regarded as an essential supplement to your course-book. At the beginning of your course it will be wiser and more convenient to use a collection of passages chosen by an experienced editor or tutor but eventually you should aim at making your own selection from your wider reading.

ASPECTS INVOLVED IN BUILDING VOCABULARY

Before you embark on your programme of vocabulary-building it is as well to understand exactly what learning an item of vocabulary means. It will help you when studying new words and when recording them in a learnable form. It is clear from the way that many students record vocabulary to be learnt that knowing a word in the foreign language is a more complex process than they realise.

What is involved will differ slightly according to whether the word is intended to become part of your *active* rather than your *passive* vocabulary. Nevertheless if you have successfully learnt a new word it will imply that you have mastered a number of aspects:

(a)   You will be able to *recognise* its spoken or written form.
(b)   You will be able to *recall* it from your memory, *pronounce* it acceptably and, in writing, be able to *spell* it correctly.
(c)   You will be able to *relate* the word correctly to an idea or object.
(d)   You will have learned the *grammatical elements* which belong to the word and enable you to fit it correctly into a sentence. For example, if it is a noun you will know its gender: le problème du chômage; if it is a verb you will know which preposition follows it: cet enfant risque de tomber, elle apprend à nager, and so on.
(e)   You will know whether the word is *appropriate* in a given situation or context, that is to say whether it is formal or familiar.
(f)   You will know which other items of vocabulary the word may *collocate* with (i.e. which it will "go with"). For example:

 * Le terrain de camping se couvre de caravanes, (not "roulottes").
 * Le tracteur s'arrêta devant la barrière du champ (not "la grille").
 * Cet enfant apporte beaucoup de satisfaction à ses parents (not "amène").
 * Il faut faire attention en traversant la rue (not "franchissant").

(g)   You will understand the *connotation* of a word and will therefore know whether it has overtones of approval or disapproval. In the following sentences, for example, the words underlined in pairs are similar in meaning but have different connotations:

 * Tous les élèves ont ricané/ri.
 * Assis à la terrasse d'un café, il lorgnait/regardait toutes les femmes qui passaient.

Although points (a) to (f) might suggest that *knowing* a new word involves perhaps more than you realised, it by no means follows that *remembering* it is going to be that much more difficult. Experiments on the learning of vocabulary have shown that asking yourself meaningful questions about a word and processing it actually help you to remember it.

Points (e) to (f) further underline the importance of learning vocabulary in a meaningful context. It is the context which really presents in a learnable, recallable form those aspects of a new item of vocabulary described in (e) to (f). Instead, therefore, of recording lists of new words to be learnt it is more effective to ensure that the new material is contained in continuous passages or at least complete sentences. Your vocabulary notebook should be not so much a list of words (only very elementary vocabulary can be safely learned in this way) but rather a collection of extracts and illustrative examples.

USING A SHORT PASSAGE FOR VOCABULARY-BUILDING – AN ILLUSTRATION

A major part of your vocabulary-building should be based on the study of *short written passages*. The following passage has been worked as an example of how a text may be studied intensively in order to extend knowledge of vocabulary. It is advisable that when studying such a text that you go further than underlining the new words and looking them up in a French–English dictionary. It is very important *to do something* with new material to be learnt, to process it and if you can, become actively involved with it. Experience shows that if material to be learnt not only means something but means something to the *learner* then the material is more effectively stored in, and recalled from, the memory.

You must first of all choose a text for study with some care, asking yourself whether it is relevant to the lexical areas which you will be required to cover. If it is too obscure, too technical or too specialised or if it is top-heavy with terms that you do not recognise, then turn to something else. The following passage is suitable because the vocabulary and subject-matter are typical of the French which you might be asked to recognise or use in an A-level translation or essay paper.

Remember that it is important to study and learn vocabulary in context. You will therefore approach the text you have chosen not as a random collection of words (to be looked up in the dictionary) but as an arrangement of words which form a continuous, organised piece of writing and a coherently developed argument. You might then usefully follow the following steps:

1. Begin by reading through the passage which follows carefully until you have grasped the *central idea or argument*. Try to express this idea, in French, as if you were explaining the gist of the passage to someone who had not read it.

Etre le témoin d'un accident de la route, c'est brutalement prendre conscience que 'cela n'arrive pas qu'aux autres', d'autant qu'une conduite prudente ne garantit même pas d'échapper aux facteurs impondérables. Qu'un fou du volant croise son parcours ou que son moteur vienne à défaillir et tout automobiliste peut basculer, d'un moment à l'autre, dans le camp des victimes impuissantes.

Il ressort, si l'on s'en tient aux prévisions statistiques, que ce risque est de l'ordre d'un sur deux cent cinquante. La réalité, quant à elle, apparaît autrement effrayante. Dans soixante quinze pour cent des cas, les accidentés ne doivent s'en prendre qu'à leur propre façon de se comporter au volant: mauvaise appréciation des distances, réflexe tardif, coup de volant trop brusque, vitesse excessive, nervosité. Telles sont les conclusions des enquêtes réalisées, entre autres, par la Prévention Routière pour qui la fautre de conduite constitue bel et bien la cause principale des accidents.

Il reste pourtant que la totalité de ces défaillances humaines se voit subordonner à un fléau plus meurtrier encore: l'alcool. Responsable d'un accident sur trois sur le réseau routier français, l'alcool tue. Plus de trois mille des accidents mortels provoqués chaque année sur les routes de France ont pour cause un excès de boisson. Il ne faut plus se résigner à recevoir le salaire de l'horreur!

2. You might briefly *summarise* the passage as follows:
Certains conducteurs sont plus susceptibles que d'autres d'avoir un accident de voiture parce que la cause principale des accidents est le conducteur lui-même, et surtout le conducteur qui a bu de l'alcool.

3. Make use of your dictionary. Once you have grasped what the writer is saying and doing then study of the vocabulary can begin. There will be words which you have not understood or words which you have only half understood and words which you *think* you have understood (possibly because they resemble the English term). You will need to consult a dictionary. Because it is important to exploit the text for vocabulary-learning purposes it is best to use a French–French dictionary (such as the *Larousse Dictionnaire du Français Contemporain*) and if you can, an illustrated monolingual dictionary (such as *Littré*). Use these tools to help you to define, in French, the *meaning* of a new word; note those *synonyms* which could replace it in the text and above all note the *example sentences* containing the new word which the dictionary provides.

4. Concentrate on *thematic vocabulary* in the passage: it is such vocabulary which is the more effectively reinforced by context. It may be of two types:

(a) vocabulary which comprises terms which relate to the *content* of the passage (and to what the writer is saying);
(b) vocabulary which comprises terms which relate to the *structure* of the passage (and to what the writer is doing).

In the text we are studying here (a) would include those terms which relate closely to driving, vehicles and accidents, e.g.:

> Un accident de la route/un accidenté/le témoin d'un accident/la conduite prudente/un automobiliste/un fou du volant/leur façon de se comporter au volant/un fou du volant croise son parcours/son moteur vient à défaillir/la mauvaise appréciation des distances/le réflexe tardif/la vitesse excessive/un excès de boisson/la nervosité etc.

(b)   would include those words and phrases which express cause:

> La faute de conduite constitue la cause principale des accidents/l'alcool est responsable d'un accident sur trois/les accidentés ne doivent s'en prendre qu'à leur propre façon de se comporter/provoquer un accident/les accidents ont pour cause un excès de boisson etc.

All of these terms have been taken from the text but it is useful to find further illustrative examples in the monolingual dictionary (having first decided that the term is useful and should become part of your active vocabulary):

un témoin: personne qui a vu ou entendu quelque chose et qui
        peut le certifier
        Elle a été témoin d'une scène touchante, de leur
        dispute.
        L'entrevue des chefs d'Etat a eu lieu sans témoins.

The examples will show you how to use the word with grammatical accuracy: Elle a été (tense) témoin (no article) d'un accident (témoin followed by de). They will also help you to understand which words "témoin", when used in this way, may collocate with:

        Elle a été témoin d'un accident.
                d'une entrevue.
                d'une dispute.
                d'une scène.

but not

    **   Elle a été témoin d'un film à la télé.
    **   Elle a été témoin du Président qui arriva à Orly.
**These sentences are ungrammatical
All of this information is essential if you wish to reuse the word correctly.

5. Rearrange new words in sentences of your own creation. Experiments have shown that if the learner rearranges new words in sentences of his *own* creation (rather than try to learn them from a list) then memorisation of them is more efficient. In a test based on the above passage students who simply concocted "fantasy" sentences (un accident sur trois se produit par un excès de bonbons; un accident sur trois se produit par la faute de mon grand-père) learned more efficiently than those who tried to learn the words from a random list.

6. Pay particular attention to, and try to understand, *structure*

words, i.e. words which indicate that the writer is *doing* things. These may include introducing an example, or indicating that the meaning of something is to be explained, or pointing out that something is obvious, or showing that he is introducing an opposing point of view, or reaching a conclusion, and so on. From the present text you would select: Il ressort que, telles sont les conclusions, il reste pourtant que. These are words which help to present an argument and you will need a stock of such terms for your own essay-writing.

7. Study *synonyms* in the text. A way of using the text as a point of departure from which you widen your lexical knowledge is the study of synonyms. If you look up the word s'empêcher in the *Dictionnaire du Français Contemporain* you will find se retenir given as a synonym; sage, averti, prévoyant are given as synonyms of prudent. If it is possible to use these alternatives in the original sentence then clearly you will be adding to your vocabulary. However, synonyms should be treated with some caution and it is advisable to learn only those which you can be sure of as possible substitutes for the word in the original passage (and you will be sure because the dictionary examples make it clear or because you have checked with a native speaker or tutor). As there is much truth in the claim that there is no such thing as a true synonym, it is probably more valuable to try to establish the *differences* between *near-synonyms* so that you can use both terms with precision. Concentrate for example, on the *difference* between le spectacle/la vue; un conducteur/un automobiliste; une défaillance/une faute; réfléchir/se concentrer, etc.

8. Study the *thematic vocabulary* in the text. Doing this helps to form clusters of words which are then easier to memorise; memory appears to have a "snowball effect", with like adhering to like. It is helpful to use this principle to build on the "family" of the word and to extend vocabulary in this way. If the new word is a verb then check the dictionary to see if there is a corresponding adjective or noun which belongs to the word-family. Follow a similar procedure if the new word is an adjective or a noun. Words taken from the text above will give:

> La route: routier, accident routier, un bon réseau routier, la circulation routière, etc.
> Un conducteur: conduire, il conduit sa voiture avec beaucoup de maîtrise; il conduit très prudemment.
> défaillir: une défaillance; une défaillance d'attention peut provoquer un accident; tout conducteur demeure à la merci d'une défaillance mécanique.

9. Use the dictionary examples carefully to build *further sentences and phrases* which will expand the thematic vocabulary contained in the text. It is worth noting that by being able to make these *transformations* (e.g. from verb to noun, from adjective to noun, etc.) you not only increase your vocabulary but also find further ways of constructing sentences. For example, the nominalisation of se comporter in:

● Il risque d'avoir un accident parce qu'il se comporte d'une façon très dangereuse au volant.

This will produce:

● Il risque d'avoir un accident en raison de son comportement très dangereux au volant.

10. Produce a *plan* of the structure of the text. When you have thoroughly studied the vocabulary of the text and have recorded definitions, examples, synonyms and useful "transformations" (e.g. verb transformed to noun, etc.) in your vocabulary notebook, it is time to turn your attention to the *way the argument or the ideas in the passage are presented*. Read the text again carefully analysing the main developments of the argument or the main stages in the author's chain of thought. The passage on pp.44–45 has three main divisions: which correspond to the three paragraphs.

Think of a *subtitle* for *each section* and of a *title* for the *whole passage*, then note down the ideas which are developed in each section. This analysis will produce a plan such as the following:

● La plupart de accidents de la route se produisent par la faute du conducteur:
  (a) Tout conducteur risque d'être victime d'un accident:
     (i) la conduite prudente ne garantit pas contre le fou du volant, une défaillance mécanique;
     (ii) le risque est de l'ordre d'un sur 250.
  (b) Mais c'est presque toujours la faute du conducteur lui-même:
     (i) dans 75% des cas il s'agit d'une erreur humaine;
     (ii) conclusions des enquêtes de la Prévention Routière.
  (c) L'alcool est responsable de la plupart des accidents:
     (i) un accident sur 3, plus de 3 mille accidents provoqués par l'alcool;
     (ii) conclusion: il ne faut pas se résigner.

Working on the passage in order to produce a plan will help you to remember new vocabulary and the plan itself can be used as a means of practice and revision. When you have completed the intensive study put the original passage aside and attempt to reconstruct it orally or in writing using the plan and your vocabulary notes for guidance. By doing this you will begin the process of making passive vocabulary (that which you merely recognise) part of the stock of terms which you are able to use actively. As you can compare your own version with the original it means that you have available a self-correcting exercise which can be used as a means of revision on subsequent occasions.

A STEP FURTHER

ARRANGE YOUR STUDY MATERIAL FOR REVISION AND SELF-TESTING

When you have completed the work on a text you will need to arrange your study material so that you are able to revise and test what you have learnt. You can of course list the new expressions on one side of your vocabulary notebook with the English equivalent entered against them on the other side of the page. However, it will help you to revise the lexical item more efficiently and fully (i.e. with consideration for those points listed on p. 43) if you test your knowledge of it in other ways as well and if possible in context.

(a) You will have noted the dictionary definition of most of the new items of vocabulary. You can record the new word on one side of the page against its definition in French entered on the other side of the page and test yourself by finding the word to fit the definition.

(b) The dictionary examples and sentences from the original text can be arranged as a self-testing device. Write the example sentence on one side of your book leaving the target word blank:

> J'aime voyager avec lui, c'est un conducteur
> très_____. (prudent)
> La Prévention Routière a effectué_____
> sur les causes des accidents de la route. (une enquête)
> Il a été_____de leur dispute, il a tout
> entendu. (témoin)
> On voyait des_____de toutes sortes:
> camions, taxis, voitures, autobus. (véhicules)

(c) You can extract a short passage from the original text, leaving certain words blank:

> Etre le_____d'un accident de la route, c'est brutalement
> prendre_____que cela n'arrive pas qu'aux autres d'autant
> qu'une_____prudent ne_____même pas d'échapper aux
> facteurs_____.

You will find that testing yourself in this way will make the task of learning and revising vocabulary more interesting. Also the very process of arranging and thinking about the tests themselves will help you towards a better understanding and recall of the words that you are aiming to learn.

FURTHER READING

Collected passages for intensive study:

S. Lee and D. Ricks. *Penguin French Reader*. Penguin
G. J. P. Courtenay. *Les Meilleures Pages du Figaro*. Longman
G. J. P. Courtenay. *Encore du 'Figaro'*. Longman
A. Deville and R. Steele. *Textes pour Aujourd'hui – Extraits de Elle*. Didier
E. Dangon, F. Weiss et al. *Lire en Français*. Hatier
Dictionaries:
> *Dictionnaire du Français Contemporain*. Larousse
> *Dictionnaire du Français Langue Étrangère*. Bordas
> *Collins-Robert English–French, French–English Dictionary*. Collins.

Chapter 5

The essay in French

GETTING STARTED

The essay or free composition is a major feature of the A-level or post A-level examination and accordingly is awarded a substantial proportion of the total subject mark (between one-fifth and one-sixth). Writing an essay in French is a complex and therefore demanding activity which requires competence in a variety of skills. It tests the accurate use of a knowledge of vocabulary which should relate to a wide range of non-specialist subject areas. It requires the ability to construct grammatically accurate sentences and to arrange material in a coherent and logical order in French in a way which would be acceptable to a *native speaker*. In addition to all this, the student is expected to have a flow of ideas and to invent the content of the essay.

When getting started on preparation for the essay in French it is therefore essential to build the appropriate foundations early in your course, making sure from the beginning that your general language work and your reading in French is made to feed into your essay-writing. Ask yourself whether the grammar work in your course-book enables you to practise structures useful in narrating, in describing people and places, in expressing opinions, in presenting an argument and counter-argument, in enumerating reasons for and against, and in emphasising points and reaching a conclusion. For these are some of the *functions* which need to be performed when writing an essay and they should be practised over a period of time (some of these structures are discussed in this and the following chapter). The acquisition of vocabulary should also take place progressively and should be planned to cover a wide range of everyday topics (see Ch. 4). Your course-book will probably cover a certain number of themes but you should make certain that a sufficiently wide range is provided. You might begin by checking your course-book against the topics included in the past essay questions listed below. Treat the texts merely as a list of relevant themes, to be *extended* by further reading. In other words, you should begin your examination preparation by organising your language study so that it always has a purpose: in this instance the improvement of your essay-writing in French.

ESSENTIAL PRINCIPLES

REQUIREMENTS OF THE EXAMINATION

It will help you to organise your work effectively if you have a clear idea from the outset of exactly what will be required of you in the examination and an understanding of what the examiner will look for when assessing the essay in French.

An opportunity to display what you know

If you began by looking at the *examiners' reports* on the way in which candidates perform in the essay paper you might not feel very encouraged. Too many candidates produce disappointing work in this part of the examination and examples of outstanding or good work are too infrequent. There is, however, a very positive lesson which can be drawn from the examiners' criticisms. Those essays which fall below the required standard or those which are satisfactory but undistinguished are often unsatisfactory or unimpressive *because the student has not responded fully to the possibilities of what is largely an open-ended exercise.* The essay paper with its choice of titles is intended to give candidates the opportunity to display their knowledge of vocabulary and structures and their ability to communicate in written French. Examiners are fond of pointing out that whereas the prose is designed to find out what the candidates do not know, the essay is there to give them the chance to show *what they do know.* There is a good deal of truth in this but many candidates do not appear to be aware of the fact that the essay is intended as a showcase in which they are expected to display knowledge of idiom and of a variety of vocabulary and structure. It is a fact which should be firmly grasped at an early stage in your preparation for the examination. In this paper you will be given a good deal of *freedom* to display your knowledge of French and your essay-writing skill. Ensuring that you have something worth displaying should therefore be one of your main objectives when preparing for the examination.

The ground to be covered

When working towards the examination it is also essential to have as clear an idea as possible of the ground to be covered, which will involve having some idea of the standard of essay-writing which you are *currently* able to reach and of that which constitutes a successful A-level essay. For most students the ground to be covered will be that which lies between O-level and A-level and this raises the often repeated question of whether a good O-level essay would be awarded a pass at A-level. It is not possible to give a hard and fast answer, but it may be said that while the good, accurately written O-level essay may be judged satisfactory at A-level, it would not be awarded a high mark. It is clearly not an adequate model to aim at. To enable you to appreciate the difference between an O-level and an A-level essay, model A level essays are provided later in this chapter and in the next chapter. It will suffice to point out at this stage that the good O-level essay should ideally be a *starting-point*. It will be necessary to progress to a greater level of complexity in expressing ideas, both in narrating and describing, and to a point where a considerably wider range of vocabulary and grammatical structures can be used accurately and spontaneously.

Although you will be expected as an A-level candidate to be more ambitious in handling French, it is still necessary to follow the recommendation that you should write *within the limits* of your knowledge of the language. There is no place for invention or experiment. To maintain a satisfactory standard of accuracy you should use only vocabulary which has been thoroughly learnt and structures which you are confident of using with precision. However, the point to be made is that the limits within which the A-level candidate writes his essay are expected to be much less restricted than those which are acceptable at O-level. The task facing you throughout your A-level course will involve progressing systematically beyond the O-level essay, with the aim of constructing sentences and paragraphs with an increasing degree of sophistication, but always working towards the new from what has already been soundly grasped.

GENERAL CRITERIA OF ASSESSMENT

Study of the model essays below will provide useful examples of how a good essay should be written but it will be of help to you if you are familiar with the general criteria on which assessment of an A-level essay is usually based. Such criteria should also be used to guide your preparation and practice prior to the examination.

What then will the examiner be looking for? The guidance provided in syllabus regulations published by the Examination Board is always rather limited but should of course be noted. Candidates are usually required to write between 250 and 400 words of continuous French on one title selected from a choice of 5–6. Note that the prescribed *minimum* number of words varies from one Examination Board to another: the exact number should be checked in the syllabus regulations published by the Board. The titles may call for narrative, descriptive, discursive or documentary writing and possibly the writing of dialogue. There may also be the recommendation that there should be evidence in the essay of accurate grammar and syntax, apt and varied vocabulary and appropriate French idiom and that the argument or discussion should be carefully planned, developed and illustrated.

Problems relating to specific types of writing (e.g. narrative, descriptive, discursive, etc.) will be examined below and in the following chapter but it is necessary first to consider the essay under the headings of "Content", "Planning", "Grammatical accuracy", "Use of vocabulary and idiom" and "Style and fluency". It is certain that the marking-scheme for the essay will be based on some or all of these aspects and in some schemes a specific proportion of the marks will be allotted to each. It is therefore appropriate to examine each heading in turn and to consider the questions that the examiner will ask in assessing the work. It will also be possible to elucidate some of the points which should guide your preparation for the essay as well as those that you should have firmly in mind on the day of the examination.

Content of the essay

When your essay is assessed it will be read a number of times but in the first instance the examiner will need to satisfy himself that the content is *relevant to the title chosen*. Irrelevance could be a serious fault in the work. If, for example, only one-third of the material is relevant, then it is quite probable that the essay will then be marked out of one-third of the total mark. There are a number of factors which lead to irrelevance and you should understand them in order to avoid them.

1. Irrelevance may result from trying to adapt a previously written and well-rehearsed essay on a similar subject. A title such as the following: <u>Si l'on proposait d'installer une centrale nucléaire dans votre région seriez-vous pour ou contre une telle proposition?</u> raises the question of pollution and it is quite likely that the subject will have been discussed and prepared during the course. However, it would be very unwise to repeat a pre-learned essay which is basically a *general* discussion of pollution and its effects on the environment: it is likely that you would digress to describe aspects of pollution which have nothing to do with nuclear power stations. Clearly, the problem of pollution could be used in an argument directed against the installation of a nuclear power station and therefore material which you have learnt in a different context could be reused. The point is that it must also be *rehandled* to fit into a rather different essay with a different angle. An essay should not contain material which *could* be relevant; that material must be clearly *shown* to be relevant. To take another example: if the essay title invites you to discuss the decisions which you will have to make on leaving school then it would be appropriate to discuss choice of employment. The pitfall to be avoided would be the digression into a general discussion of unemployment. The examiner will be impressed only by genuine decisions, those which you as a school-leaver are likely to have to take. To check that your essay is relevant, ask yourself when you have written a practice essay whether anyone reading it without having seen the title would be able to reformulate the title on the basis of what you have written. That is what the examiner may well ask.

2. Irrelevance often results from a superficial consideration of the title: the candidate focuses on a "cue word", "chômage", "violence", "la femme", "pollution" and fails to follow the direction of the question set. It is therefore essential if the essay is to be fully relevant, *to analyse the title* in order to discover whether there is more than one aspect which must be treated.

The form in which the title is presented may vary quite widely from the brief, open-ended title (Les villes neuves, Oxford, 1977, or Un orage, London, 1984) to the more complex title which has more than one part to it. For example:

(i) Au cours d'un voyage que vous avez fait seul(e) à l'étranger, vous avez perdu tout votre argent. Comment avez-vous réagi à cette situation? Racontez comment vous avez pu rentrer chez vous. (London, 1979)

(ii) Analysez les arguments pour et contre la télévision. Quelle est votre opinion personnelle?

It is essential when tackling questions which are structured in this way to show a clear response to every part of the question; the various elements should *not* be considered as *optional* suggestions. If you were writing an essay on the first title, for example, you would be expected to include some account of: (a) travelling abroad; (b) losing money; (c) your reactions to that loss; and (d) how the journey home was accomplished. The omission of one of these elements could result in the needless loss of a quarter of the total mark.

The second question has been carefully framed to make it clear that the candidate is expected to deal with: (a) arguments for; (b) arguments against; and (c) he is invited to express a personal opinion. It is not necessary that equal treatment should be given to each aspect, but each should certainly be given due consideration if the essay is to qualify as entirely relevant.

Interpreting the question involves not only identifying its parts but reaching a clear understanding of the meaning of the title. It would be inadvisable to embark on an essay title unless you were confident of its meaning and particularly of the meaning of the keywords contained in it. The following are essay titles which candidates have misinterpreted:

(i) L'importance du pétrole pour les pays occidentaux.
(ii) La vraie maladie de l'époque où nous vions, c'est la hâte.
(iii) L'influence exercée par la publicité sur la vie moderne est-elle bonne ou mauvaise?

Keywords were misunderstood: "hâte" as hate, "pétrole" as petrol and "publicité" as publicity and essays were written which were largely irrelevant.

The first step therefore, in tackling the essay is to understand and analyse the title and to follow its prescriptions. If you are asked to discuss the influence which school has had on the formation of *your* character, then do not simply discuss *one's* character in general. If you are required to examine the most important decisions in your life, the discussion should include more than *one* decision, and if you are asked to discuss the role of sport in France, it is not sufficient to discuss the role of sport in general. Read the question carefully and give attention to the details.

The purpose of the essay is to test the candidate's ability to communicate ideas or to narrate a series of events in accurate idiomatic French. How important are the ideas or the content of a narrative and how much attention will the examiner give them? The answer is that of course the content is important but that the examiner will base his assessment on a number of factors, with content being only one of them. The other factors will be *grammatical accuracy, knowledge of vocabulary and idiom*, and *arrangement and stylistic qualities*. Together these are certainly more important than content alone. You should aim at a certain level of complexity and detail as the expression of ideas which are over-simplified does not allow you to display the range of vocabulary and structure which will gain credit. On the other hand, accurate use of the language should not be sacrificed in an attempt to write at an intellectual or imaginative level which is beyond your powers of expression. It is unlikely that original ideas or interesting incidents will compensate for French which is inaccurate and anglicised. What you should aim at is a *balance* between language and content. If that balance is maintained and you are able to produce an essay which is virtually free of error, in which there is a good range of vocabulary and structure used to express mature ideas or to narrate interesting events, then the essay will undoubtedly be placed in the very highest category.

Planning the essay

The examiner will look for evidence of planning in the essay. Basically, a well-planned essay is one in which the ideas are organised in such a way that they are communicated clearly and logically to the reader. In the A-level language essay an adequate plan need be no more complex than a brief introduction leading to the logical development of three or four main points, followed by a conclusion. Ideas should be complete and clearly structured, paragraphs should be coherent and linked. In short, there should be an obvious progression from introduction to conclusion which demonstrates that the candidate has overall control of what he or she has to communicate.

It is probably true to say that planning, to the examiner, will be more evident because of its *deficiencies* than because of its merits. You should therefore be aware of the main defects and take steps to avoid them. Ensure that the introduction is a genuine introduction to the material which follows and not a well-rehearsed, all-purpose one which is not really relevant. It is particularly the narrative essay which is often marred by the unnecessarily long, semi-relevant introduction. Because of its ready-made nature it contains banal generalities and therefore, particularly if it is too long, it simply reduces the opportunity to display the apt vocabulary and idiom which will gain credit.

Repetition is also a symptom of the poorly planned, rambling essay and should be avoided. Repetition of the ideas will create the impression that the direction of the argument has not been thought out, and endless repetition of vocabulary and key phrases given in the title will only convince the examiner that the candidate's range of expression is too limited to deal adequately with the topic.

Repetition is also a characteristic of the unsatisfactory conclusion, the one which is not a concluding statement towards which the essay has progressed in a logical fashion but a recapitulation of points already discussed which adds nothing to the development of the argument. It will be seen as a rather desperate attempt to "pad out" the essay in order to reach the minimum number of words required.

Grammatical accuracy in the essay

The importance of achieving a high standard of grammatical accuracy in the essay cannot be overemphasised. It is usually made clear in the syllabus that the essay must be written in grammatically and syntactically correct French and it is certain that a substantial proportion of the marks will be awarded for grammatical competence. However, the comments in examiners' reports suggest that satisfying this requirement is not easy and most students would probably agree that reaching a high standard of accuracy is likely to be their greatest stumbling-block. Accuracy is important but it does not necessarily follow that an essay with grammatical errors in it, even a number of grammatical errors, will not gain a high mark. It depends on the nature of the errors and the examiner will recognise serious and less serious errors. It is important that you should distinguish them too so that in your preparation you can give priority to eliminating those mistakes which are going to lose most marks. The two main categories of error are:

(a) what may be called *incidental* errors, those which candidates make on odd occasions, and which probably result from a lapse in concentration (for example, adjective agreements which are *sometimes* incorrect); and

(b) errors of *competence* which indicate that the candidate has a basic misunderstanding of the grammatical category in question (for example, the imperfect tense used with such uncertainty that it is clear that its function has not been clearly grasped).

It is, of course, the second type of error which is a main characteristic of the poor essay. If there are many errors of this type it is unlikely that other qualities in the essay (such as good ideas, a lively story) will compensate for them. The less serious type of error can be compensated for by evidence of grammatical competence elsewhere, good choice of vocabulary or the attempt to display a variety of structures. The examiner will try to get your mistakes into perspective; you should do the same when going through marked work, analysing your errors and organising your revision.

Your aim will be to have a sound knowledge of all grammatical categories in order to produce accurate French in your essay. There are however, certain categories to which you should give particular attention because they prove to be such a frequent source of error. As they are so frequently misused by candidates the examiner is likely to give the way they have been handled close consideration when assessing the essay. They are:

(a) Verbs

Knowledge of the form and endings of regular and common irregular verbs; subject–verb agreement; use of tenses, particularly of the imperfect and past historic (or perfect) in narrative essays and of the conditional and imperfect (i.e. in "si" clauses) in discursive essays; the modal auxiliaries (devoir, pouvoir, etc.).

(b) The articles and the partitive	The definite article in its particularising and generalising function, its combination with "de", the use of the partitive (in other words understanding the alternation of les/des, des/de, etc.).
(c) Prepositions	The correct choice of preposition following certain verbs, adjectives and nouns; government of verbs (e.g. demander à quelqu'un de faire quelque chose, etc.); prepositions before names of places.
(d) Genders	Knowledge of the gender of nouns in common use and of those in which the ending provides a reliable indication of gender (e.g. la nation, le bonheur, le gouvernement, etc.).
(e) Pronouns	The ability to distinguish the use of il est/c'est; agreement of the pronoun and related noun; the ability to distinguish between direct and indirect object pronouns; the freedom with which pronouns are used to replace nouns in order to produce natural, fluent French.
(f) Adjective and participle agreement	The rule governing adjective and participle agreement is probably the most frequent example of the grammatical rule being understood but inconsistently applied. Candidates will usually remember to apply the rule if noun and adjective are in close proximity: de graves problèmes, notre vieille voiture, une décision importante. They frequently neglect the rule if noun and adjective are separated: la décision de passer trois ans à étudier à l'université est très importante; la grève des mineurs a rendu ces problèmes encore plus difficiles à résoudre; il est arrivé dans une voiture noire qui était couverte de boue. As candidates so frequently lose marks through haphazard application of the agreement rule, the advice must be that you should thoroughly understand its use in a wide variety of examples, determine the cause of your own mistakes and give particular attention to checking your work to ensure that agreements have been accurately made. The grammatical errors discussed above are not the only ones which occur in the essay but they are the most frequently occurring and are characteristic of the essay which falls below the required standard. It is therefore important to eliminate them from your own work.
Use of vocabulary and idiom in the essay	Under this heading the examiner will look for a range of apt vocabulary and idiom, that is for confident use of terms which are particularly relevant to the subject chosen. The good essay will show knowledge of those key terms which are essential to an intelligible exposition of the argument or to the clear description of a situation which is prescribed in the title. If, for example, the candidate has chosen to write on les causes des accidents de la route, the examiner would expect to find accurate use of vocabulary such as vitesse excessive, route trop étroite, virage dangereux, mauvais état de la route, défaillance mécanique, un excès de boisson, etc. and indeed the use of a variety of such terms would be positively rewarded. In a good essay there would not be undue repetition of vocabulary. It would not be an impressive essay in which each new point were introduced by: Une autre cause des accidents est . . ., but variety in the

use of expressions of cause would obviously be given credit: la plupart des accidents sont provoqués par; c'est une faute de conduite qui se trouve à l'origine de presque tous les accidents; un accident sur trois se produit par la faute de l'alcool; bon nombre d'accidents routiers ont pour cause un excès de boisson, etc.

The importance of building up a substantial vocabulary to cover a wide range of topics cannot be too frequently stressed. Precise use of a variety of expressions will improve the essay as an exercise in communication and impress the examiner. Ensure therefore that your vocabulary is not limited in scope, repetitive, over-simplified or worse, anglicised and invented. These are terms commonly found in examiners' notes appended to essays which are not of satisfactory standard.

Style and fluency in the essay

Here the examiner will consider the combined effect of planning and arrangement, grammatical accuracy and precise use of vocabulary and idiom. The central questions which he will have in mind are:

1. Does the essay read in a way which would be acceptable to a native speaker?
2. Has the essay been put together so that meaning is consistently clear?

The essay which has a high level of grammatical and lexical accuracy and says what it has to say in a way that an educated French person might say it, will be very highly rewarded. The less satisfactory essay will lack coherence; it may give the impression that it has been constructed line by line without any real sense of direction or communication; sentence patterns and word order may be noticeably anglicised: not basically ungrammatical perhaps, but simply awkward and un-French.

There are other considerations. The level of language or register should be *appropriate*. That is to say that the standard narrative or "discussion" essay should *not* be written in colloquial style. You should avoid using slang or familiar expressions (unless they were part of a dialogue inserted into a narrative essay and were appropriate). Some candidates are tempted to use in their essays what they have heard French people *say* without first making sure that it is also what they would *write*.

ASSESSING THE ESSAY IN FRENCH

When the examiner assesses your essay he will probably use a grid similar to the following in order to grade the work. You should use the grid to help you assess the standard of your own essay-writing and to understand what needs to be improved.

| Excellent (80–100%) | Extremely fluent French. Impressive range of structure and vocabulary. Good knowledge of idiom. Virtually free of error. Could be the work of a near-native speaker. |

Very good (70–80%)	Not quite as impressive as the above in terms of fluency and range. Very few errors and normally not more than the occasional serious grammatical error.
Good (60–70%)	French carefully handled. Reasonably fluent with a fair range of vocabulary and idiom. Not many errors and normally not more than four or five serious grammatical errors. Likely to be a grade A candidate.
Safe (50–60%)	Fair range of vocabulary. Some use of idiom but not particularly ambitious. Reasonably sound grammar. Correct verb forms and agreements on the whole. Knowledge of morphology basically sound. Too many errors for a "good".
Satisfactory (40–50%)	Grammar rather shaky, style clumsy, a little anglicised but comprehensible. Accuracy inconsistent but evidence of basic grammatical knowledge. Some weakness involving verbs and agreements. Vocabulary mainly accurate but limited and/or repetitive. Little idiom.
Less than satisfactory (30–40%)	Similar to above but greater frequency of errors. Nature of error shows there is lack of basic competence. Poor use of verbs and tenses, the article/partitive and prepositions. Too many errors in vocabulary; gender errors and inventions. Anglicised. Weak idiom.
Weak (20–30%)	Many errors in grammar, idiom and vocabulary. Meaning too often obscure. Very anglicised but some redeeming features (e.g. some success in communication, examples of correct structure, some apt vocabulary, etc.).
Very weak (0–20%)	Hardly a sentence without serious error. Much basic incompetence. Heavily anglicised. Meaning obscured.

Chapter 6

The narrative essay

The narrative essay will involve an account of real or imaginary events. It may include description of settings, objects or people and the expression of the personal reactions of characters who feature in the story, or of the writer. It may include dialogue. The way in which the essay title is framed sometimes makes it clear that certain or all of these elements are required.

In this first example: Etant parti(e) faire une longue promenade en montagne, vous avez perdu votre chemin et vous avez été obligé(e) de passer la nuit à la belle étoile. Racontez votre aventure et décrivez les paysages que vous avez vus (London, 1983), the title requires the narration of a series of events and actions together with some description.

In this second example: Un incendie a éclaté dans un grand hôtel où vous passiez la nuit. Quelles ont été vos réactions? Comment avez-vous pu être sauvé(e)?, the title requires the candidate to give an account of a series of actions and a description of emotions and reactions such as alarm, fear, determination, etc. It would of course be acceptable to include dialogue in such essays and indeed the title may specifically require the inclusion of dialogue or that the story be told in dialogue form.

Consider this third example: Un vieux Français raconte à son petit-fils quelques-unes de ses expériences en zone occupée pendant la guerre (AEB, 1983). Whether description or dialogue is prescribed or not, to include them will provide variety and enable you to demonstrate a range of narrating skills, which if well handled will impress the examiner.

To prepare yourself for handling a *narrative* account you should be aware of its main technical features so that they can be practised. Above all, it will consist of a *sequence of actions* and this implies a knowledge of verbs and the use of tenses. You should understand the distinction between a narrative tense (past historic or perfect) and the imperfect; you should have in your active vocabulary a range of verbs of actions and movement; you should have accurate knowledge of the morphology of such verbs, particularly in the third and first person.

ESSENTIAL PRINCIPLES

TENSES

Accurate handling of tenses is related to the planning of the narrative, to the arrangement of events and action in the story. It is very important to have a clear notion of the order of events before you begin to write and this order should be established as you write your plan. If you are clear in your mind about how the story moves forward, you will be more likely to handle tenses accurately and to make the correct choice between a narrative tense and the imperfect. Remember that a narrative tense is required whenever you intend that the action of the story should move another step forward and that a series of verbs in a narrative tense implies a series of consecutive actions or events in the story you are narrating. If you are simply enumerating a sequence of past actions which are completed in chronological order, then a narrative tense is what is needed.

In the following passage the verbs, with one exception, are in the *past historic* because *they depict events which happened one after the other*:

> Il se tut aussitôt; et nous restâmes plongés dans un silence plus terrifiant encore. Et soudain tous ensemble, nous eûmes une sorte de sursaut: un être glissait contre le mur du dehors vers le forêt; puis il passa contre la porte, qu'il sembla tâter, d'une main hésitante; puis on n'entendit plus rien pendant deux minutes qui firent de nous des insensés; puis il revint, frôlant toujours la muraille: et il gratta légèrement; puis soudain une tête apparut contre la vitre du judas, une tête blanche avec des yeux lumineux comme ceux des fauves.

A verb in the *imperfect* does *not* form part of the sequence; it does not indicate that the central narrative has moved a step further. Instead it will denote *an incompleted action*; it will describe "what was (already) happening".

As far as tenses are concerned it is important to bear in mind that they relate to *how* the narrative is arranged. You have control of the narrative, therefore structure it logically and make certain that narrative tenses and imperfects convey the meaning which you intended. Begin to decide on the way you will use tenses as you plan your essay and concentrate on the arrangement of your material. If you do not have a firm grasp of "what happened next" and of "what was already happening", you will not convey any clear meaning to the reader.

The following passage illustrates some of the main problem areas which candidates encounter when handling tenses in a narrative account:

La jeune fille attendait dans un coin de la pièce. Elle avait peur et elle commençait à avoir froid. Jamblier, un petit homme grisonnant, vêtu d'un tablier qui lui descendait aux pieds, traînait ses savates sur le sol bétonné. Parfois, il s'arrêtait court et son regard se fixait sur le loquet de la porte. Pour apaiser l'impatience de l'attente, il prit une serpillière qui se trouvait sur une chaise, et pour la troisième fois, lava la grande table de chêne. Entendant un bruit de pas, il se releva et voulut ouvrir la porte mais sa main tremblait si fort qu'il ne put saisir la poignée.

La porte s'ouvrit pour laisser passer un homme court et trapu. Il portait une valise dans chaque main et il était sanglé dans un pardessus marron si étroitement ajusté qu'il faisait saillir ses muscles puissants. Il y eut un silence. Enfin, Jamblier s'avança et indiqua la table. Le visiteur y posa les deux valises. A cet instant, un bruit de pas et des cris se firent entendre dans le couloir. La porte fut ouverte avec violence et une dizaine de soldats allemands s'élancèrent dans la pièce.

(Adapted from *Traversée de Paris* by Marcel Aymé. Gallimard)

1.   As any story requires a setting and as the action is likely to begin with the interruption of something that was happening, it is often necessary to open the narrative (or a new phase in the narrative) with description of place, characters or setting, as in lines 1–5 of the passage above. If the story is written in the *past* the tense used for this description is of course the *imperfect*. Most candidates understand this in theory but are too vague when deciding which elements are descriptive. Ask yourself carefully whether a detail is properly descriptive or whether it can be seen more logically as a movement forward in the narrative. If you are not sure then substitute something that you *are* sure about.

It is also important that you make clear the *transition* from description to narration. The transition should be justified by the sense and by the rest of the sentence. In other words make use of adverbs, adverbial phrases and clauses of time to indicate that the story is progressing and to show the reader that he should be thinking in terms of a sequence. In the passage above, words and phrases such as et pour la troisième fois, Entendant un bruit de pas, Enfin, A cet instant help to indicate that the narrative is now moving forward in a sequence which justifies the past historic tense.

2.   Ensure that your choice of tense has not led to an illogical or improbable statement. Ask yourself why the sense and the context would not allow the verbs in these sentences taken from the passage to be in the past historic:

- vêtu d'un tablier qui lui descendait aux pieds;
- (Jamblier) traînait ses savates sur le sol bétonné;
- une serpillière qui se trouvait sur une chaise;
- il portait une valise;
- il faisait saillir ses muscles puissants.

"un tablier qui lui descendit aux pieds" would seem to imply that the apron fell down to his feet at that moment; "il fit saillir ses muscles puissants" would mean that the overcoat (suddenly) made his muscles bulge, and these meanings would fit poorly into the context. Think carefully about the meaning of the verb in a given context when you are choosing the tense.

3. Give particular attention when writing narrative to the tense you use for être in passive constructions and for avoir (il y a). Many candidates would automatically write Il y avait un silence and La porte était ouverte avec violence but it is clear from the context that it is a question of events which form part of a sequence. One might write: Puis, il y eut un silence or Puis, la porte fut ouverte avec violence.

4. Be careful with tenses when handling the modal auxiliaries (devoir, savoir, pouvoir, vouloir). A change of tense can change the meaning. Be sure of your intended meaning. Compare the following sentences:

- Il se releva et voulut ouvrir la porte (he tried to open the door).
- Il se releva parce qu'il voulait ouvrir la porte (he wanted to open the door).
- Sa main tremblait si fort qu'il ne put ouvrir la porte (he could not open it, he failed to).
- Il sortit par la fenêtre parce qu'il ne pouvait pas ouvrir la porte (he was unable to open the door).
- Je sus à 6 heures ce qui était arrivé (I found out at 6 o'clock).
- Je savais à 6 heures ce qui était arrivé (I already knew at 6 o'clock).
- Lorsque la guerre éclata je dus retourner à Paris (I had to and I did).
- Je vendis mon appartement parce que je devais retourner à Paris (because I was in the position of having to return).

Accurate use of the narrative and imperfect tenses depends in the first instance on your having structured the events of the story clearly. Controlling in your mind the logical sequence of the action will also help to ensure that the pluperfect tense is used when required. Too frequently candidates who simply construct the story sentence by sentence without reference to an overall conception of the sequence of actions, overlook the logical need to indicate that something *had already happened*, that something took place when something else *had finished*:

- Voulant descendre au premier étage j'essayai d'ouvrir la porte mais quelqu'un l'avait fermée à clef.
- Lorsque le mécanicien eut réparé la voiture, Jacques partit à toute vitesse en direction de Paris.

STRUCTURES USEFUL IN PLACING EVENTS IN SEQUENCE

As a fundamental requirement in writing a narrative account is that of arranging the action intelligibly in time, it is important that your language work should equip you to handle spontaneously a variety of structures which enable you to sequence the events and stages of the narrative. Make a note of such structures (in a complete sentence) when you come across them in your course-book or in wider reading. Aim at compiling your own glossary and collection of examples which will include those given under the headings below.

(a) Adverbs and adverbial phrases of time	• Au bout de deux heures . . . • Trois jours plus tard . . . • L'équipe de sauvetage travailla du matin au soir. • Au cours du spectacle, il y eut une panne d'électricité. • Léon ouvrit la porte et descendit dans la rue. Puis il mit son imperméable et en releva le col. Ensuite il tira de sa poche une lettre qu'il lut attentivement. Enfin il se dirigea vers la bouche de métro. • Le chauffeur s'arrêta un instant, puis sortit de sa poche un flacon et reprit ensuite son chemin. • Soudain/subitement/tout à coup/bientôt une lampe s'alluma, puis deux, puis trois.

(b) Conjunctions

Make sure that you are able to handle the main temporal conjunctions accurately. They are:

• Quand, lorsque, comme, pendant que, à mesure que avant que
• dès que, après que, aussitôt que, à peine

Remember that comme, pendant que, à mesure que when used to indicate that an action was taking place, will require the imperfect tense:

• Le téléphone a sonné comme je quittais la maison.
• Pendant que j'attendais à l'entrée, une grosse voiture noire s'arrêta devant l'hôtel.
• A mesure que la nuit tombait les passants devenaient plus rares.

Avant que will require the subjunctive:

• Avant qu'il eût le temps de sortir dans le couloir, les trois hommes descendirent l'escalier.

Dès que, après que, aussitôt que, à peine used in a narrative written in the past historic, and intended to indicate that an action had happened immediately before the next action happened, will require the past anterior:

• Dès que/aussitôt qu'il eut enlevé ses chaussures il plongea dans l'eau.
• A peine l'arbitre eut-il paru sur le terrain que la foule siffla.

It is also useful to remember that instead of repeating the conjunction (e.g. to introduce a second subordinate clause after et) it is possible to replace it by que:

• Quand il descendit le lendemain à la petite gare et qu'il vit son ami qui attendait à la sortie . . .

64

(c) The present participle

Used carefully, the present participle and the gerund (i.e. "en" with the present participle) can add variety to the way the narrative is sequenced. It can alternate with a co-ordinate clause introduced by et or with a temporal clause introduced by <u>pendant que</u>, <u>comme</u>, <u>quand</u>, etc.:

- En arrivant à la gare il se dépêcha de trouver une cabine téléphonique (= lorsqu'il arriva à la gare,...).
- Relevant le col de son imperméable, il partit sous la pluie (= il releva le col de son imperméable et il partit sous la pluie).

The two examples which follow give a better idea of how the present participle and gerund can provide variety of structure in a passage of narrative:

En me rendant compte que (= quand/au moment où je me rendis compte que) mes compagnons ne me suivaient plus, je m'arrêtai. Déposant mon sac à dos (= je déposai mon sac à dos... et) qui était devenu très lourd, j'en retirai la carte que Jacques m'avait prêtée. Je l'étalai sur mes genoux, essayant en vain de trouver (= et essayai en vain de trouver) la route de Bordeaux.

En montant dans le bateau (= pendant que/comme je montais...) je me cognai la tête qui se mit à saigner, mais heureusement je ne perdis pas connaissance. Je me dirigeai vers l'avant et m'assis à côté de mon frère. A cet instant une grosse vague déferla sur la proue, renversant (= et renversa...) un des marins qui tomba à la mer. Se levant d'un bond, mon frère lui jeta (= mon frère se leva d'un bond et lui jeta...) une corde qu'il réussit à attraper.

(d) Absolute clauses

Temporal clauses introduced by <u>quand</u>, <u>lorsque</u>, <u>aussitôt</u>, <u>dès que</u>, may alternate with absolute clauses;

- Les policiers disparus, il se rendit chez les voisins (= une fois que les policiers eurent disparus,...).
- Devenu grand, il résolut de rejoindre son père (= quand il fut devenu grand,...).
- Libérés en 1945, les deux frères regagnèrent leur pays natal (= lorsqu'ils furent libérés en 1945,...).
- L'orage dissipé, les invités retournèrent à la salle à manger (= lorsque l'orage se fut dissipé,...).
- Une fois le père mort, les fils se partagèrent la propriété (= aussitôt que le père fut mort,...).
- Sa résolution prise, elle quitta Bordeaux (= lorsqu'elle eut pris sa résolution,...).
- La vaisselle rangée, elle passa dans la chambre d'Antoine (= lorsqu'elle eut rangé la vaisselle,...).
- Les cigarettes achetées, il s'attabla devant moi et commença de relire la lettre (= lorsqu'il eut acheté les cigarettes,...).

(e) Nominalisation

A temporal clause may also be replaced by a noun construction:

- Jean-Paul, lors de sa venue à Paris, s'inscrit à la Faculté des Lettres (= Jean-Paul, lorsqu'il vint à Paris,...).
- A sa sortie de la prison, Latour s'installa à la compagne (= lorsqu'il sortit de la prison,...).
- Dès le retour/le départ de son père...
- Au moment de son arrivée/de sa disparition...
- Lors de sa maladie/son mariage/sa naissance...

(f) Participle phrase in apposition

- Arrivé au coin de la rue, Simon héla un taxi (= lorsqu'il fut arrivé...).
- Remonté au sixième étage, il rentra chez lui et ferma la porte à clef.
- Revenu au jardin, il affecta de les ignorer.
- A peine assise, Madame Dufour entra dans le vif du sujet.
- Venu pour chercher son amie, Charles interrogeait le barman.
- Grimpé dans un arbre, Carolus tira sur les policiers.
- Rentré chez moi, je téléphonai à l'aéroport.
- Descendu pour acheter des croissants à la boulangerie d'à côté, je remarquai une voiture de police stationnée dans la rue de Londres.
- Sorti pour faire un petit tour avant de se coucher, mon père rencontra un jeune Anglais qui avait perdu tout son argent.

USEFUL STRUCTURES

In conveying action and movement

It is highly likely that any narrative account that you will be asked to write will involve action and movement. Sound preparatory work in acquiring the appropriate vocabulary (see Ch. 4) and practice of the structures illustrated above, will enable you to produce a controlled, lively account that will impress the examiner. You will notice that in the model answer provided on pp.71–72 that quite simple variations in the structure of sentences together with well-chosen verbs of movement can result in French which sounds like French and is enjoyable to read.

In conveying conflict and tension

While the essay in French is not marked according to its literary merit (but clearly if it did have literary merit it would be highly rewarded) it is nevertheless an advantage if the story is readable and lively. This is clear from the examiners' comments which appear at the end of scripts. Remarks such as "A well-told, interesting story", "A lively account", "Interesting details, quite a dramatic account", indicate that the candidate's work has been marked up for the quality of the story-telling. However, what should be emphasised again at this point is that it is not realistic to regard the essay as the exercise in creative writing which it would be if the candidate were writing in his or her mother tongue. The examiner will not be impressed by attempts at imaginative or original use of language if the result is inaccurate, non-French. The first priority remains accurate handling of structures and accurate use of vocabulary. However, the good candidate will be able to fulfil these fundamental requirements and succeed in producing an essay which is interesting and readable.

It is possible to write a narrative essay with such qualities using relatively limited means. A narrative which has been planned to include three or four phases which lead progressively to a denouement and generate some dramatic interest will have the ingredients for a successful essay at A-level. An elementary requirement of a good story is that it should be constructed to create tension or conflict. Conflict between people, between people and events or circumstances. Such elements may well be prescribed in the essay title, e.g.:

- Imaginez que vous vous trouvez dans une ville au moment où il s'est produit un tremblement de terre. (London, 1979)
- Dans un pays dont vous ignorez la langue vous vous trouvez séparé de vos amis. (Cambridge, 1980)
- Vous êtes sur le point de partir au cinéma quand vous recevez une visite inattendue. (Cambridge, 1981)

If they are not then it will make the story more readable if you introduce them and describe the feelings and reactions of those people involved (such descriptions may be specifically asked for in the title, e.g. Un(e) réfugié(e) arrive pour la première fois dans son pays d'adoption. Imaginez ses réactions et ses émotions. (London, 1983).

As part of your preparation for the essay you should concentrate on those structures which French writers commonly use when noting the feelings or reactions of characters involved in the story. You could, for example, make use of:

(a) *An adjective used in apposition*
   - Interloqué, je regardai la liste qu'il m'avait remise.
   - Gérard, muet de peur, regardait les flammes qui dévoraient la salle à manger.
   - Bouleversés, ils restèrent immobiles, l'oreille tendue.
   - Tenaillés par la peur, les cinq voyageurs s'étaient réfugiés dans l'autobus abandonné.
   - Accablé, Jean-Pierre se retira dans un coin.
   or
(b) *Avoir + un geste, un mouvement.* For example:
   - Il eut un geste d'impatience et monta dans sa chambre.
   - Il eut un geste/mouvement de dépit.
   - Il eut un geste/mouvement de lassitude/de surprise/de résignation, etc.
(c) *Appropriate vocabulary.* You should also make a conscious effort to widen your knowledge of:

(i) the vocabulary of *emotions and reactions*, e.g. expressions conveying

surprise	respect	anxiety
satisfaction	fear	discontent
sadness	pride	gratitude
admiration	anger	bewilderment
indignation	pity	hostility, etc.

and of

(ii) the vocabulary required to express *conflict*, e.g. terms which denote

contradiction	prohibition
disagreement	refusal
impossibility	refuting
necessity	threatening
obligation	obstacle, etc.

EXAMINATION QUESTIONS

1.
Votre famille a toujours été très riche, mais par suite d'une série de désastres elle se trouve soudain très pauvre. Racontez comment vous avez fait face à cette catastrophe. (Oxford, 1980)

2.
Vous êtes auteur de romans policiers. Ecrivez le commencement d'un de vos romans. (Oxford, 1980)

3.
Au cours d'un voyage que vous avez fait, seul(e) à l'étranger, vous avez perdu tout votre argent. Comment avez-vous réagi à cette situation? Racontez comment vous avez pu rentrer chez vous. (London, 1976)

4.
Imaginez que vous vous trouvez dans une ville au moment où il s'est produit un tremblement de terre. Racontez les événements auxquels vous assistez. Décrivez la scène et les incidents. (London, 1979)

5.
Un incendie a éclaté dans un grand hôtel où vous passiez la nuit. Quelles ont été vos réactions? Comment avez-vous pu être sauvé(e)? (London, 1980)

6.
Parti(e) en ville pour faire des achats, vous avez été témoin d'une attaque à main armée sur une bijouterie. Racontez cet incident et expliquez comment vous avez réussi à faire arrêter les voleurs. (London, 1982)

7.
Vous avez été à bord d'un avion qui a dû faire un atterrissage forcé en pleine montagne. Faites le récit de cet événement en expliquant comment vous avez été sauvé(e). (London, 1982)

8.
Un orage. (London, 1984)
9.
Un voyage peu commun. (Oxford, 1977)
10
Vous avez travaillé pendant vos vacances pour gagner de l'argent de poche. Où et dans quelles conditions? A part l'argent, quel profit en avez-vous tiré? (Cambridge, 1981)

AN OUTLINE ANSWER

Pendant que vous étiez en vacances dans une capitale étrangère, une grève générale s'est déclarée. Quelles ont été pour vous les conséquences de cet événement? Décrivez comment vous avez réussi à regagner votre pays d'origine. (London, 1984)

CONTENT

The title has been worded to include a number of elements:

- holiday in a foreign capital;
- a general strike;
- the consequences for you (should include more than *one* consequence);
- how you managed to return home.

Identifying the various parts of the question is the first step in tackling the essay.

An advantage of the structured question is that it provides you with an outline plan and indicates what you should write about. A disadvantage may be that it is an invitation to display knowledge of more than one vocabulary area. You should be prepared to respond to each element in the title, and within the limits of your linguistic knowledge you should put yourself imaginatively into the prescribed situations in order to make them as convincing as possible. Provide details which show that the events do take place in a *foreign* capital and indicate that you were not just there but that you were there on *holiday*. The problems encountered thereafter are caused by a general strike. Do more than announce the fact in a single sentence: give details and, if you can, make them part of the story. Do this to add interest and realism and to show that you can command the required vocabulary and structures. Similarly, you are expected to do justice to an account of the way the strike affected you and to invent convincing details of the journey home. It would not be necessary to treat each of the four elements in equal detail and at equal length but on the other hand it would be unwise to neglect one element or to give it only perfunctory attention.

Remember, when you are deciding what to put into the essay, that you could include description (e.g. of a strike-bound city) and some dialogue.

PLANNING

As you plan the essay concentrate on the sequence of events and the tenses that you will use. Your main narrative tense may be either the past historic or the perfect. Be clear in your mind about the point in time at which you wish the narrative sequence to begin. You could, for example, begin with description of how you *were spending* your holiday which was then interrupted by the strike and its consequences. Make the transition from the descriptive tense (imperfect) to the narrative tense clear to the reader. If you wish to refer to events which occurred *before* the narrative sequence starts (i.e. to why you *had decided* to spend such a holiday, how you *had travelled*, where you *had already been*, etc.) then you will use the pluperfect tense. Later in the essay you may include further description (e.g. of what *was happening* when you walked through the streets, went to the airport, etc.). Once again, think about what you are doing and arrange the tenses accordingly.

VOCABULARY

The title requires knowledge of vocabulary to do with holidays, travel, strikes and personal reactions and feelings (e.g. anxiety, annoyance, frustration) experienced in a difficult situation. Other essential vocabulary will include expressions of time and place and the expression of cause and effect, for it is necessary to situate the story and to make it intelligible to the reader. Use your knowledge to provide the kind of detail which will make your story interesting and convincing. If, having analysed the title, you feel that you have only vague knowledge of the lexical areas prescribed, then you should think of choosing another title.

DRAFTING THE ESSAY

It is advisable to write your essay plan and notes in French in order that your mind should work in French from the beginning. It is usually helpful to write down phrases or items of vocabulary in the form that you will use when you write up the essay. In this way you are more likely to generate further ideas/language by association. What you should *not* do is to write out the whole of the essay in rough first (at least, not if you are writing under examination conditions) or write out the whole of the essay in English and then translate it.

OUTLINE PLAN

The plan of the essay, in this case, might reasonably follow the order of events presented in the title:

1. An opening paragraph which explains the situation and sets the scene (but guard against the use of an all-purpose introduction to a general "holiday" essay).
2. The situation is interrupted by the strike, its consequences and attempts to deal with them.
3. A solution to the problem is discovered.
4. An account is given of the journey home.

1. Je passais quelques jours à Paris – musées, expositions, théâtres. J'étais accompagné de… L'hotel se trouvait à… Nous étions en France depuis… Nous avions fait un tour en Bretagne, etc.
2. Rentrés à l'hôtel, nous entendîmes annoncer à la radio qu'une grève générale était prévue.
   Pas d'eau, pas d'électricité, pas de transports publics, rues presque désertes;
   Il nous restait seulement 500 francs, nous commençâmes à nous inquiéter.
   Nous essayâmes de faire de l'auto-stop, sans succès.
   Manifestations, grévistes portant des pancartes;
   À la gare il y avait des piquets de grève, etc.
3. Une idée lumineuse, un touriste belge à l'hôtel, on l'avait aidé.
   Il accepta de nous emmener à Ostende.
4. Le voyage jusqu'à la frontière belge;
   Autoroute sans payer, employés du péage en grève;
   Très peu de voitures, aucun poids lourd;
   À Ostende, le ferry à destination de Douvres.

A TUTOR'S ANSWER

Racontez une histoire originale – imaginée ou réelle – intitulée "la Peur". (London, 1981)

Si j'avais le talent de Guy de Maupassant j'écrirais une belle histoire au sujet de la peur qui vous ferait dresser les cheveux sur la tête. N'ayant pas ce talent-là, je me contenterai de raconter une aventure qui m'arriva à une époque où, petit garçon de dix ans, j'habitais une région reculée dans le Yorkshire. Un soir, juste avant Noël, mes parents me demandèrent de promener notre chien avant de me coucher. Bien qu'il fît très froid dehors, j'acceptai pour faire plaisir à mon père. Juste avant Noël, il faut essayer un peu de contenter ses parents!

Notre maison était située dans un endroit isolé qui se trouvait à deux kilomètres d'un petit village. Comme il faisait noir comme un four ce soir-là, je décidai de prendre le chemin qui menait au village. C'était un petit chemin bordé de chênes et toujours désert le soir. Je partis en marchant d'un pas allègre. Le chien me suivait en tirant sur la laisse. Il était très gros le chien et n'aimait pas la marche rapide. Je l'encourageais; il me regardait d'un oeil méfiant. Arrivé sous les arbres, je n'entendais même plus le bruit de mes pas puisque le vent hurlait et faisait tomber des feuilles mortes. C'était comme des doigts invisibles qui touchaient mon visage. Il me semblait que je n'arriverais jamais au village. Inquiet, je pressai le pas, m'enfonçant dans l'obscurité. Puis, soudain, le chien s'arrêta. Je tirai la laisse mais il regardait fixement devant lui, les oreilles dressées, refusant absolument d'avancer. Enfin, il se retourna si rapidement que je laissai tomber la laisse et le chien s'enfuit à toute vitesse. C'est à ce moment-là que je connus la peur. Il y avait quelque chose qui se tenait dans les ténèbres, quelque chose d'affreux qui me guettait, qui m'attendait. Je ne le voyais pas, je le sentais. Avec une terreur croissante, je commençai à marcher rapidement en jetant des regards derrière moi. Enfin, pris de panique je me mis à courir. Je sortis du petit bois, dévalai un talus, sautai un fossé, un buisson, une clôture et arrivai, essouflé, devant la maison de mes parents.

J'entrai dans le jardin et jetai un coup d'œil dans la niche du chien. Il dormait là, bien au chaud! Ce n'était pas la peur de l'inconnu qui lui avait fait prendre la fuite: il avait simplement eu envie de retrouver sa niche aussi rapidement que possible et de se coucher.

FURTHER READING

P. Bellmare et J. Antoine. Histoires Vraies vols 1–5. C'est Arrivè un Jour vols 1–3 (Livre de Poche edition 1)
P. Lyon (ed). Penguin Parallel Texts. French Short Stories. Penguin.

Chapter 7

The discussion essay

GETTING STARTED

The type of essay in which you are asked to discuss, argue or explain will involve rather different language functions from those found in the narrative essay. This does not mean that you do not need to narrate when you are involved in a discussion. It may be very appropriate to recount a personal experience or to describe an incident or scene in order to reinforce an argument, but there are also other important functions which you should be able to handle. They include:

(a) the expression of comparison and contrast;
(b) the expression of cause and consequence;
(c) the expression of hypothesis;
(d) reporting and commenting on the views of another person;
(e) enumerating points;
(f) the expression of obligation;
(g) the expression of a personal opinion;
(h) indicating a conclusion.

   This list is not exhaustive but it shows what you need to do most frequently when you are putting together an argument or a discussion. Often the essay title will specifically require the candidate to perform one or more of these functions. For example:

- Comparez les avantages et les inconvénients du rail et de la route comme moyens de transport. (London, 1982)   (comparison and contrast)
- A votre avis quel devrait être le rôle de l'enseignement supérieur dans une société de loisirs? (JMB, 1981)   (obligation)
- Quelles sont les causes de la violence dans la société d'aujord'hui, et quels en sont les remèdes? (London, Syllabus B 1985)   (cause and consequence)
- Quelles mesures prendriez-vous si vous étiez ministre de l'environnement? (London, 1981)   (hypothesis)

Examiners' reports will very often point out that too many candidates were not able to handle tenses accurately in "si" clauses (si j'étais ministre de l'environnement je ferais voter une loi…, etc.), that they did not know the tenses of "devoir" or "falloir" or that they could not use alternatives to "parce que" and "puisque" when expressing cause.

Preparing for the essay is therefore not just a question of building-up a good stock of vocabulary around likely topics, although this is important. It is also a question of acquiring the vocabulary and structures which are used when carrying out certain functions.

ESSENTIAL PRINCIPLES

(a) COMPARISON AND CONTRAST

As you are looking at comparison and contrast with a view to essay-writing it is most useful to think in terms of the paragraph rather than the sentence. Read the following paragraph in which the writers: (1) compare Brittany and Denmark; (2) contrast the north and the south of England.

1. Nombreux sont les géographes qui ont signalé les ressemblances entre la Bretagne et le Danemark. Ces deux pays, situés sur le bord occidental de l'Europe, regardant vers l'ouest, sont ouverts aux mêmes influences maritimes. Les Bretons, tout comme les Danois, sont marins et pêcheurs. Les deux pays se ressemblent également par leur climat et leur relief. Leur superficie et la densité de leur population sont pareilles, aussi bien que leur faune et leur flore. Le littoral du Finistère a sa réplique dans la côte du Jutland; un habitant d'Esbjerg ne se sentirait pas dépaysé à Lorient ou à Concarneau. Enfin, l'économie de la Bretagne autant que celle du Danemark, est fondée sur l'agriculture. L'industrie lourde (sidérurgie, chimie lourde) reste absente.

2. Le nord-est de l'Angleterre est plus dur, plus positif, plus froidement intellectuel que le reste du pays; le nord-ouest, plus 'celtique', plus proche de l'Irlande, a plus de douceur, de chaleur, de poésie. Mais dans ces ceux régions, les rapports humains sont beaucoup moins froids, beaucoup plus amicaux que dans le sud (. . . . .) On n'est pas, dans cette Angleterre, tenu à distance par une sorte de courtoisie indifférente; au contraire, on y est chaudement, cordialement accueilli. Les enfants sont traités avec plus d'affection, les liens familiaux sont plus étroits. Les rapports humains sont moins formalistes, moins fondés sur la réserve et la peur d'autrui. Le nord, d'une façon générale, ne semble pas craindre tout ce dont le sud se protège: il ne craint pas les grands mots et les grandes idées et ne pratique pas l'*understatement*, il ne craint pas les grosses plaisanteries, le gros rire, et les comiques les plus populaires du music-hall sont des gens du nord. On travaille dur dans le nord, que ce soit à Manchester, ville du coton, et dans le grand port de Liverpool pour le Lancashire, ou à Sheffield, ville de l'acier et dans les grands centres industriels de Leeds et Bradford pour le Yorkshire, mais l'énergie va de pair avec la joie de vivre. (. . . . .) Que nous sommes loin du sud austère, frugal, surveillé, distingué, respectable!

(Adapted from *Grande-Bretagne* by Jean Bailhache, Editions du Seuil)

Note those terms which are used to make explicit comparisons and contrasts:

- Les deux pays se ressemblent par leur climat et leur relief.
- L'économie de la Bretagne, autant que celle du Danemark, est fondée sur l'agriculture, etc.
- Le nord est plus dur que le sud.
- Le nord-ouest a plus de chaleur que le sud.
- Les rapports humains sont moins formalistes.
- Au contraire, on y est chaudement accueilli.

Also note the way in which contrast or comparison is implied:

- Un habitant d'Esbjerg ne se sentirait pas dépaysé à l'orient.
- Le nord ne craint pas les grands mots et les grandes idées, etc.

(b) CAUSE AND CONSEQUENCE

In the essays that you write you will be frequently called upon to explain, to make judgements and to give your reasons, to examine causes, and whenever you are arguing a point of view you will need to justify your arguments. You should be certain therefore that you can express cause and consequence accurately and that you can avoid over-use of a limited number of expressions. You should have no difficulty in using "parce que", "puisque", "comme" and "car" (but check the dictionary or grammar-book if you are in doubt) but you should have a more varied repertoire.

Remember that *cause* may be expressed by:

1. A present participle:
   - Roulant parfois six heures sans repos les conducteurs de camions sont souvent victimes de fatigue.
2. An adjective or a past participle:
   - Fier de sa nouvelle voiture de sport, il la montrait à tous ses amis.
   - Fatigué après une longue journée de travail, un conducteur risque de s'endormir au volant.
   - Contraints de rester à la maison, les vieillards mènent parfois une vie très solitaire.
3. Using "du fait de", "sous l'effet de", "à force de", "en raison de", "à cause de", "étant donné", "faute de", "grâce à" followed by a noun:
   - Du fait de son grand âge mon grand-père ne sort plus de la maison.
   - Sous l'effet de l'alcool les réflexes d'un conducteur sont souvent tardifs.
   - A force de patience on peut résoudre tous les problèmes.
   - En raison des/à cause des/étant donné les circonstances la police a dû relâcher le suspect.
   - Grâce à l'intervention du ministre il sera possible de monter une nouvelle campagne de prévention routière.

In your own reading find passages such as the following one which deals with the causes of road accidents:

Il apparaît, si l'on considère les résultats d'enquêtes effectuées par la Prévention Routière que la cause principale des accidents de la route n'est ni le mauvais état des routes où les défaillances des véhicules, mais bien le conducteur lui-même. A l'origine d'environ soixante-quinze pour cent des accidents on trouve une faute de conduite: mauvaise appréciation des distances, réflexe tardif, vitesse excessive, imprudence. Mais parmi les causes de ces défaillances il en est une qui les recouvre toutes par sa fréquence: l'alcool.

Un accident sur trois se produit par la faute de l'alcool. Sur les dix mille morts que provoquent chaque année les routes de France, plus de trois mille ont pour cause un excès de boisson. C'est une proportion trop importante pour laisser indifférent.

The principal means of expressing *consequence* are as follows:

- pour que
- afin que
- de sorte que
- de façon que
- de manière que
- de crainte que   *followed by the subjunctive*

For example: Il a garé la voiture de sorte que l'agent de police ne la voie pas.

- pour
- afin de
- de manière à
- de façon à
- de crainte de
- de peur de   *followed by an infinitive*

For example: Il a arrêté la voiture de manière à voir l'arrivée de l'ambulance.

Make sure that these terms are part of your vocabulary. Find examples of their use in a French–French dictionary and check their grammatical use in your grammar-book.

(c) EXPRESSING HYPOTHESIS

Many essay titles call upon you to describe "what you would do if . . .":

- Quelles mesures prendriez-vous si vous étiez ministre de l'environnement? (London, 1981)
- Si l'on proposait d'installer une centrale nucléaire dans votre région, seriez-vous pour ou contre une telle proposition? (JMB, 1980)

When you are arguing a case or discussing problems it is often necessary to develop a hypothesis over one or two paragraphs. Many candidates are uncertain of the use of tenses:

Past: Si j'avais travaillé j'aurais gagné de l'argent.
Present: Si je travaillais je gagnerais de l'argent.
Future: Si, un jour, je trouvais un emploi, je gagnerais de l'argent.
(*Check in your grammar-book if you are not certain*)

Others are not able to sustain the structure throughout a whole paragraph or throughout an essay. It is therefore very important to remember what you are doing and to keep the "si j'étais . . . je ferais" pattern constantly in mind, as does the writer of the following passage:

> Le développement de la civilisation industrielle a augmenté les bruits dans une telle proportion que l'on peut parler d'une véritable pollution sonore. Si j'étais ministre de l'environnement j'aurais des pouvoirs qui me permettraient de m'attaquer à ce problème. Tout d'abord, dans les villes, où le bruit des voitures est un véritable fléau, je ferais construire des écrans, buttes de terre ou murs en béton, pour protéger les habitations en bordure des voies à grande circulation. J'imposerais des limites de vitesse plus sévères et j'interdirais le passage de poids lourds entre six heures du soir et sept heures du matin. Ensuite, j'introduirais de nouveaux règlements de construction afin d'améliorer l'insonorisation des bâtiments. Enfin, je monterais une campagne pour faire comprendre aux propriétaires de chaînes Hi-Fi, de radios et de télévision, de chiens, de tondeuses à gazon et de tronçonneuses qu'il ne faut pas importuner ses voisins et qu'il faut respecter le droit au silence.

(d) REPORTING AND COMMENTING

If as part of your essay you are arguing a case you are quite likely to want to refer to an opposing point of view in order to counter it:

- Le premier ministre a annoncé que le gouvernement prendrait de nouvelles mesures pour lutter contre le chômage.

It is useful to have in your vocabulary a number of those verbs which can be used to report other peoples' ideas and opinions:

déclarer	prétendre
avertir	assurer
penser	soutenir
être d'avis	annoncer
estimer	protester
juger	prévenir
affirmer	professer

By choosing the right verb or phrase you can show that you are going to contradict or attack the point of view that you are reporting, e.g.:

- Siméoni <u>prétend</u> que la Corse n'a jamais été qu'une terre de colonisation (and you imply that Siméoni is wrong).

77

- Siméoni   voudrait nous faire croire
            se plaît à croire
            s'obstine à croire   que la majorité des
            semble croire   Corses sont d'accord
            semble persuadé   avec lui (but that is not
                                     the case).

Useful phrases include:

- à tort
- au mépris de toute évidence
- contrairement à la raison
- contre toute raison

These can be added to the reporting verb so that you can begin your counter-argument:

- Il soutient, contrairement à la raison, que la conquête de l'espace apportera des bénéfices à toutes les nations de la terre.

When you have reported the opposing point of view you can introduce your counter-argument with "mais", or "en fait":

Pendant les années soixante les savants voulaient nous faire croire que les centrales nucléaires ne présentaient aucun danger. Or, les accidents survenus dans les réacteurs de Windscale et de Chernobyl ont démontré que les scientifiques sont bien capables de se tromper.

(e) ENUMERATING POINTS

By clearly enumerating the points that you make you will add force to your argument and give your paragraph and your essay a satisfactory shape. Using the following "markers" will help you to enumerate the stages in an argument or a sequence of points:

en premier lieu   d'abord/tout d'abord
en second lieu   ensuite
en dernier lieu   de plus
                     en outre
                     enfin

Pourquoi tant de Français continuent-ils à voter communiste? D'abord, le parti leur paraît l'instrument le plus efficace dans le lutte contre le patronat. Ensuite parce que le parti communiste, grâce au dévouement des militants et des cadres, est beaucoup mieux organisé que les autres partis. Enfin, les luttes du XIXe siècle ont donné au prolétariat français un sentiment d'isolement tragique, qui n'a pas entièrement disparu. Voter communiste, c'est presque une question d'honneur: abandonner le parti serait commettre une sorte de trahison.

(f) EXPRESSING OBLIGATION

Essay titles frequently ask you what you think should/could be done concerning certain issues, what remedies should be applied to solve certain problems, e.g.:

- "On ne devrait pas punir les jeunes criminels, on devrait punir leurs parents". Discutez. (London, 1981)

You should ensure in the first instance that you can handle the tenses of "falloir", "devoir" and "pouvoir". Too many candidates are uncertain of these verbs, particularly in the conditional (il faudrait, on devrait, etc.). You should also find other expressions which denote necessity and find paragraphs in which the writer is pointing out what should be done:

On a mille fois énuméré les remèdes à l'alcoolisme. A l'école, dans les entreprises, partout et de toutes les façons, il faudrait expliquer les méfaits de l'alcool et favoriser la consommation de jus de fruits. Il importe de faire prendre conscience aux gens et surtout aux jeunes des désagréments qu'engendre l'alcoolisme. Ensuite, il faudrait améliorer l'action médicale à l'hôpital, dans des services spécialisés, avec l'aide de médecins qui auraient reçu un complément de formation en hôpital psychiatrique. Mais ces remèdes ne pourraient, tout seuls, guérir le besoin d'alcool. Seule une action politique et sociale de grande envergure, qui offrirait à tous des perspectives d'avenir, distrairait les Français de leur quête des "paradis artificiels".

Other phrases which express what is necessary or required include:

- il convient de
- il s'agit de
- il est question de
- il est indispensable/essentiel de
- il est de première nécessité de   *followed by the infinitive*

Note also the use of "nécessiter", "s'imposer", "exiger":

- Pour s'attaquer à ce problème la plus grande prudence s'impose.
- La solution de ce problème nécessite/exige la plus grande prudence.

(g) EXPRESSING A PERSONAL OPINION

Many essay titles invite you to express your own opinion about the subject to be discussed. You should make sure that you have the vocabulary and knowledge of grammar to be able to express:

admiration	doubt
anger	hope
approval/disapproval	indignation
astonishment	regret
concern	satisfaction
certainty	shock
disappointment	surprise
displeasure	sympathy

Remember that certain verbs or verbal phrases that you use to express an opinion, a feeling or a doubt require the use of the subjunctive in the clause introduced by "que", e.g.:

- Je suis fâché/mécontent qu'elle soit revenue.
- Je m'étonne/je m'indigne/je regrette que tant de conducteurs soient imprudents.

Note: Je crois/je suis sûr/je pense que ce parti peut gagner l'élection; but

Je ne crois pas/je ne pense pas/je ne suis pas sûr que ce parti puisse gagner l'élection.

(h) INDICATING A CONCLUSION

The conclusion to the essay is important because it is your last word on the subject and your last chance to make a good impression. If it is well handled it will convince the examiner that you have good control over both language and ideas and, if the rest of the work is up to standard, it will help you to to achieve a high mark.

What is a good conclusion to a discussion or argument? It should first and foremost be seen as a coherent part of the discussion that precedes it and not as something which is simply tacked on at the end. It is not enough to produce a formula which claims that the last few lines of your essay are a conclusion (e.g. En conclusion on peut dire . . ./Concluons par affirmer . . ./Toute réflexion faite, on peut dire . . .). Examiners will not be impressed with these phrases if they are not used meaningfully, particularly as some candidates tend to over-use them at this stage of the essay. A conclusion will have a meaningful function:

- if it recapitulates *briefly* the points that you have discussed not for the sake of recapitulation but in order to pull the various points together to form a final statement; or
- if it recalls the main line of your argument in order to add one final, important point; or
- if it opens out the discussion and invites the reader to think about future or wider implications of the points that have been discussed; or
- if it provides an answer to a question (even if the answer is that there is no answer) the pros and cons of which you have been considering throughout the essay.

The most effective way of learning to write satisfactory conclusions is to study the way that good French writers go about it and collect a number of models. By all means learn those words and expressions which help to form concluding statements (e.g. On voit par ce qui précède que/Il résulte de ce qui précède que/On peut conclure en disant, etc.) but learn them in a context so that their function is clear.

Study the concluding paragraph of the following passage asking yourself what the writer is saying *and* doing, and how the paragraph relates to the discussion which has gone before.

Pour une majorité de Français et même d'Européens, c'est la natalité débridée des populations du tiers-monde qui est la seule cause de leur misère. Ces gens sont pauvres, affirme-t-on, parce qu'ils font trop d'enfants.

Certes, les pays du tiers-monde connaissent un taux d'accroissement démographique qu'il faudrait ralentir. Nul voudrait nier que le surpeuplement soulève des problèmes énormes. Il y a pourtant un fait incontestable qui ne retient pas suffisamment les planificateurs de la vie chez les autres: les hommes et les femmes des pays pauvres ont besoin d'enfants pour vivre et pour se garantir un bâton de vieillesse; s'ils ont besoin de faire beaucoup d'enfants c'est qu'ils en perdent beaucoup. Ainsi, si l'on veut diminuer la fécondité il est parfaitement clair qu'il faut commencer par faire baisser la mortalité et notamment la mortalité infantile. Pour s'en convaincre, il suffit de lire le rapport présenté par la Banque mondiale à la conférence de Bucarest. Là-dessus les experts sont formels: "Chaque fois qu'il s'est produit une baisse importante de la fécondité dans les pays en développement, cette baisse a été précédée d'un recul de la mortalité."

Il est donc infiniment regrettable que, sur ce point, gouvernements et autorités religieuses manquent de réalisme ou de bonne volonté. Leurs efforts se portent surtout sur des programmes de stérilisation forcés ou sur la distribution gratuite de pilules avec promesses de récompenses pécuniaires. Mesures impuissantes qui tombent même dans la barbarie. Il ne s'agit point de contraindre ni d'acheter le consentement des gens mais d'assurer leur adhésion active en s'attaquant aux facteurs qui commandent la décision de faire des enfants. L'essentiel est donc de multiplier les efforts pour améliorer les conditions de vie des plus pauvres et d'augmenter en même temps le revenu monétaire des familles pour que l'enfant ne soit plus une source de revenus indispensable.

EXAMINATION QUESTIONS

1.
"Ce qui gâche la vie dans une société industrialisée comme la nôtre, c'est le bruit." Discutez. (London, Jan. 1986)

2.
L'auto-stop devrait-il être prohibé? Examinez les divers aspects de cette question. (London, Jan. 1985)

3.
"Les jeunes ne s'intéressent pas à la politique; ils ne méritent pas le droit de vote à l'âge de 18 ans." Que pensez-vous de cette critique? (London, June 1984)

4.
"L'homme a si bien maîtrisé la nature qu'il est en train de la tuer." Discutez. (London, June 1983)

5.
Quelle invention, à votre avis, a fait le plus de bien à l'humanité? (Cambridge, 1983)

6.

"Le sport international, au lieu de rapprocher les peuples, les a dressés les uns contre les autres." Discutez. (Oxford and Cambridge, 1984)

7.

Comparez le système des transports en France et en Angleterre. (Oxford and Cambridge, 1984)

8.

"L'âge de l'ordinateur est une perspective effrayante." (Oxford and Cambridge, 1985)

9.

Les étudiants devraient-ils payer eux-mêmes leurs études supérieures? (JMB, 1982)

10.

Certains prétendent qu'on ne peut pas être heureux sans un confort matériel assez important. Etes-vous de cet avis? (JMB, 1983)

11.

L'éducation pour le loisir, luxe ou nécessité? (Oxford, 1984)

12.

Les personnes âgées: minorité oubliée de nos jours? (Oxford, 1982)

13.

Notre vingtième siècle est un siècle brutal et cruel. Est-il pire que ce que nous apprend l'histoire du passé? Discutez. (Cambridge, 1982)

14.

Les enfants sont faits pour être vus et non entendus. (Welsh, 1976)

15.

Quels sont les métiers les plus dangereux, et pourquoi le sont-ils? (AEB, 1983)

OUTLINE ANSWERS

Think through the following question using the notes provided below. Tackle some of the other past questions in a similar fashion.

- Quelles sont les causes principales des accidents de la route?
- Quels moyens devraient être mis en œuvre pour les éviter?

1. Make sure that you have understood the question. Deal with *all* of the question. Look carefully at every word.
2. Find ideas. Draw on personal experience, think of examples, ask yourself questions.
3. Get your ideas in order and begin to formulate a plan:
   - route trop étroite
   - excès d'alcool
   - trop grande vitesse
   - éclatement d'un pneu
   - réflexe tardif, etc.
   (a) Causes imputables au conducteur lui-même (alcool, vitesse, réflexe tardif, etc.);

(b) Cause imputables au véhicule (freins défectueux, éclatement d'un pneu...);

(c) Causes imputables à l'état de la route (verglas, route trop étroite...).

4. Classifying the ideas will have helped construct a plan: the main part of the essay could be divided into three.

How will you introduce the subject? How will you conclude? (with a final main point, e.g. l'alcool? With a suggested solution to the problem? By underlining the importance of the problem?)

A TUTOR'S ANSWER

"S'il ne faut pas prohiber tout à fait le tabac, il faut du moins en interdire l'usage dans tous les endroits publics." Discutez. (London, 1986)

S'il est vrai que le tabagisme suscite aujourd'hui dans le public une certaine émotion, il faut pourtant avouer que bon nombre de nos concitoyens restent indifférents devant un problème social et médical qui risque toujours de s'aggraver. Ils n'écoutent pas les médecins qui constatent que les services hospitaliers sont encombrés de malades dont la déchéance physique est provoquée ou considérablement aggravée par l'usage du tabac. Ils ne se laissent pas émouvoir par le fait que les dépenses engendées par les effets nocifs du tabac grèvent lourdement le budget de la Sécurité Sociale. Aux cris d'alarme des médecins, aux protestations des ministres, ils répondent que dans un pays démocratique on a bien le droit de fumer ou de ne pas fumer et qu'il s'agit là d'un choix tout à fait personnel.

Il est donc évident que, malgré les tentatives pour faire prendre conscience des méfaits du tabac, malgré la certitude des chiffres qui montrent qu'un fumeur a vingt fois plus de chances de mourir d'une maladie pulmonaire ou d'une crise cardiaque, il y aura toujours un pourcentage assez élevé de gens qui continueront à fumer. Mais les fumeurs ont-ils bien le droit d'abîmer leur santé et de courir volontairement le risque d'une mort prématurée? Devrait-on interdire totalement la vente et l'usage du tabac pour conserver la santé de ceux qui refusent d'en avoir soin eux-mêmes? C'est là une question qui n'admet pas de réponse facile: les fumeurs, tout comme ceux qui boivent de l'alcool ou qui pratiquent des sports dangereux ont bien le droit de jouir de certaines libertés personnelles, même au péril de leur santé ou de leur vie.

Pourtant, il n'est pas question de proscrire tout à fait l'usage du tabac mais seulement d'en interdire l'usage dans les endroits publics. Proposition raisonnable et juste, car les non-fumeurs autant que les fumeurs ont des droits qu'il faudrait sauvegarder. Ils ont le droit de voyager dans un train ou dans un autobus, de manger au restaurant ou de prendre un verre au café sans être gênés par la fumée de cigarettes et de cigares, d'autant plus qu'il est maintenant démontré que la fumée est nuisible pour toute personne qui la respire, qu'il s'agisse du fumeur lui-même ou de la victime innocente qui se trouve près de lui.

Il est donc évident qu'il faudrait interdire l'usage du tabac dans tous les endroits publics – autobus, trains, cinémas, restaurants – où la dissipation de la fumée ne s'effectue pas rapidement. Si les fumeurs tiennent à exercer leurs libertés personnelles qu'ils le fassent en plein air de sorte qu'ils n'empêchent pas leurs concitoyens d'exercer les leurs.

A STEP FURTHER

Every teacher and examiner will tell you that you will improve your essay-writing by reading. One should add that reading will be particularly beneficial if it is done with a purpose. What has been said in the preceding pages will have given you an idea of what to look for when you set out to read a newspaper or magazine. Remember that you should be concerned with what the writer is *saying* – in other words the subject he is writing about – and also with what he is *doing* – that is the way in which he is using the language. Make sure that your own reading prepares you for the type of subjects which are most frequently referred to in examination questions and for the language functions which the essay titles will require you to be able to handle.

FURTHER READING

Technique of essay-writing:

G. Vigner. *Ecrire et Convaincre*. Hachette
G. Niquet. *Ecrire avec Logique et Clarté*. Hatier
G. Niquet. *Profil Formation-Français*. Hatier
G. Niquet. *Structurer sa Pensée. Structurer sa Phrase*. Hachette

articles dealing with social, political and cultural topics of the 'discussion' essay type appear in the following weekly publications:

Le Point	(available in many newsagents and through
L'Express	European Schoolbooks,
Le Figaro Magazine	Croft St.
Le Monde Dimanche	Cheltenham GL 53 0HX)

The Profil actualité and Profil dossier series (Hatier) has many titles which relate to frequently occurring essay subjects, e.g.
        Les Françaises Aujourd'hui
        La Réduction des Inégalités
        La Famille en Question etc.

Chapter 8 — Translation into French

GETTING STARTED

How well you do prose translation will depend largely on how much work you have put into your vocabulary-building, language exercises and reading in French. It is a skill which you may not be asked to practise extensively at the beginning of your language course as many tutors feel quite rightly that translation into French is an advanced skill which is best delayed until the student has an adequate command of structure and vocabulary. Most teachers would agree that while prose is a good test of your knowledge of French, it is not necessarily the best means of extending that knowledge. You should be prepared therefore to concentrate on other language work first as a preparation for the prose. Getting started on prose translation means getting started as soon as possible on building up a good working vocabulary and on improving the quality of your written French through other language exercises.

However, it is important to understand from the beginning what to expect when it comes to the examination so that you can organise your work efficiently. Consult the syllabus to ensure that the examination which you are intending to sit does have a prose (some Boards offer alternatives) and look at past papers to find out what kind of English passage is usually set. If you read through the selection of past questions on p. 93–95 you will soon realise that the passages are of different types. In question **2** there is an example of a passage which the syllabus regulations (if they are that detailed) would term as "non-literary". In such a passage the subject-matter is likely to relate to current affairs and to social, economic, political and cultural aspects of modern life. You will recognise in it the kind of writing that you would find in newspaper articles, periodicals and non-fictional books which comment on, report and analyse topics of contemporary interest. Passages for questions **3** and **4** could be called "literary" and contain the kind of writing to be found in a modern novel, short story or similar work of fiction.

It would be wrong to exaggerate the differences between literary and non-literary French or English and misguided not to include material of *both* types in your reading programme. However, if you can be sure that the passage that you will be set will be of one type rather than another then it is clearly in your interest to direct your reading and vocabulary-building towards the area which is most relevant.

Your course-book will probably contain passages in the appropriate register but you will need to supplement them from your own reading. When you are working out your reading programme for the course, it is therefore important to know what your needs are going to be as far as the prose is concerned and to make sure that you are laying down the right foundations.

Finally, so that you know exactly what you are aiming at, check the syllabus to see how many marks are allocated to this particular test, how long the passage is and how much time you are given to do it in.

ESSENTIAL PRINCIPLES

The difficulties involved in doing prose translation should not be minimised: at an advanced level it is certainly a sophisticated exercise which demands a good knowledge of many elements of both languages. It is a test of grammatical accuracy and of precise knowledge of vocabulary. It is likely to force you to use a range of structures and terms which on other occasions (e.g. in conversation, writing free composition, etc.) you could choose to avoid if you were uncertain about how to use them correctly. There is a great deal to be kept in mind when you are tackling this exercise, particularly in the examination. It is true to say that many candidates do not always discipline themselves to be sufficiently mentally alert to avoid errors which they do not usually make when there is less pressure, when the difficulties are less concentrated and when there is more time for thought.

AVOIDANCE OF ELEMENTARY ERRORS IN THE PROSE

It is because they are aware of the difficulty of this test and perhaps because their first attempts at translation have been returned liberally covered in red ink that candidates are apprehensive about this part of the examination. The fact that they are facing a test which appears to be designed to find out what they do not know, that they are likely to make mistakes and that these mistakes are all going to lose them marks, understandably undermines their confidence. If you find yourself in this position it is important to understand the problem of errors and to get the facts into perspective. Always remind yourself that the errors which lead to a poor result are mainly *elementary* errors. Candidates do not fail the prose because they have not grasped the finer points of the language or cannot understand "difficult" grammatical rules. They do badly because they accumulate many basic errors and because they are inaccurate in using structures and forms which they have once understood and learnt but which have since become unfamiliar through lack of practice and revision. The first step therefore in preparing for the prose is to ensure that your working knowledge of basic structures and forms is sound. You cannot afford to neglect what is elementary simply because it is elementary or because "we did that in the second year".

If, when you begin to practise prose translation, your prepararatory language work has been sound, you will make few errors and you will be able to handle most structures instinctively. However, it would be unrealistic to assume that you will not make mistakes and it will not be advisable to rely purely on instinct. Think carefully about your work before you hand it in for marking and make a point of doing something constructive about errors when you go over work that has been returned. Classify the errors that you seem prone to make so that you know exactly what kind of remedial action you need to take. Check subsequent proses to see whether this action has had any effect. If you have made no progress then get the advice of your tutor. If you organise yourself in this way it will give you more incentive to look through a translation carefully before handing it in.

You will need to train yourself in this critical, reflective approach to your prose work. It is useful to finish the work well before the time when you are required to hand it in so that you have the opportunity to put it aside and then review it a day or two later as objectively and critically as the tutor or examiner who is going to mark it. Establish a list of priority points (e.g. forms of irregular verbs, genders, prepositions following a verb, etc.) which need attention before the day of the examination. Even if you do not have enough time to work through all the items on your revision list, what you do manage to get through could very easily make the difference between a pass or a fail, a good performance and one which is merely satisfactory.

CRITERIA OF ASSESSMENT FOR THE PROSE

It will help you to prepare for the prose if you understand the principles according to which the test is marked. It will help you to get the problem of accuracy into the right perspective and will enable you to self-correct your work more realistically and effectively.

The prose is most commonly marked according to a deductive system. A pool of marks is allotted (say 140 for a passage containing 240 words) and deductions are made for *each error*. The total number of penalty points is then converted to a positive mark. (Some schemes allow for the award of additional bonus points for a translation which shows particular merit). Such a system of marking obviously underlines the need to strive for accuracy with every word you write. The omission of a word or what may seem to you like a careless slip are likely to incur a penalty. The lesson is to be *precise* and to give attention to detail because your work will be marked in exactly the same way.

However, you should not be too alarmed by the way the prose is marked; the system will seem less punitive if you remember that there are safeguards built in to the marking-scheme to prevent over-penalisation. Consequential and repeated errors are not penalised and it is customary to divide the passage into sections (probably 4 sections for a passage of 240 words) with a fixed maximum number of deductions which can be made for each section. It means that all is by no means lost if you get into difficulties with just one section of the passage. It is helpful to remember this if you are unlucky enough to be faced with a passage which gives you all sorts of problems in the opening lines. You should not panic as some candidates do. You cannot lose all of your marks however badly you do the opening section, so it is important to keep your head and tackle the rest of the passage with the knowledge that you still have a chance of reaching a reasonably good mark.

When marking, the examiner will distinguish between serious and less serious types of error.

The *more serious errors* will certainly include:

1. Incorrect grammatical forms. For example, the wrong form or ending of a verb, the wrong form of an adjective or of a demonstrative pronoun, the wrong plural form of a noun. In other words you would be making serious errors if you did not know that "vouloir" had the forms "il voudrait", "ils veulent", that the plural of "le travail" is "les travaux", that the feminine form of "nouveau" was "nouvelle" or that "celui-ci" had the forms "ceux-ci", "celle-ci", etc.
2. Failure to observe basic grammatical rules, relating, for example, to the agreement of adjective and noun or of noun and pronoun, the use of the definite and indefinite article and of the partitive, the choice of prepositions or conjunctions, the basic use of tenses.
3. Vocabulary errors where the term chosen conveys a completely wrong meaning; wrong genders; words which contain more than one spelling mistake.
4. Words which are omitted because of an oversight or are deliberately left blank.

The *less serious errors*, which are more lightly penalised, would include:

1. A choice of vocabulary which is approximately correct in meaning.
2. Use of language which is not grammatically incorrect but which is clumsy and not genuinely French.
3. A word which contains no more than a single spelling mistake.

Minor errors would also include omission or misuse of accents or hyphens or the misuse of a capital letter. However, a word of warning is necessary here. If the omission of an accent changes the meaning of a word (e.g. mur/mûr, tache/tâche) or it indicates a grammatical change in the word (e.g. bien qu'il fût/il est arrivé, etc.) then this is likely to be considered as a serious error.

It is important to bear these principles in mind when you are going through corrected proses and analysing your own mistakes. It will help you to get your priorities right when you draw up a list of revision or remedial points.

It may seem rather alarming to you that in the prose translation every word you write seems to be under scrutiny. You can reassure yourself for two reasons. Firstly, the passage will not be littered with pitfalls or contain unreasonable difficulties, and secondly, examiners will accept more than one version (in some cases quite a number of versions) of any phrase or sentence, provided that it is grammatically correct. There is never just one right "answer" which the examinee is expected to find and it is likely that he will be given some credit for a near-miss. When the following section, taken from a recent examination prose, was marked, a number of different "correct" versions would have been allowed and credit would have been given for reasonable approximations.

> When Helen realised that she was walking over the Colonel's land she felt uneasy. Perhaps she should go back, she said to herself.

In addition to any other acceptable translation which the candidates may have thought of but which he had not, the examiner would have allowed:

> Lorsque/quand Hélène s'aperçut/se rendit compte qu'elle marchait sur les terres/le domaine/la propriété du Colonel elle se sentit inquiète/mal à l'aise/gênée/elle éprouva/sentit/ressentit de l'inquiétude/de l'appréhension. Peut-être devrait-elle rebrousser chemin/retourner sur ses pas, se dit-elle.

Some credit would also have been given for:

> Lorsque Hélène comprit qu'elle traversait ses champs elle se sentit anxieuse.

Note that the terms underlined are not accurate enough to be entirely acceptable.

A SYSTEMATIC APPROACH TO PROSE TRANSLATION

You will practise prose translation as part of your course-work, probably as regularly as once a week. It is best to tackle this exercise only when a good deal of preparatory work has been successfully covered as it is perhaps most useful as a means of practising, testing and refining what you have already learnt. It is not the most efficient way of learning new vocabulary or of assimilating new structures. If you find that you are continually looking up words in the dictionary and that putting sentences together is a struggle which leaves you searching through the grammar-book, then you will clearly not have done enough preparatory work to enable you to cope realistically with prose translation. If this is the case then you would do well to follow the advice given in the final section of this chapter. You will also be using what many language teachers call the "look-up-bang-down-

and-forget" method of language learning. Ideally you should be able to feel that the exercise enables you to reactivate and manipulate language which you have already practised and absorbed.

Although, when you work on a prose, you should be drawing on language which you can use with instinctive accuracy, it is also important to treat the exercise as one which requires thought and concentration. You will certainly improve your prose work during the course and in the examination if you build the following points into a *systematic approach* to the exercise.

Reading the passage

Before you begin to translate into French it is essential to read the *whole* of the passage. If you are sure about the information in the original and the order in which it is presented you are less likely to make mistakes in the French. The line-by-line approach adopted by many candidates can easily lead them into error as the grammar of any sentence may well be partly determined by what has gone before and by what comes after. For example, in any passage in which there is a sequence of events it is important to have that sequence clear in your mind if you hope to use tenses correctly. Understanding the sense of the whole passage will also determine the correct use of the article and partitive. If there are people involved then it is obviously necessary to know and to keep in mind the fact that they are male, female, or plural as, throughout the passage, this will govern grammatical points such as agreement of adjective and noun, of subject and verb and of noun and pronoun (all frequent sources of error). Having the facts of the passage clear in your mind will ensure that you do not translate it (it could be "il", "elle" or "ce"), they (ils or elles), that of (celui de, celle de), etc. without realising which nouns these pronouns relate to.

Reading the passage will make situations and context clear, which is important if you are to make the appropriate choice of vocabulary. For example, the situation may require "apercevoir" rather than "voir", "se retourner" and not "tourner", "amener" rather than "emmener", "la rue" and not "la route", "la chaussée" and not "la route". It pays dividends therefore to read the original carefully. This means not just reading the words but "reading into" the passage so that you can picture what events take place and so that, in a discursive passage, you can grasp the points and developments of an argument or discussion.

Translating the passage

The prose tests the candidate's ability to render *precisely and correctly* a passage of English into French. The important word is "precisely": it is not sufficient to convey the gist of the English passage. It is here that you should be particularly careful in the way you heed the often repeated warning that the translation should not be too literal. The advice is, of course, sound and elementary but some candidates, presumably because they are anxious to demonstrate that they are following it, will recast or even add to the original in order to produce what they sometimes mistakenly consider to be a version which is "more French". It is true that recasting a sentence is sometimes permissible or even necessary to produce better, more natural French and meaning may be rendered by transposing structures (e.g. by rendering a verbal construction by a nominal construction in French). The following translations show that a degree of recasting can result in good French which conveys the meaning of the original with sufficient precision:

- As she walked out of the room she took a key from her pocket.
  Comme elle sortait de la pièce elle prit une clef dans sa poche. En sortant de la pièce elle prit une clef dans sa poche.

- As soon as he returned to the village he telephoned his mother.
  Dès qu'il fut retourné au village il téléphona à sa mère.
  Dès son retour au village il téléphona à sa mère.

You should, however, be cautious about radical recasting, changing word order or the order of phrases and subordinate clauses, unless you are certain that there is a need for it and that it is the most effective way of rendering the meaning of the English. For example:

- Helen walked rapidly down the steps carrying a large jug of water in front of her.

This sentence can be adequately translated without any recasting:

- Helen descendit rapidement les marches, portant devant elle une grande cruche d'eau.

Unnecessary changes might distort the meaning of the original:

- Rapidement, portant devant elle une grande cruche d'eau, Helen descendit les marches.

"Rapidement" is given an emphasis which "quickly" does not have in the English sentence and therefore the sense is slightly changed.

The candidate who indulges in wholesale recasting not only runs the risk of distorting the meaning of the English, but in the process of rearranging phrases and clauses often overlooks some element in the sentence and leaves it untranslated.

You are asked for a precise translation, not a loose one, and a loose translation can also result when candidates attempt to make what they have written "sound more French" by adding words unnecessarily. In a recent examination candidates added "très", "bien" and "petit" where they were not needed, presumably because they thought that the French used these words a lot and that they were adding a touch of authenticity:

- Elle avait (bien) peur d'habiter toute seule.
- Il commanda une (petite) tasse de café au comptoir.
- Votre fille est (très) jolie.

In fact they lost marks because they had added to the meaning of the English.

Another cause of loose translation is paraphrase. Candidates often resort to it when they do not know the French for a word in English. It must be said that a neat paraphrase which conveys the meaning of the original and fits correctly into the sentence is very often acceptable and some (if not all) credit will be given for it. Past candidates who did not know a closer translation of "rocky", "overcast" and "middle-aged", successfully offered "un chemin couvert de cailloux" for "un chemin rocailleux", "un ciel couvert de nuages" for "un ciel bouché" and "un homme ni jeune ni vieux" for "un homme d'un certain âge". However, it is advisable to avoid a lengthy paraphrase or definition to replace a single word for which you do not know the French. When this happens the candidate writes an extra number of words which often invite further errors and often misconstructs the whole sentence in the attempt to fit in the paraphrase. If you are forced to fall back on a paraphrase it is as well to be brief. You should also be particularly careful with the grammar of the sentence in which it occurs.

Relating to your other language work

When you practise prose as part of your course-work it is important *to relate what you are doing to the rest of your language work*. Use your own vocabulary notebook as far as you can. If, for the purpose of vocabulary-building, you have studied texts in which the subject-matter is similar to that in the text you are going to translate, then reread those texts and try to reactivate language which you have already learnt. Cultivate the habit of retrieving words from your memory and of thinking of words in context.

You will, of course, use a dictionary to look up words that you have not met before. It is essential to use a dictionary which is adequate for your needs. It is advisable to use a French–French dictionary (such as the *Larousse Dictionnaire du Français contemporain*) in addition to an English–French dictionary (such as The *Collins–Robert* or *Harrap's New Standard French and English Dictionary*). In this way you will have access to a greater number of example sentences containing the French word that you are seeking and you will give yourself further guidance as to whether the word is appropriate in the context in which you wish to use it, and useful illustrations of the way in which it fits grammatically into a sentence. When you look up a word, read the entire section in the dictionary if you can until, by comparing examples and taking note of the indications given, you have an understanding of the register of the word (is it familiar or formal, etc.?), its meaning and the contexts in which it can be used.

The small pocket dictionary is not suitable for this work. It is probably the use of such a dictionary combined with an attempt to translate the English word for word which leads to such errors as "Le bal commença à évier" (= The football began to sink) and "Dans le vestibule il y avait une odeur de polonais" (= In the hall there was a smell of polish).

Checking your work

Nowhere is the advice "check your work before handing it in" more applicable than to the prose. Ideally you should be able to produce French with spontaneous accuracy but experience shows that candidates cannot afford not to subject their work to *thorough, reflective checking*. Careful checking, which implies much more than simply reading the work through, requires practice which should begin as soon as you start to do prose translations for your course-work. Most students are able to correct an error once it has been pointed out to them. The difficulty is spotting the error in the first place. When the translation is neatly written out it is easy to persuade yourself that there is nothing wrong with it. Clearly it will help if you use a method of reviewing your work which makes you read critically. Look for specific types of error (those which experience tells you that you are prone to make): agreement of adjectives, verb endings, genders, prepositions following a verb. Make sure that concentrating on an obvious difficulty in a given sentence has not led you to overlook less obvious problems. Analysis of candidates' scripts shows that this frequently happens. The candidate spots the difficult point (e.g. the need to use the subjunctive or a past anterior), deals with it successfully and then goes on to make elementary errors in the rest of the sentence. You should check very carefully the whole of the sentence in which you have identified a "trouble-spot".

Your final reading should be made in order to check that you have considered every word in the original passage. Careless omissions occur too frequently, particularly under examination conditions, and marks are lost needlessly. Check first to ensure that *no sentence has been omitted* (it can easily happen when the translation makes perfectly good sense without the missing sentence), and secondly to make sure that *no single word has been overlooked*. There are certain English sentences which very frequently lead to omissions: they are those which contain rather a high number of apparently insignificant words. In a recent examination the following sentence gave rise to frequent omissions:

- They both suddenly remembered that the new manager often stayed very late in the office on a Friday."

Candidates lost marks because they simply overlooked words (such as "both", "new", "often", "very") which they would have had no difficulty in translating.

RECENT EXAMINATION QUESTIONS

Read through these passages in order to give yourself practice in fully grasping the ideas or situation and in anticipating the kind of problems discussed in the previous section of this chapter. Questions **2** and **4** have been translated for you. It will be useful to attempt the question yourself and then to compare your versions with the fair copies provided.

1.

De Gaulle understood better than most politicians the importance of radio and television. During the Second World War, the act which established his prestige as the saviour of France was the appeal he made on the radio, on 1 June 1940, that the French should resist the invader. Later, when he was President, he went on using both radio and television in his efforts to persuade and influence people.

Perhaps the finest examples of his belief in the power of the media are the famous press conferences, of which seventeen took place during his years at the Elysée. Described as "the absolute weapon of the régime", those conferences received the greatest possible publicity on radio and television as well as in the newspapers. Since important policy decisions were revealed in them, they would have been significant for that reason alone; what made them impressive, however, was de Gaulle's personal style.

Like an actor, he knew how to use voice and personality effectively, thus exerting enormous influence on the way people received his message. The projection of his personality won him enemies as well as friends. Perhaps more significant was the fact that the conferences provided proof that television especially had emerged as a powerful political force, particularly if under governmental control. This was illustrated in May 1968, when, initially, the government refused to allow any details of the events to be given on the State channels, although the press and the commercial stations were providing information for the public. (London, Syllabus B. Unpublished thesis, University of Bradford 1983.)

2.

In the spring of 1981, when the Left won control of the government of France for the first time in twenty-three years, it was thought that the hopes of May 1968 would finally be realised, through what was called Mitterrand's 'gentle revolution'. The student revolt that had eventually spread throughout the entire French nation during that spring filled with hope had failed to produce authentic social change. When the French people was asked to choose a new government, it had elected a solid Gaullist majority that would, at best, produce only modest reforms with the aim of satisfying the demands of both students and workers in industry.

But May 1981 was to be different. The parties of the Left would seek to carry out the reforms which it had already established in its Common Programme in 1972. The Mitterrand government began its programme with the nationalisation of important sectors of the economy. In this way it sought to increase government control in those domains. However, this action forced the government to introduce new austerity measures in 1983 and 1984, in the hope of slowing down inflation in France.

It was clear in 1984 that the President's austerity plans were worrying some of the more radical members of his own party, such as Edmond Maire, who declared himself to be particularly concerned about the high level of unemployment. However, it seemed obvious at that time that Mitterrand would continue as President until the election in 1988. (London Syllabus B, 1986. Adapted from *Contemporary French Civilization*, Vol viii, Nos. 1 and 2).

3.

We are told that London is one of the most difficult places for meeting people. This is the case with all big cities. Solitary souls join evening classes and clubs, all because it can be so hard to find someone to talk to in the course of a day. Of course not many would go as far as Dorothy Parker when feeling a sudden need for company: she placed a notice bearing the word "Gentlemen" on her hotel room door.

But I have found, accidentally, a simple way into other people's homes and lives. It all began when I needed some pieces of furniture for a country cottage a little while ago. Looking through the advertisements in the local paper I found some unbelievable bargains.

There was a bed. "That's a good bed, believe me", said the owner, gently patting her divan, "my little boy has slept on it since he was a baby." Just as I was leaving, her "little boy" came home from work: six foot tall, enormously fat and nearly fifty.

"My husband hates this divan so much that he said either this thing goes or he goes", was another lady's frank explanation for a sale.

"We are emigrating to South Africa", an elderly couple said aggressively. "There is no more freedom in this country."

(Cambridge, 1981. *London Standard* 1981)

4.

We were in the habit of bathing every day at a beach called the Baths of Tiberius. Having left the main road, we would wander through orchards and vineyards, till we came to the cliff-top, from which a narrow, winding path led to the sea. The next day, while we were making our way towards the water's edge, my friend said: "Look, there's Wilson back again." We stumbled across the pebbly beach and, as we approached him, Wilson noticed us. He was lying on a towel, pretending to read a book. We were hot after our walk, so we undressed quickly and plunged into the sea. Hardly had I got out of the water than Wilson sat up and waved. I lit a cigarette and went and sat down beside him.

"Did you enjoy yourself?" he asked, closing the book. "Was the water warm?"

Evidently he wanted to talk.

"Lovely", I said. "It's the best beach I know."

"It's unbelievable," he went on, "but some people think those buildings over there were the Baths of Tiberius." He pointed towards some ruins half submerged in the water. "How ridiculous! It was just one of his villas, you know."

I did know, but it is always best to listen when someone wants to offer you information. It does no harm and gives them pleasure. Wilson laughed heartily.

"Funny emperor, Tiberius. What a pity they're saying now that all those stories which are told about him are completely untrue."

(London, 1983. *Somerset Maugham: Collected Short Stories*)

TUTOR'S ANSWERS

2.

Au printemps de 1981, lorsque la gauche obtint le contrôle du gouvernement de la France pour la première fois en vingt-trois ans, l'on crut que les rêves de Mai 1968 allaient enfin se réaliser, au travers de ce que l'on appela "la révolution tranquille" de Mitterrand. La révolte des étudiants qui avait fini par se répandre dans toute la nation française lors de ce printemps débordant d'espoirs n'avait pas réussi à produire un changement social authentique. Lorsqu'on avait demandé aux Français de se prononcer sur le choix d'un nouveau gouvernement, ils avaient élu une forte majorité gaulliste qui devait, au mieux, ne mettre en oeuvre que quelques modestes réformes visant à satisfaire les doubles revendications des étudiants et des travailleurs de l'industrie.

Cependant, Mai 1968 devait s'avérer différent. Les partis de gauche allaient tenter de mettre en place des réformes qu'ils avaient déjà élaborées dans leur Programme Commun de 1972. Le gouvernement Mitterrand commença la réalisation de son programme par la nationalisation d'importants secteurs de l'économie. Il visait ainsi à accroître le contrôle du gouvernement dans ces domaines. Cette action obligea pourtant le gouvernement à adopter de nouvelles mesures d'austérité en 1983 et 1984, afin de ralentir l'inflation en France.

Il ne faisait aucun doute en 1984 que les plans d'austérité du Président suscitaient l'inquiétude, au sein de son propre parti, de quelques éléments les plus radicaux tel Edmond Maire, qui se déclara particulièrement troublé par les taux élevés du chômage. Mais, à ce moment-là, il paraissait évident que Mitterrand exercerait ses fonctions présidentielles jusqu'aux élections de 1988.

4.

Nous avions l'habitude de nous baigner tous les jours sur une plage qui s'appelait les Bains de Tibère. Ayant quitté la grande route nous errions à travers des vergers et des vignobles jusqu'à ce que nous arrivassions en haut de la falaise d'où un sentier étroit et sinueux conduisait à la mer. Le lendemain, pendant que nous nous dirigions vers le bord de l'eau, mon ami me dit: "Regarde, voilà Wilson qui est revenu!" Nous traversâmes en trébuchant la plage de galets et, comme nous nous approchions de lui, Wilson nous aperçut. Il était étendu sur une serviette, faisant semblant de lire un livre. Nous avions chaud après notre promenade, ainsi nous nous déshabillâmes rapidement et plongeâmes dans la mer. A peine fus-je sorti de l'eau que Wilson s'assit et agita la main. J'allumai une cigarette et allai m'asseoir à côté de lui.

"Vous vous êtes amusé?" demanda-t-il en fermant le livre. "L'eau était bonne?" Evidemment, il avait envie de parler.

"Délicieuse", dis-je. "C'est la meilleure plage que je connaisse."

"C'est incroyable," reprit-il, "mais il y a des gens qui croient que ces bâtiments là-bas étaient les Bains de Tibère." Il montra du doigt des ruines à moitié submergées sous l'eau. "Que c'est ridicule! Ce n'était qu'une de ses villas, vous savez."

Je le savais bien, mais il vaut toujours mieux écouter lorsque quelqu'un veut vous offrir des renseignements. Cela ne fait pas de mal et cela leur fait plaisir. Wilson rit de bon coeur.

"Drôle d'empereur, Tibère. Quel dommage que l'on prétende

maintenant que toutes ces histoires qui se racontent à son sujet sont complètement fausses."

A STEP FURTHER

If you need extra practice in prose translation you can, of course, work on past papers or find your own English passages and work on them by yourself. However, it is not always easy to find someone to mark the work and go through it with you. It is easier and indeed more profitable to work on the retranslation of passages which you have translated from the French yourself.

Retranslation is most effective if you link it to the intensive study of texts described on p. 44–49. When you have completed the intensive study of a passage as part of your vocabulary-building programme, you can translate the passage, or better still a simplified or slightly rearranged version of it, into English. After an interval of two or three days, attempt to translate it back into French using the original passage and your own intensive study notes to self-correct your work. You will find that your retranslation will not necessarily take you back exactly to the text you started with but this in itself will help you to understand the technique of translation and the nature of language.

It is very valuable to make your translation practice emerge naturally from your own reading and language-learning programme. You can ensure that you are working on texts which are totally relevant to your examination needs and you will be using translation as a productive revision exercise and one which teaches you to retrieve words and phrases from your memory rather than from the dictionary. With a little experience you will be able to build into the target passage and therefore into the English passage intended for retranslation, those points on which you need to test yourself.

It is also useful to work on parallel English–French texts. It is quite easy to obtain in paperback editions (Gallimard folio, Penguin, etc.) a range of French or English translations. It is always best to work initially on an original French passage using it for intensive study and then to use the English translation for retranslation practice. If you do this rather than attempt immediately to translate or retranslate into French, you will be carrying out a productive language exercise rather than just setting yourself a test. You will also be in a better position to look critically at the translator's version and you will learn that even a professional translation can often be improved upon.

FURTHER READING

S. W. Segger. *Thèmes Modèles*. C.U.P.
See Gallimard Folio and Penguin catalogues for works translated from French to English/English to French.

Chapter 9   Reading comprehension

GETTING STARTED

You will already be familiar with reading comprehension in one form or another because it is a very frequently used language exercise at all levels: a text in French is studied closely and its vocabulary and structures are practised through a series of questions and answers. However at an advanced level, although the format may be similar (a passage of French followed by a number of questions), reading comprehension is likely to demand more sophisticated skills and a wider reading vocabulary and understanding of structures than the "questions on the text" that you are probably used to. The reading comprehension test may well be less familiar and more challenging than you have assumed and you would therefore be advised to prepare carefully for it.

The first step is to find out as much as you can from the syllabus and from past papers about the type of passage and questions which will be set. The syllabus regulations will probably give only brief indications such as "The intention of this Paper is to test the candidates' ability to understand a passage (or passages) of quite complex contemporary French in a non-literary register" (London, Syllabus B) or "The passage will be in the form of a narrative with elements of analysis and dialogue" (AEB), but what it says can guide you to the *main type* of reading material which you should use when preparing specifically for this paper. This is important because the most useful way in which you can prepare for the test is to read as extensively as you can and to develop your comprehension skill through practice. Extensive reading, of course, should become an activity which is the foundation of all your language work and it will therefore be valuable to read a wide variety of texts. However, if the reading comprehension test in the examination is clearly going to be of a specific type (e.g. a non-literary passage or a passage of narrative) it is essential to work on plenty of passages of the appropriate type. A passage of argument or discussion in a non-literary register will present different analytical problems and require a somewhat different approach from a passage of narrative and dialogue.

The syllabus regulations will give you information about the time allowed for the test and the length of the passage (or passages). If you consult past papers (there may be none available if the Board has only recently introduced reading comprehension, but ask for specimen papers) you will have an idea of the type of questions which you will be required to answer. There is a variety of possible question types: multiple choice questions, gapped sentences for completion, "true or false" questions and of course, Why? What? How? questions. At A-level the questions are usually set and answered in English on the grounds that it is the candidates' comprehension ɗf French which is being tested rather than their ability to write it.

Sometimes the syllabus will give quite detailed information as to the number and type of questions: "There will be not less than 6 and not more than 10 questions on the passage. Some of these will test comprehension of specific elements, others gist comprehension, and they may require the candidate to draw inferences from surface content of the passage" (AEB). Find out what you can. It will give you confidence and a more defined sense of purpose. If only a little information is given there is no cause for alarm. If you follow the advice in this chapter it will help you to improve your comprehension skills generally and to prepare yourself for tackling different question types. Indeed, it is a wise approach to be ready for a number of possibilities.

These preliminary investigations will enable you to begin to set up a reading programme designed to support not only your practice in reading comprehension but the rest of your language work. Extensive and intensive reading are essential for training in reading comprehension but they are also vital for vocabulary acquisition and for familiarisation and revision of grammatical structures. The reading in French that you do to develop your comprehension skills will also help you to improve your essay-writing in French together with your prose and translation work.

ESSENTIAL PRINCIPLES

CRITERIA OF ASSESSMENT

Before considering in detail what is involved in applying and developing the skill of reading comprehension, it is as well to discuss briefly the way in which the test is usually marked and to mention some of the common pitfalls which candidates should learn to avoid.

The purpose of the reading comprehension is to assess the ability of candidates to express their understanding of a passage of written French. As it is a test of comprehension candidates are not expected to translate directly from the original but to express themselves clearly in their own words in order to answer the questions on the text. The main requirement is that *all* relevant information should be given and that precise information or explanation should be provided. Penalties are incurred therefore when necessary details are omitted or where the answer is imprecisely or poorly expressed to the point where the information required is really incomplete. Excess information does not usually lead to a penalty unless its inclusion vitiates the correct answer.

When the test comprises a number of questions (normally between 6 and 10) on a piece of continuous French (usually a passage of 500–600 words) the marks will probably not be distributed evenly to each question. The number of marks carried by an individual question will depend on the amount of information which must be retrieved from the text in order to provide a satisfactory answer. The number of marks carried by each question is sometimes printed on the question paper.

REASONS FOR POOR PERFORMANCE

When candidates do not do well in the reading comprehension test examiners find that it is mainly for one or more of the following reasons:

1. Candidates try to translate sentences from the text instead of reading it and processing it in order to identify relevant points and ideas. This can lead the candidate to miss the point or to produce half-meaningful English which may falsify the answer.
2. Many candidates appear not to have had sufficient training in reading texts of the right length and of sufficient complexity. They have therefore not developed the skill of identifying and following the main theme of the passage and of picking out and remembering its points and counter-points. Instead they adopt a piecemeal, line-by-line approach and as a result misinterpret points or miss them altogether.
3. Candidates do not always give sufficient attention to the rubric. They may therefore fail to read the text with precise comprehension.
4. The passive or reading vocabulary of too many candidates is not sufficiently wide. Some candidates have not developed the strategy of using context and global understanding of the passage to help them discover the meaning of lexical items which they do not recognise.
5. Candidates do not read the questions on the text carefully enough, particularly those questions which ask for precise information. The result is a general answer which will not score full marks. All terms of the question should be taken into consideration.
6. Some candidates have not understood the nature of the test and spend time commenting on the text in vague terms or on agreeing or disagreeing with opinions and ideas expressed in it.

These, of course, are faults which you should make sure of avoiding. Some of them would never arise if candidates had a better understanding of what reading comprehension really involves. Making clear what it involves is the purpose of the section which follows.

ACTIVITIES FOR IMPROVING YOUR READING COMPREHENSION

Extensive reading

There are a number of reading skills which you can learn which will help you to tackle the reading comprehension efficiently. These will be discussed below, but the best way to improve your performance in this test is to ensure that you read regularly and as widely as possible in French. If you read frequently in your own language you will probably not find it difficult to motivate yourself to read in French. You will be able to transfer some of your reading interests from one language to the other.

If you are not an enthusiastic reader you should ask yourself why and see whether you can cultivate an interest in reading in French. Remember that there is a range of reading material which is appropriate now that you are studying French at an advanced level. It is to be found in newspapers, advertisements, illustrated magazines, instructions, short stories, poems, novels, plays, biographies, reference books, encyclopaedias, books on geography, history, science and so on. Select topics which interest you and try to read with a purpose. If you are studying other subjects make an effort to read books on that subject in French. Set yourself tasks which will motivate your reading. If you can buy regularly, or have access to, a French newspaper such as *Le Figaro* or *Le Matin*, or to a French magazine such as *Elle, Le Point* or *L'Express*, use it to follow up a topical theme or to document a place or person of interest. Read French to find out information and you may find that you want to read more French.

What is proposed here is *extensive reading*, rather than intensive reading (which also has an important place in your language work but is a different activity) which would involve you in analysis of grammar and vocabulary. Your primary objective when you embark on a programme of extensive reading is to read with interest and with fluency. Foreign language learners tend not to read in this way. They have often developed the habit of concentrating on every word instead of taking in groups of words and blocks of meaning. It may be of course that they are forced into this approach simply because the text contains too much unknown vocabulary and too many unfamiliar structures. More often the apparent inability to read with fluency is the result of old habits which persist because the reader does not realise that it is *not necessary* to understand every word and that it is worth tolerating some uncertainty as to the meaning in order to maintain the thought process involved in continuous reading and to prevent interest from flagging. At first you will find it taxing to get through a short story, a novel or a long newspaper article but sometimes it is important to keep going even if you have only a rather hazy idea of what the novel or article is about. Remember that when you are reading to improve fluency it is better to avoid over-use of the dictionary. Meaning can often be inferred from the context and by reading on you will often come across clues which will elucidate troublesome vocabulary. When you meet words that you do not understand it is valuable to go through a process of inferring or intelligent guessing instead of, or at least before, checking the word in the dictionary. It is an important way of developing your comprehension skill. It will mean, of course, that you do not read each section of the text at the same speed but this does not necessarily mean loss of fluency. It is quite normal for a fluent reader to read certain sentences and to read some parts of the text more slowly than others.

In the initial stages you will need to be discriminating in your choice of texts. A certain amount of difficulty is tolerable and, if your attitude is relaxed, will not prevent you from making reasonable progress; but clearly some reading matter will be too inaccessible and is best discarded or left until later. To begin with, in order to have reading material which *does* allow fluent reading, you could make use of simplified versions of authentic texts such as the series Textes en Français Facile published by Hachette. You could also try textbooks and junior encyclopaedias intended for younger native French readers. If you can have access to a French newspaper or periodical concentrate on the easier sections such as reports of events in the news about which you already have a background knowledge or on the Courrier des Lecteurs which provide shorter, less complex passages of French until you have the confidence to read more generally. If you have difficulty in locating and selecting authentic material of an appropriate standard then consult your tutor and the suggested reading at the end of this chapter.

Fluent or even semi-fluent reading of a range of material will help you to develop those comprehension skills which are essential for dealing successfully with the reading comprehension test. Such reading will also become a very important part of your general language-learning programme. It is the most effective way of building up an extensive receptive vocabulary, of rehearsing known but half-forgotten lexical items and structures and of generally keeping in use language that you have already learnt. This is a major difficulty for the learner who is not living in a French-speaking environment. Reading fluently is also a way of acquiring a feel for what is grammatically correct and of assimilating syntactic patterns. Setting yourself clear reading goals and establishing good reading habits is something that you cannot afford to neglect.

Intensive reading

When it comes to tackling the type of passage set as a reading comprehension test you will be required to read it *intensively*. Nevertheless your extensive reading, particularly if it has been directed towards finding out information, will stand you in very good stead. You will be used to identifying main points and to separating them from less significant detail; you will also be more able to read rapidly or to scan a text in order to retrieve a specific piece of information. When it comes to the reading comprehension test these are useful skills. When you work on the passage set you will need to read it a number of times, closely and analytically, and then rapidly scan it as you search for the information asked for in the questions. Extensive reading will also have improved your background knowledge or your "knowledge of the world". When such knowledge corresponds to that of the writer you will be able to deal with assumptions which are left inexplicit and with those lexical items which do not mean very much unless you are aware of the reality to which they refer. Examples of such terms are: les collectivités locales; une caisse de sécurité sociale; le social; le nucléaire; la cohabitation. The words *seem* easy enough but without some background knowledge the reader may well ask: "What exactly do they mean?"

The format of the paper may vary from one Examination Board to another but what you are most likely to meet is a passage of narrative or discussion of 500–600 words followed by a number of questions.

When you start work on the passage read it first continuously, without lingering over details which are not immediately understood, in order to arrive at an overall understanding of the passage. It is best to work *from* a global understanding *to* the understanding of smaller units: paragraphs, sentences and then to individual words. In this way you will have an outline of the text in your mind from the beginning. Knowing the context will help you to elucidate specific parts of the text which, initially, may have caused difficulty. Remember that the examiner will have approached the text in this way when setting the questions and that most questions will be designed to test not just individual sentences but sentences in context.

If you are not working under exam conditions and you are practising reading comprehension on a passage of your own choosing, it is a good idea, before you study the text closely, to try to anticipate what the writer is going to say. First read through the text rapidly in order to get an overall view of its main points. Then write down the questions that you think the text should answer. Finally you study the text closely, looking for the answer to your questions. Predicting information contained in the text will help you to read with a purpose and working out your own questions will give you some insight into the way an examiner might approach the passage when setting questions on it.

Any text that you may be faced with, in the examination or elsewhere, will inevitably contain vocabulary that you do not recognise and constructions that you are unable to unravel. There *are* ways of dealing with specific difficulties of this nature and they are discussed in Chapter 12. However, it is important to realise that there is more to understanding a text than understanding separate words and structures or even separate sentences.

| Types of meaning | To comprehend a text fully you must practise "reading into" it and in order to do this effectively you should be aware that any given sentence can have more than one type of meaning. |

1. Firstly, there is the meaning that a sentence can have on its own, i.e. its *independent* or *propositional* meaning:
    Nous sommes aujourd'hui deux milliards et demi de terriens.

2. Secondly, a sentence which is part of a text will also have a *contextual* meaning which is created because the sentence is related to other sentences which precede and follow it. It then takes on a function which derives from the writer's reason for using it. When it stands alone the sentence in French above has no function, but it takes on a function when it follows another sentence:

> Il est important de reconnaître qu'il y a une limite au peuplement de la planète. Nous sommes aujourd'hui deux milliards et demi de terriens.

Here it is a justification of the first statement and part of the writer's argument. The relationship between the two sentences would, of course, be more clearly indicated if they were joined by "parce que" or "car" but you will often find that the relationship is not marked explicitly. The reader interprets it by referring to the context and through his global understanding of the text.

3. Thirdly, there is the type of meaning which a sentence can carry and one which a reading comprehension question may require you to interpret, namely the meaning that *reflects the writer's attitude or feelings*:

> Avec 8, 43 sur 20, Christine avait été jugée "irrécupérable" par ses professeurs. A 9, apprirent peu après ses parents, elle aurait été admise à redoubler. Admirable certitude des chiffres!

The closing sentence which is to be taken ironically, expresses the attitude of the writer who is not at all convinced that marks are as precisely reliable as Christine's teachers were apparently prepared to believe.

Every sentence can have these *three* kinds of meaning and if you aim to understand a text fully you should be prepared to interpret all three meanings. Ask yourself what a writer is saying in a sentence but also ask yourself what he is doing (i.e. is he giving an explanation, providing an example, establishing a reason, introducing a contradiction, etc.?) by placing it in relationship with other sentences. Aim to discover what attitude the writer is conveying by using the sentence in the way he has used it.

The fact that a sentence can have these different meanings can be of positive help when you are interpreting a text as one meaning can lead you to infer another. For example, you would probably have understood from the rest of the passage that the writer was being ironic in the final sentence of the above quotation. Even if the meaning of the two preceding sentences had eluded you, you would have at least been able to infer that Christine had suffered rather harsh treatment because of her marks and the thread of the writer's argument would not have been lost.

Points to check when trying to infer meaning

If the meaning of part of a reading comprehension passage escapes you there are a number of points that you can check.

    1. Use the approach described in Chapter 12, to help you disentangle the *syntax*.

    2. Check those words which are used to indicate the *function* of a sentence, i.e. those which tell how a writer is using a sentence and what he is doing with it:

cependant	en effet	en revanche	ainsi
mais	en fait	d'autre part	ensuite
toutefois	d'ailleurs	enfin	
néanmoins	en outre	or	
pourtant	par ailleurs	en somme	

Words such as these (they are sometimes called "markers") indicate that the sentence is carrying out one of a number of possible functions such as expressing an opposition, making a concession, giving an example, sequencing, specifying, resuming, commenting, focusing attention, passing from one point to the next, enumerating or concluding. It is not possible to provide an exhaustive list of such words or even of the functions that they mark but the important point is that you should be aware of them. Identify them in your reading and use them in order to read a text with full comprehension. They provide useful clues. For example, in the following sentences:

- Cette histoire semble invraisemblable; elle est <u>pourtant</u> vraie.
- Si les objectifs n'ont pas totalement changé, on note <u>en revanche</u> une nette divergence sur les moyens d'y parvenir.

If you had not understood "invraisemblable" the word "pourtant" gives you a clue because it tells you "invraisemblable" is opposed in meaning to "vraie", and if you had not grasped "une nette divergence sur les moyens d'y parvenir" "en revanche" would tell you that it goes against the meaning of the first part of the sentence in some way enabling you to decipher the meaning of the whole sentence, or at least to reach enough understanding of it to be able to deal with a comprehension question.

    3. Check what are called the *reference words* in the text. They are those words which tell the reader that he has to find their meaning in another part of the text. The pronouns il, elle, elles, le, la, les, lui, leur, eux, y and en are obvious examples:

- Lorsque le directeur m'a demandé des renseignements sur la conférence de presse du Président je lui ai dit qu'elle avait été remise au lendemain.
- Quand tu le verras, dis à Paul de me téléphoner.
- Le bâtiment se trouvait près du port et l'odeur des poissons y pénétrait.
- Si les autres veulent partir je ne peux pas les en empêcher.

Other words of this type are the relative pronouns qui, que, quoi, dont, a preposition with lequel, où, ce qui, ce que, ce dont, ce à quoi and the demonstrative pronouns celui-ci, celui-là, cela, ceci, ce.

When you study a text, examine the way in which these terms relate backwards or forwards to other parts of the text. If the meaning of a sentence or paragraph eludes you, make sure that it is not because you have misunderstood the function of one of these reference words. It is good practice to ring such terms when you read a text and to link them visibly to other elements in the passage to which they refer.

4. The use of words to indicate the function of a sentence and reference words are two of the elements which make a text hang together and work as a process of communication. There is another factor which makes a text cohesive: a writer will use different words to refer to the same thing at different points in the text. These words may be synonyms of the word already used but often they will add to the meaning as well as providing a substitute term. It is therefore possible to talk of a *synonymic development* which runs through a text. If you are aware of it and can identify it this will help you to follow the sense of the passage.

The following words and phrases all taken from a text on over-population represent what we have called the synonymic development of the text:

> La croissance de la population... l'extraordinaire développement de l'homme... la multiplication de l'espèce humaine... la prèdominance de l'homme sur la terre... l'accroissement démographique... ce problème... ce danger... le peuplement de la terre... le nombre des individus, etc.

It is a useful task to set yourself to trace such a development when reading a text. It will help you to grasp the way in which the ideas are organised and developed through different paragraphs and will improve your ability to relate one part of the text to another.

TYPES OF QUESTION SET FOR READING COMPREHENSION

The questions which follow the reading comprehension passage are nearly always put and answered in English as questions on the text. However, comprehension may be tested in a number of other ways. You may be required to *summarise* a given section of the text, to *tabulate information*, to *explain precisely* a section of the text in your own words, to *give the gist* of a selected number of lines or possibly *to write a brief report* on the passage. It is as well to check the syllabus to find out exactly how comprehension will be tested.

1. Questions on the text may be of different types.
The first and simplest type is the direct *reference question*. It is simple because the answer can be reached by translating (or by "lifting", if the answer is in French) the relevant part of the text without "organising" the material in any other way.

> Pourquoi tant de Français continuent-ils à voter communiste? D'abord, probablement, parce que le parti leur paraît l'instrument le plus efficace dans la lutte contre le patronat, pour la défense des intérêts des travailleurs. De façon directe, par son action et celle de la CGT – sa filiale – dans les combats pour les

salaires, la sécurité et les avantages sociaux. De façon indirecte aussi, par la peur qu'il inspire aux chefs d'entreprises et aux pouvoirs publics. Le pourcentage des voix communistes aux élections a fini par devenir une côte d'alerte: s'il s'élève, patrons et gouvernements sentent qu'il faut "faire quelque chose" pour les ouvriers, lesquels ont fort bien compris cette situation. D'autre part, l'admirable dévouement des militants et des cadres n'a pas d'équivalent dans les autres partis, lesquels ressemblent plus à des comités de politiciens professionnels qu'à des organisations de masse: cela aussi maintient l'attachement au PC. Enfin, l'intégration morale de la classe ouvrière dans la nation est probablement en retard sur son intégration matérielle. Les terribles luttes du XIXe siècle, les massacres de Juin 48 et de la Commune ont donné au prolétariat français un sentiment d'isolement tragique, qui n'a pas encore entièrement disparu. Voter communiste, c'est presque une question d'honneur, de dignité: abandonner le parti serait commettre une sorte de trahison.

(*De La Dictature* by Maurice Duverger. Julliard)

A direct reference question and answer relating to these lines would be:

Q: Why do so many French people vote Communist?
A: Because the Communist Party seems to be the most effective way of fighting the employers.

Such a question tests only literal comprehension and is not the type of question that you should expect at A-level.

2. Another type is the *inference question*. To answer it you will have to relate different sentences or parts of the text, reorganise the information contained in them and examine the text to see what if any, implications there are. It is a question of not only reading the lines but of "reading between the lines". It may be necessary to refer to information which is scattered quite widely throughout the text in order to make a deduction or to check that your deduction is correct. The following are inference questions set on the passage above:

Q: Why is the Communist Party an effective party organisation?
A: Because it is a party which has a mass membership and has loyal and hard-working party workers and officials.
Q: Why should the working class feel a sense of honour and dignity in supporting the Communist Party?
A: The working class feel a sense of honour and dignity in voting Communist because it is an act of solidarity and loyalty; events in recent history have made them feel that they stand apart from the rest of the nation therefore they feel that they must stand together.

3. The third type may be called the *interpretative question*. It requires you to not only understand the text but to interpret it in the light of wider knowledge or of common sense.

– Nous parlions de Mlle Lagarde.
Simon s'agita.
– On se connaît elle et moi depuis un an!
– Je sais.
– Elle est sensationnelle! dit-il et il se mit à froisser l'extrémité de sa cravate. Pauline, c'est la jeune fille la plus... elle est merveilleuse! Vous verrez...
– Simon, tu te rends bien compte que dans une petite ville comme Sault, un grand garçon ne peut pas fréquenter une jeune personne sans que les gens bavardent.

(*La Parade* By Jean-Louis Curtis. Julliard)

Q: What is Simon's attitude towards his mother when she questions him?

A: He is ill at ease and hesitates to assert himself.

Here it is necessary to understand the literal meaning of the French and to use common sense to understand that this behaviour (fidgeting, playing with his tie, etc.) is a sign of nervousness and uneasiness.

4. Finally, there is the *evaluative question*. It is the one which involves you in making a judgement about the writer's attitude and about what he is trying to do in the text. You could be asked to describe the author's opinion of the facts that he is relating or explaining, even though that opinion is not explicitly stated in the text. Questions of this kind are perhaps the most advanced of all as the reader has to analyse his response to the text and discover the objective reasons for it. The way in which the ideas are presented, i.e. the author's style, will help indicate whether he is being ironic, flippant, indignant and so on.

The comprehension questions set in an examination are likely to involve a *mixture* of these types and any one question could require both literal comprehension and a measure of inference or interpretation. What the different types should show you above all is that reading comprehension will need considerably more than a literal, sentence by sentence, understanding. The skill being tested is the ability to read the text as connected French and to be alert to all its levels of meaning.

POINTS TO NOTE IN THE EXAMINATION ROOM

When you tackle reading comprehension *under examination conditions* you should remember the following points:

1. Do not be in too much of a hurry to get to the questions. Study the text intensively in the way described on p. 105. When you feel that you have worked your way sufficiently into the passage, try to establish a rough plan of it by identifying the main developments of the argument or the main stages in a chronological account, depending on the type of passage. These divisions will not always correspond to the paragraphs in the passage, you may find that two or even three paragraphs will relate to one main idea. It is useful *to indicate the natural divisions visually* by bracketing them together on the paper. Then, in each division, *underline the key sentence*, the one

which seems to contain the central idea. It is also helpful to *ring those words which signpost the various stages in the argument* or the account. Your plan may be somewhat "rough and ready" but working on it will improve your understanding of the passage and help you to hold it in your mind.

2. Once you have the "feel" of the passage, study the questions carefully and pay attention to every word. If the question asks for "causes", "advantages", "factors" in the plural then expect to find more than *one*. Use the clues which are in the questions. Sometimes the way in which the question is framed will indicate that you may have to make an inference or a supposition in order to reach the answer. (e.g. Why does the factory *seem* to be important? What *appears* to be the French view?)

It will help if you have practised interpreting questions set on past papers; you will be used to some of the terms which examiners use (factors, attitude, indications, evidence, etc.) to avoid giving too much of the answer in the question.

Read the English carefully. A question such as "What *motivates* Y's attitude?" is not the same as "What *is* Y's attitude?" and if you think about it the question on p. 107, "Why *should* the working class feel a sense of honour etc.?" is slightly different from "Why *do* the working class feel a sense of honour?" If a question really does seem ambiguous then indicate in your answer that it could reasonably be interpreted in two ways.

3. Make brief notes in rough for each answer. Until you have read the passage with complete understanding it may seem that some questions overlap. As subsequent readings improve your grasp of the passage you may well find that what you have jotted down for one answer is more applicable to another. It is therefore best to work through *all the questions in rough* before you start to write on the answer paper.

It is usual for the order of the questions to follow the order of the text (the examiner will not have jumbled them deliberately to confuse you) but you should not assume that having taken an answer from say the first few lines that you can forget about them. They may have further relevance. This is why it is important to have a global view of the text.

4. Remember that you are required to give all relevant information in answer to a question. When you have identified the relevant point in the text always read on to see whether there are further elements which should be included. The information which you are seeking may be scattered. Sometimes, of course, it is difficult to decide whether the extra information is necessary or not. This need not give you cause for too much concern. The inclusion of non-essential details is not likely to be penalised unless it distorts the answer.

5. Express your answer as clearly and as simply as you can and ensure that it says what you mean. Concentrate on answering the question and do not be satisfied with locating what seems to be a

relevant section of the text and translating it into English. You are likely to miss the point.

Certain questions will specifically ask you *not* to translate. For example: In your own words, explain the ideas in paragraph X; Without translating, outline the points made in paragraph Y. This does not mean that you are not allowed to use the English equivalent of some of the words in the French, it means rather that you should make clear your understanding of the essential points without struggling with the niceties of translation and that the examiner is not looking for an answer in clumsy "translationese".

EXAMINATION QUESTIONS

You will find below two A-level reading comprehension passages. The first is narrative and dialogue and is in a literary register; the second deals with a contemporary issue and is in a non-literary register. Study the passages and the questions bearing in mind what has been said in the earlier part of this chapter and in paragraphs 1–5 above.

a)

Read the following passage carefully and then answer in English, giving all relevant details, the questions which follow it:

Quand, sur la recommandation de la directrice de son cours, Anne avait reçu une convocation des Papeteries réunies, une joie conquérante s'était emparée d'elle. Elle s'était présentée à l'heure indiquée. Mais à peine franchie la grille, elle s'était trouvée, sans bien savoir comment, dans un petit bureau triste et sombre où d'autres candidates attendaient anxieuses, assises sur le bord de leur chaise… Il n'y avait plus de siège. Elle avait dû rester debout jusqu'au moment où une porte s'était ouverte sur une grande femme revêche qui les avait interpellées.

– Pour le poste de sténodactylo… Nous allons faire un essai… Si vous voulez bien me suivre…

Dans une salle, des machines à écrire étaient préparées. On leur avait distribué un texte. Il lui avait fallu un prodigieux effort de volonté pour dominer sa nervosité, éviter des fautes de frappe et, un peu plus tard, retrouver en sténo sa vitesse habituelle.

L'épreuve finie, la femme les avait sèchement remerciées:
– On vous écrira…

Elles s'étaient retrouvées dehors toutes les six, se regardant avec un peu de méfiance et un curieux sentiment de gêne qui ressemblait à la honte.

– Ils disent toujours ça, avait soupiré une petite boulotte qui ne devait pas en être à sa première tentative, et ils n'écrivent jamais.

Ils avaient écrit cependant, un imprimé rempli d'une main hâtive. Une visite encore avant de signer sa lettre d'engagement. Un salaire moins important qu'elle ne l'avait espéré, mais qu'elle avait accepté, trop heureuse, après cette attente, d'avoir la place.

Anne ouvrit la porte de l'appartement, traversa l'entrée obscure et pénétra dans sa chambre dont elle claqua la porte. Elle chercha ses pantoufles et courut vers la cuisine où Louise s'affairait. Elle saisit sa mère dans ses bras, l'embrassa avec fougue et s'écria:

– Ça y est, maman, ça y est! Je suis acceptée! Je commence demain!

– Quelle chance! dit Louise. J'espère que tout le monde sera gentil pour toi.

– Naturellement, ma douce! On ne va pas manger ta fille, répondit-elle, taquine. Et, tu sais, c'est une grosse boîte... Plusieurs millions d'affaires par an... Quinze sténodactylos et neuf cents francs par mois pour débuter. Ce n'est pas si mal. Et puis je monterai en grade. Que crois-tu que père va en penser?

– Il sera content, bien sûr... Tiens, le voilà.

La porte d'entrée s'ouvrit avec fracas et Léon Moiraud entra en chantant.

– On l'a acceptée aux Papeteries réunies, dit Louise. C'est une maison sérieuse; elle commence demain.

Léon tapota la joue de sa fille.

– C'est bien, fillette. Le travail, vois-tu, il n'y a que ça. Mais il faut en profiter quand on est jeune.

A quarante-cinq ans lui n'était plus assez jeune pour accomplir cet effort quotidien. Après quelques années de dur travail comme transportateur, la guerre et quatre ans de captivité en avaient fait un autre homme. Le beau garçon plein d'allant et de drôlerie avec qui Louise avait connu quelques années de bonheur n'avait plus le cœur à l'ouvrage. Il passait au café le plus clair de son temps, jouant aux cartes ou revivant les aventures imaginaires de sa vie de prisonnier. Il n'avait gardé de sa jeunesse que sa gaieté, son humeur tapageuse et un optimisme qui croissait avec sa paresse.

Louise s'usait à faire des travaux de couture pour colmater les brèches que la prodigalité et l'insouciance de Léon creusaient dans son budget. Il ne semblait pas, cependant, qu'elle fût malheureuse. Elle accueillait les extravagances de son mari avec une indulgence que la résignation ne suffisait pas à expliquer. Bien qu'Anne eût moins d'indulgence et souffrit de vivre dans ce logement inconfortable et de voir sa mère s'épuiser à la tâche, elle s'amusait, elle aussi, de la verve intarissable de son père.

Séduisant, son père avait dû l'être. Il avait ces yeux chauds de Méridional, ce teint basané qui plaisent aux femmes. Mais ces séductions ne suffisaient pas à compenser les privations de toute une vie et l'angoisse de la misère.

Anne aussi était gaie, avait envie de rire, de chanter, et elle se sentait prête à mordre à belles dents dans les fruits dorés de la vie. Mais elle se promettait bien de ne pas tomber dans les pièges auxquels Louise s'était laissé prendre.

Ce soir, elle avait remporté sa première victoire, fait ses premiers pas sur la route qui devait conduire au succès.

(*Le Revers de la Médaille* by Pierette Sartin. Casterman)

Questions

(a) What kind of test did Anne have to carry out?

(2 marks)

(b) How many candidates were called for the post, and in what state of mind were they before and after the test?

(6 marks)

(c) What are we told about the firm to which Anne applied?

(6 marks)

(d) What evidence is there in the text to show that Anne was ambitious?

(7 marks)

(e) What else are we told about Anne?

(9 marks)

(f) How did the war affect Léon Moiraud?

(6 marks)

(g) What was Louise's reaction to these changes in her husband?

(6 marks)

(h) In what ways could Léon Moiraud be described as attractive?

(6 marks)

(AEB Specimen paper)

(b)

Read carefully the following passage, <u>which is not to be translated</u>, then answer in English the questions set on it. Your answers should be in the form of complete sentences. Tabulation may be used if appropriate. In the assessment of your answers accuracy, appropriateness and quality of language will be taken into account.

L'industrie en Europe

Berceau de la première révolution industrielle, l'Europe jouera-t-elle encore les premiers rôles à l'avenir? Pour provocatrice qu'elle soit, la question doit être posée aujourd'hui. Qui ne voit qu'au fil des ans son influence scientifique et économique, culturelle et militaire – en un mot, politique – s'érode?

Si l'Europe demeure un marché convoité, elle a été détrônée par le Japon comme principal partenaire-concurrent des Etats-Unis. Ce sont les entreprises nippones qui inquiètent outre-Atlantique, non les entreprises européennes. Sur un plan militaire, Américains et Soviétiques la considèrent plus comme un pion – certes non négligeable – que comme une entité autonome et responsable. Dans le reste du monde les jeunes Etats s'interrogent sur les capacités de l'Europe à offrir une alternative aux Super-Grands.

Attendant anxieusement de recueillir les miettes d'une reprise économique outre-Atlantique, assistant impuissante aux sauts capricieux d'un dollar plus dominateur que jamais, manipulée de sommets en sommets par un Président Reagan qui mène le bal, la vieille Europe donne bel et bien l'impression de jouer un rôle secondaire.

Ce déclin, dont on commence à prendre conscience et à

s'inquiéter dans les capitales européennes et au siège de la CEE, ne date pas d'aujourd'hui. Les causes en sont multiples. En fait, tout se passe comme si les Etats européens, à commencer par la France, n'étaient pas parvenus à maîtriser le phénomène concomitant d'une crise économique durable et de l'arrivée des nouvelles technologies électroniques.

Le drame des Dix réside dans l'étroitesse de chaque marché national et la duplication des efforts entre ses membres sur des programmes qui mettent en jeu des dizaines de milliards de francs. Vu les moyens en hommes et en argent que mobilisent les Etats-Unis et le Japon, appuyés également sur de larges marchés intérieurs, seule la coopération entre les industriels européens peut permettre au Dix de rattraper globalement leur retard. Coopération qui implique une relative répartition des tâches, une concentration des efforts dans certains domaines.

Ce concept avait présidé au début des années 70 à l'aventure d'Airbus. Mais les forces centrifuges hostiles à l'idée d'une Europe forte, indépendante des Etats-Unis, allaient, la crise aidant, l'emporter. Les vieilles rivalités entre voisins, entre groupes industriels, ressurgissaient. Depuis 1975 la coopération industrielle européenne marque le pas. Comme si chaque industriel préférait jouer son propre jeu international. Comme si, derrière les déclarations de foi européenne des gouvernements, chacun cherchait à mériter le titre de *meilleur élève de Washington* ou de *meilleur ami de Tokyo*. Quitte à affaiblir longtemps l'Europe.

Après tout, dira-t-on, il est normal que des industriels tiennent d'abord compte de leurs propres intérêts. Leur logique première n'est pas forcément de privilégier les coopérations avec leurs concurrents les plus proches. Il revient donc aux Etats, à la Communauté, de créer un cadre tel que les firmes du Vieux Continent trouvent une motivation à coopérer entre elles.

La France paraît attacher aujourd'hui le plus grand prix à la relance d'une coopération industrielle européenne, seule voie – selon elle – pour donner un second souffle à l'Europe. Le président de la République en a reparlé lors du sommet de Stuttgart.

Les esprits sont-ils mûrs? L'environnement, le climat politique et psychologique sont-ils favorables à une telle relance de l'idée européenne à partir de coopérations industrielles? Rien n'est moins sûr.

(La Coopération Industrielle: un imperatif pour l'Europè
by J M Quatrepoint, *Le Monde* 2.8.83)

Questions
1. What, according to the writer, is the crucial question facing European industry, and why does he ask it now?

(5 marks)

2. What factors does the writer see as supporting his point of view?

(5 marks)

3. What evidence does he produce suggesting the "devalued" role played by the EEC in world affairs?

(5 marks)

4. What, for the writer, are the underlying causes of the present situation?

(5 marks)

5. Indicate clearly the ideas in paragraph 5. Do not translate.

(10 marks)

6. Why, according to the writer, did the idea of unity fail, and what has characterised the political and industrial situation since 1975?

(10 marks)

7. What must EEC industries do to remedy the situation?

(3 marks)

8. What appears to be the French view?

(4 marks)

9. What is the writer's conclusion?

(4 marks)
(London, Syllabus B, 1985)

OUTLINE ANSWERS

You should work through the passages in rough as you would in the examination.

Passage (a)

1. Read it several times and try to find three main divisions. You should find that these can be subdivided.
2. Think through the questions (a)–(h). Watch for those which might require you to consider more than one part of the text, e.g. (c), (d) and (e). Are there any others? Take all parts of the question into account. In (b) for example, look for: (i) number of candidates; (ii) state of mind before; (iii) state of mind after. What is implied exactly when the question says "What are we told?" Does it mean "What does the author say directly to the reader?" or does it mean "What can we tell from the text?" In (h) you are asked about "ways" in the plural, so expect to find more than one.
3. Make brief notes for each answer. Decide whether the information in the notes is appropriate.
4. Check by re-reading the text that all relevant information has been noted.

Answers to the questions on passage (a)

(a) A test in typing and shorthand.
(b) There were six candidates. Before the test they were uneasy and tense; afterwards they experienced a kind of embarrassment which was like a feeling of shame.
(c) It was called *les Papeteries réunies* and therefore presumably produced stationery. It is said to be a large establishment with an annual turnover of several millions. It employs fifteen shorthand typists.
(d) Her ambition is revealed by her sense of triumph at being called for interview and at being offered a post in a good firm. She was confident of promotion and of increasing her salary and felt that she had taken the first steps on the road to success.

(e) She was cheerful and fun-loving and ready to enjoy what life had to offer. She was amused by her father's lively nature but less tolerant than her mother. She did not like living in uncomfortable accommodation and seeing her mother work so hard, so vowed to avoid ending up like her.

(f) The war had changed him. He no longer had any enthusiasm for work. He would spend most of his time in cafés, playing cards or reminiscing about his imaginary adventures as a prisoner of war. He had not lost his good humour, his cheerfulness or his optimism.

(g) She tolerated his behaviour and was not unhappy. She worked hard to try to compensate for the cost of his shortcomings.

(h) He was cheerful, lively and optimistic and with his warm eyes and tanned complexion he was physically attractive.

Answers to the questions on passage (*b*)

1. Will Europe play a leading role in the world in the future? He asks the question because Europe's scientific, economic, cultural and military influence is being eroded.

2. Japan has overtaken Europe economically and it is Japanese firms which threaten the United States; the USA and USSR do not consider that Europe is a military force in its own right; the rest of the world doubts that Europe is a credible alternative to the Superpowers.

3. Economically Europe depends passively on the USA, trying to profit as best it can from American economic recovery and remaining at the mercy of the dollar's fluctuations. Europe allows itself to be manipulated at summit level by President Reagan.

4. The fact that Europe cannot control a situation in which there is the problem of dealing with new electronic technology at a time of long-term economic crisis.

5. The problem is that each member country is limited to its national market and therefore operates separately in an area of spending involving millions of francs. What is required (following the American and Japanese example) is co-operation between leading industrial organisations throughout the ten countries and this would mean some division of labour with concentration on particular areas.

6. There were forces which worked against the idea of a strong, independent (and therefore unified) Europe. Old rivalries between countries and industrial groups re-emerged. Since 1975 there has been no further industrial co-operation; in spite of government claims of a belief in a united Europe there has been individual action from separate organisations.

7. The industries must co-operate with each other instead of always following the natural inclination to compete.

8. France appears to attach great importance to a renewal of European industrial co-operation as the only way of leading Europe to recovery.

9. It is uncertain that people are ready, politically and psychologically, for a renewal of the idea of Europe based on industrial co-operation.

A STEP FURTHER

Textes en Français Facile – Four star level – e.g. Simenon. *L'Affaire St Fiacre* and numerous other titles. Hachette

Periodicals (available through European Schoolbooks, Croft St. Cheltenham GL53 OHX):

Clé: *Votre Journal en Français* (articles on current affairs, sport, fashion, music etc. 4 issues per annum)

Revue de la Presse (4 page illustrated newspaper containing articles from the French daily press)

Elle (covers a range of topics of interest to women together with studies of wider issues)

See Gallimard Folio catalogue.

Chapter 10   **Summary**

GETTING STARTED

If you are entering for one of the professional examinations such as those set by the Royal Society of Arts, the Institute of Linguists, or HND Business Studies, you are likely to find that the examination includes some form of summary. This is because summary-writing is a skill which is frequently used by linguists who work in business and commerce. The full-length summary is not now a feature of A-level examinations but you might be called upon to summarise part of a passage to test reading comprehension. Even if it is not tested specifically it is a useful study skill.

There are several types of summary. It is therefore important to consult the syllabus so that you are certain of what you will be faced with. What is usually prescribed is a summary in English of a passage in French, but it could be a summary in French of a passage in French, or even a summary in French of a passage in English. You should also note the length of the passage that will be set for summary in your examination, the number of words that you are allowed to use and the amount of time which you are given for doing the exercise. All this is vital information. Since it varies from one Examination Board to another, you should check carefully the regulations which apply to you.

Summary-writing depends above all on the thorough understanding of a passage of quite complex French and on your ability to follow an argument. You must be able to identify the main points and separate them from the less significant details and to understand what the writer is doing, e.g. giving an example or an explanation, passing on to a new point, reaching a conclusion, etc. The groundwork that you do to improve your summary-writing should therefore coincide with the work that you do for reading comprehension. What you should do in order to get started on summary-writing is to follow the advice in the previous chapter on

117

establishing a reading programme (extensive reading) and on reading and understanding a passage of French (intensive reading). Just like translation into and from French, summary-writing has to be practised as a separate skill but must be based on linguistic knowledge which is acquired in a variety of other ways. Do not be surprised if summary as such is not introduced until later on in your course.

ESSENTIAL PRINCIPLES

If you are to produce a summary in English of a passage in French then what will be tested in the examination is your ability to understand the original and to reduce it to (usually) one-third of its length without distorting the meaning and without altering the opinion or the attitude of the author. In the marking-scheme a proportion of the marks will be awarded for identifying and accurately expressing the main points, and penalties will be incurred if the maximum number of words to be used is exceeded. It is usual to prescribe a lower and upper limit. For example: "Summarise the following passage in English. Your summary should be between 250 and 310 words long, in connected English. Marks will be lost if the summary exceeds the prescribed length." If your summary is shorter than the lower limit you are likely to lose marks for omitting some of the essential information.

COMMON ERRORS IN SUMMARY

It will help you if you are aware of the most common errors which candidates make in this paper.
1.   There are always candidates who lose marks because they fail to keep within the maximum number of words.
2.   Many candidates do not succeed in producing a précis which is an acceptable piece of English. If the rubric requires that the summary should be written in "accurate, natural English" or in "connected English" then it is not sufficient to write it in note-form. Many candidates are not critical enough of what they write and produce phrases and sentences of "translationese". The passage would often not make sufficient sense to the objective reader who had no knowledge of the original passage.
3.   Some summaries read as though they were a reassembly of translated phrases and sentences selected from the original. As a result the summary lacks coherence and important points are often missed.
4.   Some candidates work through the passage and mechanically reduce it without having first grasped the main points and the structure of the passage. It does not follow that because the entire passage is to be reduced by one-third that each paragraph should be reduced in the same proportion.
5.   Numbers of candidates forget or do not realise that the writer of the summary should remain objective and avoid any commentary or explanation which is not in the original.

6. It is not understood by some candidates that the summary is assumed to be a substitute for the original text and is written from the same point of view. In other words, if the original is written in the first person, the summary is also written in the first person.

IDENTIFYING 'SIGNPOSTS' IN SUMMARY

In the examination you will be asked to summarise a passage of perhaps 600 words. It is advisable to practise first with much shorter passages as this will make it easier to concentrate on reaching a global understanding, which is the important first stage in summarising any passage. Working on passages of a more manageable length will enable you to give attention not only to identifying the main ideas but to make sure that you understand the way in which they are organised. A common fault with beginners is that they often fail, particularly if the text is dense, to distinguish an argument from its counter-argument or a positive example from a negative one. Where conflicting points of view are represented in a passage, there is often a tendency to lose track of who is in favour of what. Such confusion is less likely to arise if you are used to identifying those words which act as *signposts* to the way in which the passage is organised. In the passage which follows these words have been underlined:

> Au début, on croyait que la reprise n'allait pas trop tarder. De leur côté, les entreprises ont refusé de recourir à de nouveaux 'dégraissages'. Elles ont donc maintenu des taux de production qui dépassaient les possibilités du marché et elles ont stocké leurs produits au lieu de les vendre. Mais il est évident aussi que le stockage ne peut plus continuer au rythme actuel.
> La baisse de la demande a, en effet, frappé en même temps toutes les entreprises et tous les marches. Dans le passé on a connu d'autres crises qui étaient moins graves que celle-ci parce qu'elles étaient moins généralisées. La demande baissait, par exemple, sur le marché intérieur, mais l'exploitation continuait à bien marcher; si le textile et le bâtiment connaissaient de graves problèmes, l'automobile et l'informatique étaient en plein essor. Il n'y a pas eu, cette fois, de compensation de ce genre.

Some essential terms which signpost the organisation of a text are:

et d'abord	cependant
tout d'abord	néanmoins
en premier lieu	pourtant
par ailleurs	toutefois
en outre	mais
de plus	donc
d'autre part	par conséquent
ensuite… ensuite	en définitive

There are others. You will find them in your reading; make sure that you understand them. Misunderstanding a term like toutefois, par ailleurs or even or, could alter the sense of a whole paragraph.

THE TIME FACTOR

For many students the most difficult part of summary-writing is the time factor; i.e. the difficulty of mastering the content of 600 words of complex French, sorting out the main points from the detail and writing up the summary in perhaps 1½ hours or less. Working on *shorter passages* (such as the passage above) is a way of speeding up the process of summarising. Select a passage of 200–300 words (The *Penguin French Reader* has numerous examples which are suitable). Scan it to form an *impression* of what it is about. On this basis write down the *questions* which you think the passage should answer. Study the passage again and (a) try to find a title, and (b) write a brief, two-line summary. Practice of this kind and improvement of your reading comprehension skill are invaluable ways of preparing yourself for the full-length summary completed under the time constraint of exam conditions.

READING THE TEXT

When you tackle a summary in the examination or in practice you will begin by reading the text several times. Avoid the line-by-line approach and aim at a global understanding. Ask yourself what the text is about, what is the central idea which runs through it. It is a good idea, after your initial reading, to try to sum up the passage in just a sentence or two. Do this having put the text aside. You will not need these notes for your summary but writing them and making the effort to get at the main ideas of the passage will be helpful for subsequent reading. You will make more sense of the text at the second or third reading if you read it with anticipation and points already in mind. If the text has a title ask yourself whether it is apt. If necessary adapt it to give a better indication as to what the text is about. It is preferable not to start underlining what you consider to be main points at the first reading: you are likely to make a mistake or underline too much and this could cause confusion later on.

PRODUCING A PLAN

You then work on producing a plan of the passage to be summarised. Try to identify the natural divisions in the text. If it is a narrative account then you will look at the main sequences, trying to get the essential action clear in your mind and to differentiate between the characters. If it is discussion or argument you will look for the main developments, trying to find the central ideas or the main units of thought. The natural divisions may correspond to the division into paragraphs but often you will find it necessary to group two or three paragraphs together. When you have structured the passage in this way, *bracket the different divisions* so that you can see how the text is organised.

In each division *underline the sentence or parts of sentences* which contain the most important idea expressed in that section of the text. But remember that you are not selecting sentences in order to translate them and reuse them without change in your summary; you are still getting to grips with the way in which the author's line of thought develops while trying to maintain a global view of the text.

When you begin to make your *rough notes* follow the plan of the text. Summarise each division or section in note-form. Jot down the main idea for each division and underneath make a note of the secondary points, arranging them so that you can see how they are organised around the main idea. As you do this distinguish between the main point and any examples or illustrations.

When you have carried out this operation on each division or section of the text you will have completed an overall plan. You will have carried out an analysis and a synthesis which will help you "make the text your own" and you will be ready to write the rough draft of the summary.

LENGTH OF THE SUMMARY

At this stage you will begin to concern yourself with the length of your summary. However, you should not waste time on unnecessary counting and recounting of the words that you have written. Count the number of words in your plan and then, having established previously how many words you write to a line, count the number of lines. Have in mind that it is better to produce a draft which is too long rather than too short as it is generally easier to prune what you have written than to graft on extra details in order to make up the length.

DECIDING WHAT TO INCLUDE AND EXCLUDE

When deciding on what to eliminate from a passage students are often uncertain about what to do with examples, quotations, statistics and certain stylistic features. The following points can be used as a guide-line.

(a) Examples and illustrations

Try to decide to what extent they are important to an understanding of the main argument. If the examples are numerous or the illustrations lengthy then abstract any important idea which they add to the main argument and restate it in order to include it in your summary. Otherwise retain only the most useful of a number of examples and condense the illustrations. If an illustration turns into an anecdote then be prepared to reduce it quite drastically. If it does not help to make a point clear and is really more of an ornament and a digression then leave it out.

(b) Figurative language

You are not expected to imitate the style of the original. It is advisable to abstract the idea conveyed by a metaphor or simile and, if it is important, to restate it in non-figurative language.

(c) Irony

Again, you are not expected to imitate the style of the original. If the point behind the irony is important then re-express in the form of a plain statement.

(d) Rhetorical questions

You will notice that French writers, in a passage of argument or discussion, often use rhetorical questions to emphasise a point or to attract the reader's attention. Such a device would be out of place in your summary. Convert the rhetorical question into a statement.

(e) Quotations	Convert them into reported speech and condense them.
(f) Statistics, tables, diagrams	If the statistics are essential to the argument they may be included in full; otherwise abstract the point which they are intended to make and report it. If they make no substantial point, e.g. if they are there merely to provide an interesting comparison, omit them altogether. With tables and diagrams it is usually possible to extract a relevant fact or figure or to restate the point that they are intended to demonstrate.

When you are writing up your summary (if it is a French to English summary) give careful attention to the quality of the English. Too many students are unable to free themselves from the French and as a result they produce passages of "translationese" which they would not write under normal circumstances. You should be certain that everything that you write makes good sense. It is also important that your summary should read as continuous, connected prose and not as notes (unless of course note-form is specifically allowed by the rubric). This is where it is important to have achieved a good overall grasp of the original passage and of the plan that you have made. It will help you to recompose the text in summarised form, rather than string together a succession of sentences in a clipped, telegraphic style. However when recomposing, be careful that the "link" words that you use (however, nevertheless, but, on the other hand) are justified by the meaning of the original.

EXAMINATION QUESTIONS The following passages are of the type set for summary. Work through them applying the principles described above. Your summary should consist of about one-third of the original length. Remember that summaries of excessive length are penalised in the examination.

NOS ROBOTS SOUS LES MERS

1.

Les robots, on les rencontre sur la terre, où ils remplacement de plus en plus l'homme dans les tâches répétitives ou dangereuses. On les retrouve aussi dans l'espace où, sous forme de sondes automatiques, ils explorent notre système solaire. Depuis une dizaine d'années, ils ont également envahi discrètement les fonds marins.

Cette armée de l'ombre est aujourd'hui très diversifiée, mais le plus célèbre et le plus utilisé de ces robots sous-marin, est le P.A.P. (poisson autopropulsé). Il en existe deux cent soixante-dix exemplaires, actuellement dans le monde tous conçus et fabriqués par E.C.A. une société française très discrète qui vient de lever le voile sur les engins qu'elle produit et qui a pourtant inventé le plus grand nombre de robots sous-marins de la planète.

Le P.A.P. a vu le jour en 1972 et depuis lors il passe son temps à débarrasser toutes les mers du monde des bombes oubliées lors des divers combats. Ce gros poisson jaune peut plonger jusqu'à 300 mètres de profondeur. Il est relié en permanence par un câble à un navire qui lui fournit son énergie. Équipé d'un sonar, il traque la mine, signale sa position au navire, la déplace au bout de son bras télémanipulateur quand il est nécessaire de bien la positionner puis retourne rapidement à la surface. Le navire se charge alors de faire exploser la bombe avec une grenade. Ce travail de nettoyage est régulièrement effectué dans la mer du Nord, truffée des déchets mortels de la dernière guerre mondiale mais également autour des îles Malouines et dans la mer Rouge.

Transmissions stratégiques

D'autres robots se chargent eux de traquer dans le fond des mers des objets beaucoup moins dangereux. C'est le cas par exemple de l'«Épaulard», utilisé par l'Ifremer et qui a pour fonction essentielle la chasse aux nodules polymétalliques. Cet engin est complètement autonome. Il peut descendre jusqu'à 6 000 mètres de profondeur et photographier avec son œil de cyclope le fond de la mer. Il est capable de s'arrêter devant un obstacle et de le contourner.

Le P.O.P.E. (poisson d'observation pleines eaux), dit aussi le Curieux, est, lui, moins malin. Tenu en laisse par un câble raccroché à un navire, il ne descend qu'à 100 mètres de profondeur mais il possède deux énormes projecteurs et une caméra de télévision qui lui permettent d'inspecter tout ce qui se passe sous la mer. Le P.O.P.E. est largement utilisé aujourd'hui comme surveillant général du travail des plongeurs qui installent des plates-formes *off shore*.

Le Scytale (du nom des premiers messages codés grecs) a, lui, une tâche encore plus importante, il est relié aux six sous-marins nucléaires français. C'est un petit engin qui se dirige vers la surface et déploie une antenne radio à quelques centimètres sous l'eau. Grâce à elle, le sous-marin est relié en permanence avec l'état-major militaire stratégique et le président de la République, à qui revient le droit de donner l'ordre de tirer les missiles nucléaires. Pour l'instant, cette antenne se contente de donner aux marins des nouvelles de leur famille et de retransmettre, paraît-il, les matches de foot importants!

La nouvelle génération des robots sous-marins développée ces dernières années a été essentiellement conçue pour la construction et l'entretien des plates-formes des forages pétroliers.

Nettoyage automatique

Ce sont de véritables ouvriers de la mer. L'ouverture et la fermeture d'un puits de pétrole sont déclenchées aujourd'hui par des unités de télécommande sous-marine, mais il y a plus. Des robots circulent le long des pipe-lines pour inspecter leur état, certains grimpent le long des piliers des plates-formes pour examiner la qualité des joints de soudure, d'autres encore creusent comme une charrue le sol marin pour enfouir les câbles qui transmettront les communications ou l'électricité.

La société E.C.A. a même à l'étude un véritable engin de nettoyage du futur, le robot Funi. Celui-ci glissera le long des câbles d'ancrage des plates-formes à 400 mètres de profondeur et les débarrassera de la vase et des algues. Peu à peu, les robots ouvriers vont donc prendre la place des plongeurs dans la plupart des tâches difficiles. La véritable colonisation du fond des mers passe par leur bras cybernétique.

(MARTINE CASTELLO, *Le Figaro* 24.10.85)

LA RUÉE VERS L'OR DE L'ESPACE

2.

Plus de navette pour mettre en orbite des satellites commerciaux. La décision du président Ronald Reagan, annoncée en même temps que la construction d'une quatrième navette pour remplacer «Challenger», détruite en janvier dernier, relance la concurrence sur le marché international des lanceurs de satellites.

Attendue depuis plusieurs mois, la nouvelle confirme la volonté affichée de Washington. Désormais, comme le soulignait Ronald Reagan, le rôle de la N.A.S.A. est limité. Les navettes vont servir à des fins scientifiques mais aussi et surtout militaires. Enfin, résolument tournés vers le futur, ces cargos de l'espace devront également se consacrer à la mise en place de la station orbitale américaine dont la mise en service est prévue dans les années quatre-vingt-quinze.

Dès 1983, le président Reagan avait amorcé le changement de cap de sa politique spatiale en décidant de faire vendre les fusées traditionnelles par d'autres que la N.A.S.A. et de louer à des entreprises privées les pas de tir de cette dernière. Mais la catastrophe de «Challenger» et la place prise par la fusée Ariane sur le marché des concurrents ont accéléré la concrétisation de ce projet.

En confiant entièrement au secteur privé et non plus à la N.A.S.A. le lancement des satellites commerciaux, Ronald Reagan espère relancer l'intérêt des sociétés pour le choix américain dans le lancement de leurs satellites. D'autant plus qu'il ne manque pas aux Etats-Unis de postulants.

Contrats honorés

Plusieurs firmes ont annoncé ces dernières années leur intention de se lancer sur le marché des lancements commerciaux: Transpace Carriers, Space Service, Truax Engineering, General Dynamics, etc. Toutes proposent d'utiliser des fusées existantes, Thor Delta, Atlas Centaur, Titan et même d'en fabriquer comme la «Conestoga», à partir d'un Meccano de pièces détachées. Ces lanceurs ont plus ou moins les mêmes capacités que les Ariane 1 et 3 européennes.

Mais les Américains se préparent aussi à lutter avec l'Ariane 5 des années quatre-vingt-quinze qui sera capable de placer 6 tonnes en orbite géostationnaire. Dans leurs cartons, Hughes Aircraft et Boeing Aerospace ont en projet un nouveau lanceur, le «Jarvis», conçu sur la même technologie que les fusées Saturn des vols lunaires. C'est dire qu'aux Etats-Unis on est bien loin d'avoir abandonné le marché de l'espace aux autres concurrents. Et, en attendant, assurait un porte-parole de la N.A.S.A., «*les quarante-quatre contrats commerciaux en cours seront honorés*». Certainement avec les quatre fusées actuellement disponibles: des Thor Delta, qu'il apparaît possible d'utiliser dès l'année prochaine.

Quoi qu'il en soit, cette nouvelle donne américaine vient bousculer le marché de l'espace. Celui-ci représente environ 200 satellites commerciaux (essentiellement de télécommunication) á placer en orbite avant la fin du siècle, pour un montant de 60 milliard de francs. Aujourd'hui, même clouée au sol, Ariane demeure le principal rival des Américains. Ce lanceur totalise actuellement 54 contrats dont l'ensemble représente un chiffre d'affaires de 11,6 milliards.

Une soixantaine de contrats signés

Quant aux Américains, ils comptent une soixantaine de contrats signés ou en négociations, mais ils ont déjà perdu six marchés au profit d'Ariane après l'échec de Challenger. Le lanceur européen devrait reprendre ses vols au début de 1987. Ses problèmes apparaissent en fait bien minimes par rapport à ceux des fusées classiques américaines et ce pays risque finalement de perdre encore des marchés en attendant que les firmes privées prennent la relève de la N.A.S.A.

D'autant plus qu'ill va falloir bientôt compter avec de nouveaux concurrents. La Chine avec le lancement de sa fusée Longue Marche III en juin dernier est rentrée en force sur le marché de l'espace: un contrat de lancement avec la Suède, un autre avec une firme américaine et un accord de coopération avec l'Aérospatiale. D'ici quelques années cette nation pourra rivaliser avec les Occidentaux en se montrant capable de pouvoir placer deux satellites en orbite géostationnaire. Mais plus dangereux encore est le Japon. Il vient de réussir le lancement de sa nouvelle fusée H 1 qui a mis deux satellites sur orbite. Dès 1992 avec son lanceur H 2, il sera capable de placer à 36 000 km de la Terre des satellites de deux tonnes, à des prix défiant toute concurrence assurent les Japonais. Quant aux Soviétiques, ils maîtrisent depuis très longtemps la technologie des lancements spatiaux. Pour des raisons politiques, ils n'offrent cependant leurs services qu'aux pays de l'Est.

Cette conquête n'a jamais été en fait leur véritable objectif, seule les intéresse la maîtrise de la proche banlieue de la Terre. En excluant la N.A.S.A de la compétition commerciale pour ne se consacrer qu'à des recherches scientifiques et militaires, Ronald Reagan a en quelque sorte opté pour la même philosophie.

(MARTINE CASTELLO, *Le Figaro* 18.8.86)

TUTOR'S ANSWER TO QUESTION 2

President Reagan's decision to limit N.A.S.A.'s activities to scientific and military objectives and to the launch of the American orbital space station in the 1990s will stimulate international competition concerning the launching of commercial satellites. The implementation of the new

American policy, begun as early as 1983 when commercial firms were allowed to sell traditional rockets and hire N.A.S.A.'s launch-pads, has been accelerated by the Challenger disaster and the emergence of Ariane as a rival. Several private American firms are interested and plan to use existing rockets or assemble their own. These will have the same capability as Ariane 1 and 3 but a new rocket is planned capable of competing with Ariane 5, which can put a 6 ton load into orbit. With a quarter of the present commercial contracts Ariane is the Americans' strongest competitor, but China has now entered the market and Japan, with its successful H 1 and future H 2 rocket, will become increasingly competitive into the 1990s.

A STEP FURTHER

The most important step further that you can take is to give yourself plenty of timed practice. You should try to obtain past papers for this purpose but you could also make use of *Practice in Advanced Précis Writing* (M. F. Lécuyer; Harrap) which has a wide selection of non-literary passages mostly between 600 and 800 words in length, or *Le Résumé de Texte* (P. Gaillard and C. Launay; Hatier) which includes a range of more literary passages. You will also find articles of a suitable length in *Le Monde*, *Le Monde Dimanche* and *Le Figaro*.

When you have mastered the basic principles of summary-writing it is useful to practise it on a self-correcting basis. You can always "try out" your finished summary on someone who has not read the original and who can look objectively and critically at the sense of what you have written.

FURTHER READING

M. F. Lécuyer. *Practice in Advanced Précis Writing*. Harrap
P. Gaillard et C. Launay. *Le Résumé de Texte*. Hatier.

Chapter 11

Listening comprehension

GETTING STARTED

All A-level examinations in French and most other advanced examinations now include some form of listening comprehension test. The skill also plays a part in the dictation paper and in the oral. Part of your examination preparation should therefore be devoted to improving your ability to understand spoken French. If you do this successfully you will do far more than improve your chances in just one part of the examination. If you make use of the right kind of listening material (news bulletins, radio and possibly television plays, films, talks, discussions, panel games and interviews) you will provide yourself with a valuable source of French which will help you to build up your vocabulary and to keep what you have learnt in circulation. Listening comprehension may be examined and practised as a separate skill but you should see it as an integrated part of your language learning.

Many people would argue that for anyone who is intending to use his French in real life situations, listening comprehension is the most useful of all the language skills. As a non-native speaker you are likely to do much more listening than speaking or writing. When you are in a French-speaking environment you will find that the major difficulty is not making yourself understood, it is *understanding the native speaker*. There is therefore great practical value in developing your listening ability, which is a consideration which should give you extra incentive to spend time and effort on it.

Like all the other linguistic skills listening comprehension needs regular practice over a long period of time. This need not be a source of drudgery. On the contrary, if you make yourself an active listener and if you make an effort to use a wide variety of material, listening to French can become the most enjoyable part of your learning programme. Many students are encouraged by the progress they make in this area and many find that they learn more French aurally than from the printed word.

In order to get started you will need some basic equipment such as a cassette player or better still a radio cassette recorder and a source of listening material. There is a very wide range of authentic material available commercially (see for example the catalogue published by Radio France, Cassettes Radio France). The cassettes are expensive to buy but if you have access to a language laboratory or centre with a tape library you should be able to borrow them. It is also worth making enquiries at your local public library. You might even make your own recordings from France Inter (details of French radio programmes are to be found in *Le Monde* or *Le Figaro*). The advantage of being able to use a tape library is that the tapes are usually classified according to difficulty, and *transcripts* of the recordings are sometimes available. If you have difficulty in getting hold of taped material you could always try approaching the language centre at a local polytechnic or university.

At an early stage in your course and while you are looking for material it is important to consult the syllabus regulations and past papers to see what kind of listening comprehension test is set by your Examination Board. Find out whether you are required to listen to a passage of written French which is simply read out by your own tutor (who may not be a native speaker) or to the spoken French of native speakers. Listening to prose read aloud is rather different from listening to a natural conversation involving two or three participants. If you are listening to what is basically "written" French you should be prepared for the sound of the past historic or past anterior and be ready to follow aurally longer and more complex sentences. When you are listening to genuine spoken French you should be prepared for repetitions, false starts, changes of direction in mid sentence, interruptions and all the other features of natural speech. It is obviously important to include listening material of the *appropriate type* when you are practising specifically for the examination.

ESSENTIAL PRINCIPLES

CRITERIA OF ASSESSMENT AND THE EXAMINER'S VIEW

The aim of the listening comprehension paper is to test the accuracy and extent of the candidate's *understanding* of the French. It is not just a test of hearing. The exercise inevitably involves the ability to interpret the meaning of the question, to switch from English (as the questions and answers are usually in English) to French, to select and retain the information which has been asked for and finally to return to English in order to present the answer in a satisfactory form.

The type of question may vary. Direct reference questions (the answer to such questions are directly stated in the original text) are set but inference questions are the more frequent. To answer the second type of question you must interpret what you hear and make certain deductions. The questions may test understanding of specific items in the original or of the broad outlines of what you have listened to. What is tested therefore is both detailed comprehension and global comprehension of the material that is heard. It is usual for the questions to follow the text chronologically but it is always important to reach an overall understanding of the text (which you will always hear more than once and at least once as an uninterrupted whole).

Marks are awarded according to the amount of information needed in the answer and a distinction is usually made between main points and supplementary details. In some examinations the number of marks awarded for each answer are printed in the question paper.

Allowance is made for the fact that candidates have limited time to answer each question, therefore answers are sometimes acceptable in note-form but it is always important to ensure that the answer is clearly presented.

In their reports on candidates' performance in this part of the examination examiners draw attention to the following points:

1. Many candidates appear to have given insufficient time to practising listening comprehension. The test requires specific practice.
2. There is a need for clear presentation of answers, which must be relevant. The wrong approach is to write down everything you can think of in answer to a question. The inclusion of irrelevant information is penalised if it distorts the information which has been asked for.
3. Candidates need to listen to a greater variety of texts in order to build up a wider receptive vocabulary.
4. Some candidates are not able to recognise words and particularly combinations of words spoken at normal speed although they would be familiar with their written forms.
5. It is essential to treat the exercise as more than an exercise in listening. Most candidates do not have difficulty in identifying what they hear but do not always succeed in processing it and retaining it in the short-term memory in order to answer the questions satisfactorily.
6. Some candidates have clearly not practised the art of note-taking. They attempt to take down too much information which sometimes prevents them from hearing and selecting relevant points or from reaching overall understanding of the text.

INTENSIVE AND EXTENSIVE LISTENING

There are two main types of *listening* practice which will improve your listening comprehension as a means of language learning. They are *intensive listening* which concentrates on detailed comprehension and on listening to particular features of the language, and *extensive listening* which should involve listening more widely for meaning and information. Both will help you to prepare for the listening comprehension paper, the dictation and the oral.

Intensive listening

If you have difficulty in following spoken French, it will help you in the early stages of the course to work on selected phonetic exercises. A major obstacle for the learner whose experience of the language is based mainly on written texts is that the spoken sentence can sound like a single, long word or just a succession of syllables. Students therefore complain that the French is too fast or that all they can hear is a blur of sound. If this problem arises it is advisable to study the way in which syllables and words are grouped. French tends to end syllables on a vowel (e.g. particulièrement: par-ti-cu-lière-ment; ridicule: ri-di-cule) and if a consonant follows, it becomes initial in the following syllable even if that syllable is part of the next word. The result is that words are often linked. The phrase "avec une amie" becomes (avekynami) rather than (avek-yne-amie). This phenomenon is called linking.

It is further complicated by the problem of *liaison*. This involves the pronunciation of a linking consonant at the end of certain words when they are followed by a vowel. It means that in practice many French words have two spoken forms, one containing a liaison consonant which is heard in certain combinations and a more frequent form in which the liaising consonant is absent.

By making yourself aware of linking and liaison and, better still, by practising it yourself, you will begin to distinguish sense-groups and the meaning of the sentence more readily.

Understanding where the *stress* falls in the sentence will also help you to follow a passage of spoken French. Stress falls on the last syllable of the word (the syllable is stronger and more prominent) but also on the last syllable of a word-group. As the word-group is a grammatical unit and a unit of meaning it is important to identify it when you are listening.

Intonation patterns (the rise and fall of pitch) can also indicate the limits of sense-groups in speech as well as signal a question, a plain statement, an instruction or changes in the speaker's attitude or intention which can become important clues to meaning.

A course in French pronunciation will provide practice in identifying and imitating features such as stress and intonation patterns, linking and liaison.

A further problem for the learner who is more familiar with the way that French *looks* on the printed page than with the way that it *sounds* when spoken, is that in everyday speech delivered at normal speed there are contractions of words and groups of words which cause certain vowels and consonants to disappear or become distorted. If you compare the following sentences with their phonetic transcription you will see that recognising them in normal speech could cause difficulty:

- Il te voit [itvwa]
- Tu as fini [tafini]
- Je ne sais pas [chépa]
- Deux chevaux [deuchvo]
- Je le vois [jelvwa]
- Un faux jeton [un faucheton]

Exercises which will help you to recognise such *contractions* are provided in *Le Pont Sonore* (see bibliography). If you are preparing for a listening comprehension test which aims to use authentic speech it will help you to practise these or similar exercises. *Le Pont Sonore* contains further exercises which help with aural recognition of tenses. There are also self-correcting, gap-transcription exercises on the recognition of selected items of vocabulary.

Extensive listening

Intensive listening is important but the greater part of your practice should be devoted to extensive listening based on a wide variety of oral texts so that you will develop the skill of hearing, understanding and processing information which will be tested in the examination.

As you make the transition from intensive to extensive listening you should learn not to concentrate on distinguishing the sound and meaning of every word. Instead you should aim to follow the text continuously in order to "re-create" the gist of the passage and to maintain a global understanding of what you are hearing. It is important training for the listening comprehension test in which you will have to structure the passage and retrieve items of information from your short-term memory.

It is in fact not necessary to hear *every* detail. You do not hear clearly everything that is said when listening in your own language. You will not hear everything when you attempt listening comprehension under exam conditions but it does not mean that your comprehension will not be adequate. It is good practice to listen to texts in which there is some form of natural hindrance such as interruptions, two people talking at once, hesitation or even background noise. You will learn to tolerate gaps in what you hear and to infer meaning from other clues. The text which you hear in the examination may include little or no interference of this kind but learning to cope with it is an important way of developing your own listening strategies.

Plenty of varied listening practice will also help you to build up a stock of vocabulary that you are able to recognise aurally. This is important because there is good evidence that in understanding speech we rely more on registering the meaning of words, and particularly keywords, than on the grammar of the sentence. We apprehend semantic elements first and only go back over the way the sentence is put together if there is any ambiguity. This means that you need a wide *recognition* vocabulary and that you should ensure that when you learn new items of vocabulary you learn to recognise their sound.

One way of learning to associate the written form of the word with its sound is to listen to recorded material with a transcript. Commercially produced listening materials often come with a transcript. (Cassettes Radio France produce a series of tapes plus transcript.) You should check the index in your tape library.

A useful variation on listening with a transcript which will help you build up recognition vocabulary is *gap transcription.* You follow the recording which has items of vocabulary deleted so that the learner can fill in the gaps.

Of course, it is also essential to listen to French without the support of the printed word so that you train yourself to use other clues to meaning. One very important clue is your knowledge of the *context* of what is being said because this knowledge helps you to make predictions and make sense out of what comes next. Quite a lot of what we comprehend comes not from the actual words we hear but from the context, and we hear more clearly what we expect to hear. When listening in our own language to a weather forecast, a joke or a lecture the fact that we have a vague idea of what is going to be said helps towards understanding.

Being aware of the context and creating an outline of the "script" can help you both in your listening practice and in the examination. If you are going to listen to recordings which you have taken yourself from French radio it is a good idea to work on news bulletins or programmes about current affairs. You will always have an idea of what the broadcast will be about, particularly if you have read about the topic in a French newspaper, and you will be able to make predictions and inferences from context which are an essential part of aural comprehension. In the examination you have no choice of what you listen to, but there is usually an introduction to the text and the context will be partially outlined by the questions which you have to answer. It must be remembered, of course, that knowledge of context is not based solely on what you know beforehand, it is built up as you listen and is continually used to make further predictions.

If you have access to a tape library you will find it quite easy to select a range of listening texts. They should include news bulletins, weather forecasts, radio (and possibly television) plays, interviews, advertisements, panel games, "phone-ins", speeches and recorded readings from novels and of short stories. This list will probably include the type of listening text that you will be given in the exam but check to see that you are giving yourself sufficient practice with appropriate material.

To make the most of your listening, to make it more interesting and to avoid the situation where sounds "go in one ear and out of the other", you should listen with a *purpose* and if possible link listening to a productive activity. It will help you to train for an examination where you are obliged to listen for a very specific purpose, namely that of selecting information in order to answer questions.

You will no doubt be given practice in answering listening comprehension questions as part of your course but there are other activities which you can bring to your private listening. If you listen to an interview of a well-known personality, tabulate information to build up a biographical picture of the interviewee. You could listen to a news report on a bank robbery or a hijacking and draw a plan or diagram of what happened or you could use a map to fill in information gleaned from a weather forecast. A news item describing a state visit could lead to the drawing up of an itinerary and timetable.

These activities will not only ensure that your listening is not passive but as they involve the selection of information they will improve your ability to make succinct notes (a skill which is essential for success in the listening comprehension test). Indeed note-taking and summarising the gist of what you hear should be regularly practised. If you train yourself to listen and process you will be well prepared for the examination and will not feel, as one student put it, like "a non-swimmer in a sea of sound".

USEFUL POINTS FOR THE EXAMINATION

On the day of the examination make sure that you give or have given attention to the following points:

1. It is important to be familiar with the mechanics of the test. You will have to listen and write *only* when instructed, so make sure beforehand that you know what is going to happen and when. You should also know:

- whether the questions and answers are to be in English or French and whether note-form answers are accepted;
- whether the text will be pre-recorded or read out by your tutor;
- how many times you will hear the text and whether it will be divided into parts;
- whether the instructions for the test are given in English or French;
- at what stage you may read the questions;
- at what stage you may take notes;
- how many questions there will be and how long you will have to write the answers.

2. Try to adopt a reasonably relaxed attitude when you listen to the text. Remember that the inexperienced candidate who is desperate to hear everything often concentrates too much on one part and sometimes misses what comes next or fails to reach a global understanding of the passage. If you miss words do not panic: you can afford not to understand everything clearly.

3. During the first listening try to reach an overall understanding of the text. Use the introduction or title to the text, and the questions, to help give you an idea of what the text is going to be about. It is often a help to memory if you make an effort to visualise as you listen. Try to picture a narrative account. If you are listening to an interview, imagining the positions and gestures of the speakers can help you to remember who says what and even what has been said.

4. Read the questions carefully and underline keywords to remind you what the main point of the question is. You will probably have to answer more than one question on any section of the text that you hear, therefore it is important to distinguish one question from another. In a text on immigration for example, you are likely to meet the word "immigrants" in several of the questions: but if you read attentively you may discover that in the first question you are asked about illegal immigrants, in the second about unemployed immigrants, in the third about married immigrants and so on. If you look at the questions analytically it will enable you to structure the text even before you hear it and it will be less likely to come over as a

blur of information. Working actively on the questions *before* you begin listening and answering will help you to internalise them. If you have them in your mind you will avoid the confusion of reading questions in English at the same time as listening in French.

5. You should practise note-taking so that it is a help to you. If you spend too much time writing when you should be listening, then taking notes could be a hindrance. Before the stage when you listen and write notes it is useful to number the lines of your answer sheet to correspond to the numbering of the questions. Keep your notes as brief as possible, just one or two words to help you recall the information from your memory. It is best to make your notes in French as they are intended to recall relevant parts of the text. At the note-taking stage you do not have time to start formulating an answer in English. However, if an English term occurs to you and it is brief, use it. You can also make use of simple symbols, e.g.:

- to indicate the idea of increase, growth, becoming more important, rise; e.g. population ↑
- to indicate that someone announced, stated an opinion, put forward a view, made a speech, etc. President "peace talks". If you use symbols it is best to use only a small number and to develop your own.

Practice in "listening and doing" will have helped your note-taking: you will have developed the technique of selecting information and of listening with a purpose. Also, the more you have practised listening to the linguistic patterns of French the easier note-taking will be because you will be able to choose the right moment to jot things down: when the speaker pauses, when you can predict what the rest of his sentence will be, when he is adding a detail or repeating himself rather than making a main point. With practice you will find that very brief notes are adequate. A professional interpreter's notes made for a consecutive interpretation will usually contain only a few abbreviated words of French and English and a number of symbols.

6. When you answer the questions the main requirement is to give all the relevant information. This means that it is often not enough to supply the main point; relevant supporting details are also required for full marks to be awarded for the answer. It is sometimes difficult to know where to draw the line when it comes to secondary details, but if in doubt it is usually safer to include them. As a general rule the examiner will not penalise the addition of unnecessary details unless they vitiate the main point of the answer or are simply invented. Do not expect the answer to be stated directly in the text, it may need to be inferred. However, it is unlikely in a listening comprehension that the information to be recalled will be dispersed throughout the text. The questions follow the text chronologically. It is not a test of English and you will have limited time to write down your answers but it is important that your answers are presented clearly. If note-form is allowed then make sure that the notes are not ambiguous: the examiner should not have to try to deduce what you mean.

7. A common fear among candidates is that the French will be too

fast for them to understand. Again, the remedy is practice. If you have had plenty of varied listening to a variety of authentic texts spoken at normal speed or near normal speed you will be well prepared.

EXAMINATION QUESTIONS

It is not possible to present past listening comprehension tests exactly as the candidate would experience them under examination conditions. However you have below the *transcript* of passages of French which in the examination you would listen to but not see. They will give you an idea of what is involved and of the type of questions asked but it is obviously essential to practise the test as it would be administered in the exam, perhaps with the help of another person.

1.

Vous allez entendre un extrait d'une interview avec l'auteur Jacques Lacarrière. Récemment installé dans le village de ses grands-parents, il parle des problèmes du nouveau-venu qui veut se faire accepter comme membre de cette société.

D'abord vous allez écouter une première fois tout l'extrait.

Reporter: Il semble que, quand on vit dans un village, les rapports entre les gens sont souvent dus à la rivalité plutôt qu'à la convivialité. Vous avez trouvé que cela est vrai?

Lacarrière: Les relations dans des espaces aussi restreints que ceux des villages ont presque toujours été fondées sur la rivalité, ou même sur le conflit – à cause du partage des terres et de l'occupation des sols. Les rapports qui existent entre voisins proches sont toujours difficiles, mais pas forcément agressifs, quand même.

Reporter: Le village ne se livre-t-il pas à une sorte de petite 'guerre froide', où tous les protagonistes ont plutôt intérêt à contrôler leurs animosités, puisqu'ils sont condamnés à coexister?

Lacarrière: Effectivement. Mais, en vérité, la plus grande part des rivalités villageoises provient rarement de vous, mais de vos ancêtres. C'est à dire que lorsqu'on revient au village familial – après une absence de 30 ans, comme la mienne – on n'y revient pas seul, mais chargé d'un lourd héritage. Si on a eu la chance d'avoir des ancêtres respectés et généreux, on est alors vite accepté, mais si on a eu le malheur d'avoir un ancêtre irascible, alors les rivalités demeurent. Il y a encore dans mon village des personnes qui m'évitent uniquement parce que nos grands-parents étaient ennemis mortels.

(END OF PART ONE)

Reporter: Et maintenant quelle est votre position au village?

Lacarrière: Ma position au village – indépendamment du fait que je n'y suis pas un étranger, puisque mon grand-père y a déjà vécu – était, au départ, celle d'un enfant du pays, mais qui était incompréhensible. Etre auteur ne fait pas partie des activités rurales! Il ne faut pas oublier que c'est un phénomène assez récent dans l'histoire de notre

société que des écrivains s'installent à la campagne! 'Ecrire'
n'implique aucune participation à la vie villageoise et, jusqu'à
l'invention de la télévision, l'écrivain paraissait presque comme un
oisif. Or, avec l'émergence des mass media tout a changé, puisque cet
homme mystérieux, faisant des choses qui sont de l'ordre de
l'invisible, puisque la plupart des villageois ne lisent pas ses livres,
apparaît brusquemment sur les écrans de tous les foyers, sous une
forme quasi-officielle! D'ailleurs, depuis que j'ai commencé à paraître
d'une façon assez régulière à la télévision, il est certain que l'attitude
du village à mon égard a changé. On s'est rendu compte que je n'étais
pas seulment un garçon sympathique et rêveur, mais aussi un
travailleur dont on voyait enfin les résultats!

('Mon Village en Guerre et en Paix' by G Pessis Pasternak, *Le Monde*
3.9.84)

First part
1. What does the reporter see as characterising relationships in a
   village and what reason for this is given by Lacarrière?
2. According to Lacarrière, what is often the source of bad feeling?
3. What does the reporter suggest is the determining factor in
   village life?
4. What factors determine the villagers' attitude to the newcomer?
5. Why do some villagers still ignore Lacarrière?

Second part
6. How did the villagers receive Lacarrière?
7. What accounts for their original attitude towards him?
8. In what light does Lacarrière suggest the villagers saw him before
   his television appearances?
9. How have his regular appearances on television changed their
   opinion of him?

(London, Syllabus B, 1985)

**TUTOR'S ANSWER TO
QUESTION 1**

1. Relationships are often based on rivalry. In an area as confined
   as that of a village relationships have always been based on
   rivalry.
2. Bad feeling is caused by disagreement over the distribution and
   ownership of land.
3. It is the state of "cold war" which exists. Animosity is there but it
   is kept under the surface because people are obliged to live
   together.
4. The villagers' attitude towards any newcomer is determined by
   his family's past. He is judged in the light of what his ancestors
   were like. If they were respected he is readily accepted, if they
   were not then old rivalries are likely to continue.
5. Because their grandparents had been on bad terms with his
   grandparents.

6. They looked on him as someone who belonged to the area because his grandfather had lived there but they thought Lacarrière was an enigma.

7. They were not used to having a writer living among them as writers have only recently settled in the country. A writer does not seem to have any role in the community.

8. They saw him as idle and as something of a mystery – as this was the impression usually formed about writers, but as a nice enough fellow and a dreamer.

9. Television has given him a kind of official status since he has appeared on the screen in all their homes. They are now aware that he actually does some work.

A STEP FURTHER

In order to prepare for the listening comprehension test and to improve your knowledge of French generally you should listen to as much spoken French as you can. A useful step further is to make the most of your French language assistant or of any other native speaker whose help you can enlist. Persuade them to record material that you have chosen yourself. You might include:

- Readings of stories or anecdotes (for example, some of the true stories taken from Histoires Vraies or C'est Arrivé un Jour collected by P. Bellemare and J. Antoine).
- Unscripted accounts of films, plays, personal anecdotes, jokes.
- Commentaries on visual material such as cartoon strips, photographs or diagrams.
- Descriptions of places, people or journeys.
- Explanations of how things work, of what one has to do in certain situations (e.g. catching a plane, going through customs, booking theatre tickets, taking a driving test, playing a game, etc.).

FURTHER READING

P. Pimsleur. *Le Pont Sonore*. Hachette
M. Léon. *Exercices Systématiques de Prononciation Française*. Hachette
Cassettes Radio France (75786 Paris Cedex 16 France and some of these are available through European Schoolbooks, Croft St. Cheltenham GL53 0HX)
P. Bellemare et J. Antoine. Histoires Vraies vols 1–5. C'est Arrivé un Jour vols 1–3 (Livre de Poche Edition No. 1).

Chapter 12

Translation into English

All other language work contributes towards the student's proficiency in translating from French into English. Practice at listening comprehension, intensive reading for building up active vocabulary, extensive reading for increasing passive vocabulary, and studying texts for reading comprehension. All these activities develop the skills which are essential for success in the translation paper. It does not follow, however, that this is the only preparation which is required or that translation into English, simpy because it involves writing in one's own language, is the easy part of the examination. (It is worth noting that the average mark for this paper is often lower than for the prose or essay paper.) The purpose of the translation paper is to test the candidate's ability to understand the foreign language and to express that understanding as accurately as possible in good, natural English. However, it is clear from examination scripts that many candidates see comprehension of the French as the main difficulty to overcome and therefore tend to neglect the accuracy and quality of the English. It is not sufficient to demonstrate general comprehension and to convey the gist of the passage or of a section of it (unless the rubric states specifically that this is all that is required); a precise translation and correct English are necessary at all times. You should understand that practice is essential and that there are helpful techniques which can be acquired. The candidate who does exceptionally well will have mastered these techniques, will have read and listened to a great deal of French and will have a very good command of his own language (as his performance in other parts of the examination which are written in English invariably shows). It should not be forgotten that the translation paper is a test of French *and* a test of English.

When getting started on preparing this part of the examination you should map out as far as possible the ground to be covered. Consult the syllabus and as many recent papers as you can so that you know whether you will be required to translate one passage or two, how much time is allowed for the paper, how many marks it carries and what type of passage or passages you can expect. As you will see from the selection of past papers on pp. 146–148, the French passage may be descriptive, discursive or narrative; again it may be colloquial, journalistic or literary. In examinations where two passages are set they are likely to be in contrasting styles and registers. Know, therefore, exactly what you are preparing for and ensure that your reading programme and translation practice include passages of the appropriate type.

ESSENTIAL PRINCIPLES

SUFFICIENT GENERAL KNOWLEDGE

Choosing the right passages for reading and practice will do more than enable you to cover the relevant vocabulary areas. Different types of passage (e.g. narrative, discursive, etc.) can present their own problems and you should get used to tackling them. The discursive or documentary text which deals with current affairs, for example, can often be more confidently understood and competently translated if your *general* knowledge is adequate. A text set recently for translation at A-level dealt with an aspect of the Common Market. A good many candidates would have coped much more satisfactorily if they had had some elementary knowledge of the EEC. They would not have translated "le traité de Rome" as the "Roman treatise", "la communauté" as the "Commonwealth" and they would have realised that "il vaudrait mieux repartir à Six" meant "it would be better to start again with six members" rather than "it would be better to leave again at six o'clock". If you are familiar with the subject-matter then clearly you are in a better position to understand the passage and to choose those English terms which are appropriate within the context. If, by sampling past papers, you can see that you may be asked to translate a passage which touches on subjects such as trade unions, the French educational system, the French press, Paris, the French postal system, etc. (which have all appeared in recent translation papers) then try to make certain that your reading in French and translation practice include the kind of passage which will provide you not only with the vocabulary but with the general knowledge which will help you to produce a good translation. It is not specialist knowledge which is necessary: it is a question of sufficient general knowledge, provided quite adequately in newspapers and periodicals, which will allow things to fall into place more readily when you are working on a text which deals with a contemporary subject.

It is always valuable to have had plenty of experience of the type of passage which will be set in the examination. General knowledge of the kind discussed above may not be important if you are translating a passage of narrative or dialogue from a novel but it is still essential to understand fully the situation, so that you can know what is going on. If you choose your reading material sensibly then experience will help you to become familiar with not just narrative or descriptive vocabulary but with the way in which French writers deal with description or narrative or even the way in which dialogue is presented and punctuated on the printed page. You will also be better able to judge the tone, the formality or perhaps the humour of a passage, and to get a proper "feel" of it, which is an essential step towards turning out a first-class translation.

CRITERIA OF ASSESSMENT

The translation paper tests close understanding of the passage in French and ability to express its meaning in natural English. A deductive system of marking is most commonly used where penalties for errors are subtracted from a pool of positive marks. It is usual to divide the passage into sections, each with a fixed maximum number of penalty points.

Allowance is made in marking for the fact that there is often more than one way of translating the French phrase or sentence and for the fact that a wrong translation is often not entirely wrong. The *more serious errors* (and therefore more heavily penalised) would include the total misinterpretation of a word, an omission or unnecessary addition which distorts the meaning of the original, and grammatical errors such as the wrong choice of tense or the wrong use of pronouns, prepositions or adverbs. An expression which is definitely not English or a grammatical inaccuracy in the English (even though the meaning appears to be correct) would also be considered as a more serious error. *Less serious errors* would include the use of a word or phrase which is not completely appropriate, a clumsy turn of phrase which nevertheless conveys the right meaning or an unnecessary addition which does not alter the meaning of the French.

The system of marking then, is a precise one. It reflects the importance of thoroughly understanding the original passage and the need for accuracy (and this should include punctuation and spelling) in the use of English. The translation paper, because of the way in which it is marked and the nature of the exercise itself, requires that you should give very careful attention to every word that you write.

FOUR MAJOR AREAS FOR IMPROVEMENT

When asked what worries them most about this paper students usually say that it is the problem of *vocabulary*, of simply not understanding the words or some of them. It is true that this is the most obvious cause of a poor result but it is never the only cause. *Inability to understand structures*, *inaccurate use of English* and *unfamiliarity with the techniques of translation* can also be major areas of weakness. You should therefore take positive steps to improve in all four areas throughout the course. And if it seems that you are having to fight a battle on several fronts then console yourself with the thought that if you managed to make progress in only one direction you could still improve your chances quite significantly.

Vocabulary

When preparing for the translation paper your objectives as far as vocabulary acquisition is concerned will be rather different from those required when working towards prose translation and the essay in French. Those two exercises depend on your active vocabulary. When you tackle the translation paper you will need to draw widely on the resources of your *passive* vocabulary which comprises that stock of lexical items which you should be able to recognise but which you may not be able to recall spontaneously from your memory. The learner's passive vocabulary is assumed to be considerably wider than his active repertoire and you must aim at building it up throughout the course. Working on the translations set by your tutor will help but in order to ensure that your vocabulary is sufficiently wide and varied you should follow a programme of *extensive reading* (as opposed to the intensive reading described in Ch. 3). There is advice on organising such a programme on p. 101.

The more you read the more likely you are to meet new lexical items on subsequent occasions and so consolidate your recognition of them. This is important because although it may not be necessary to establish the new word as part of your active vocabulary, it is necessary nevertheless to be able to identify it accurately and to avoid the confusion which has led past candidates to read "chaussé" as "chauffé", "honteusement" as "heureusement", "jouir" as "jouer", "épuisé" as "épousé", and so on.

Useful points to help interpret unfamiliar words

Of course, you are bound to meet words that you do not recognise in the examination, no matter how conscientiously you have worked at extending your vocabulary. However, all is by no means lost. The following points will help you to interpret a word which you are not sure of or even one which is totally new to you:

1. Read the *whole* passage again carefully. The context will often provide clues to the meaning of an unknown word and the surrounding sentences may even contain a synonym which you *can* recognise for the word which is baffling you. Generally speaking, the more important the word is to the passage you are translating, the more likely you are to accumulate evidence as to its meaning as you read on.

2. Always use your knowledge of *grammar* to establish whether the word is a noun, adjective or verb. If you can be certain of its function in the sentence then you are one step nearer to deciphering its meaning.

3. Use your knowledge of *suffixes* and *affixes*. They may indicate, for example, that a word is negative (e.g. inopportun) that it has an unfavourable meaning (e.g. un malfaiteur) or that it probably indicates a process or an action (e.g. le ravitaillement).

4. An idiomatic expression (that is, a lexical item consisting of several words with a meaning which cannot be deduced from the meaning of the individual words, e.g. y être pour quelque chose, en vouloir à quelqu'un, l'emporter sur quelqu'un, etc.) is difficult to

interpret if you have not met it before. However, if you can isolate the *semantic group* and can decide that it is indeed an idiomatic expression, you may be able to deduce the meaning from the context and you will be less likely to produce a clumsy, literal translation.

5. Some expressions are *metaphorical* (e.g. des prix qui <u>montent en fleche</u>, un hôtelier qui <u>égorge</u> ses clients). You should look for this possibility if the literal translation seems unlikely. Identify the two terms of the comparison (e.g. rising prices/arrow), consider their characteristics and try to infer the meaning of the expression. You would therefore discard "prices which rise like an arrow" and substitute "rocketing prices". It is likely that English usage will require a metaphor involving different terms (e.g. not prices=arrow but prices=rocket).

6. A further difficulty sometimes arises because certain words have more than one meaning (e.g. toujours, toucher). Once again it is important to be prepared for this possibility and to relate the word to its *context* to ensure that you have chosen the right meaning.

Structures

When the structure of a sentence makes its interpretation uncertain it is again advisable to approach the problem systematically. The "difficult" sentence is often one which confuses the student because of its length and complexity, even though the individual items of vocabulary have been recognised. The following sentences taken from past A-level papers are typical. They caused many candidates problems which could have been solved if there had been a little more reflection and method in the approach.

(a) Mais bon nombre d'écrivains prévoient un avenir que les progrès de la science et de la technologie rendront encore plus standarisé que le présent et où l'homme perdra progressivement sa liberté de choix.

(b) Rappelant que serait célébré le mois suivant le 25ième anniversaire du traité de Rome, qui avait été indiscutablement pour quelque chose dans la prospérité qu'avait connue une Europe sortie de la guerre exsangue et ruinée, le ministre poursuivit: « Pourquoi faut-il que cette célébration soit nuancée d'amertume? »

If you find yourself faced with a sentence like one of these and the meaning eludes you, first try reading it rapidly several times. A rapid reading of sentence (b), for example, will help you to connect <u>Rappelant</u> with the subject of the verb, <u>le ministre</u> which does not appear until the end of the sentence. After rapid reading ask yourself questions about what you think the sense might be and then read the sentence again slowly to see if there is any evidence that you were right. Reading the sentences which precede and follow should also provide clues to the meaning of the problem sentence.

If the sense still does not emerge clearly you can resort to a more *systematic* analysis:

1. Find the main verbs and try to establish what their subjects and objects are. Be prepared for the inversion of subject and verb, particularly after the relative pronoun "que", as this is a very frequent source of confusion. There are examples of inversion in sentence (b) above:
   Rappelant que serait célébré le 25ième anniversaire; la prospérife qu'avait connue une Europe…
2. Identify those words which belong in the same semantic group or breath group: le mois suivant, not le mois suivant le 25ième anniversaire; not la guerre exsangue et ruinée (it makes no sense to attach "exsangue" and "ruinée" to "la guerre") but une Europe… exsangue et ruinée.
3. Identify the present participles and past participles and decide with what subject or object they belong. For example, "rappelant" belongs with "le ministre" and "sortie" belongs with "une Europe" in sentence (b) above.
4. If necessary, rearrange the sentence in a more straightforward manner, using all the grammatical clues that you can: e.g. les progrès (de la science) rendront un avenir plus standardisé; Rappelant que le 25ième anniversaire (du traité de Rome) serait célébré; une Europe (sortie de la guerre) avait connu la prospérité.

Under examination conditions you may be forced into inferring the meaning of words from context or into disentangling the syntax of a difficult sentence in order to draw out the sense. However, attempts at working out the meaning of a word or sentence based on the points listed above should not be reserved for the examination. Practise deducing meaning whenever you can. When you come across unknown vocabulary while reading or doing course-work translations, do *not* immediately open the dictionary; first see how far you can decipher the sense by using only those clues which are contained in the passage. You will be training yourself in a skill which will prove invaluable on the day of the examination.

Use of English

Once you have grasped the meaning of the text you are translating there remains the essential task of expressing that meaning accurately in English. Candidates are not always aware of the importance of this part of the exercise. Although they may have reached a sound, detailed understanding of the French they are not always careful enough about the way they express themselves in English.

When the English is substandard it is sometimes because the candidates simply do not have sufficient control of their own language to avoid grammatical errors and spelling mistakes. But in the main it is the process of translating itself which leads them to invent words, to distort syntax and to produce stilted, non-English sentences which they would probably not write at all under normal circumstances. Of course, it is not easy to switch from reading and understanding a testing passage of French to expressing yourself fluently and accurately in English. It is certainly not a skill which can be suddenly produced on the day of the examination; it is a mental exercise which must be practised throughout the course.

When you work on a translation, try to think of more than one English version for any phrase or sentence. Ask yourself which version is closest in meaning to the original and then ask yourself whether it sounds natural within its context. When you have finished the work it is a good idea to put it aside for a day or two so that you can reread it and criticise it later as a passage of English. Better still, get somebody to read it who has not seen the original. You may have to admit that what you have written, or some of it, is stilted and reads like "translationese" rather than genuine English, but you will know what it is you have to improve. Try rephrasing or look for a word which is more normal in English, but always check once more to ensure that your correction satisfies the sense of the original.

It may seem rather surprising to learn that you have to work at your English when you have chosen to study French, but it will pay dividends. Faulty, imprecise or clumsy English will cause you to lose marks in the examination. As examiners' reports regularly point out, use of English is an aspect of the translation paper which many candidates seem to neglect and it contributes more significantly than many realise to success or failure in this part of the examination.

Techniques of translation

Here we will review a number of points which really are to do with the technique of translation under examination conditions. They are based on experience of the way in which candidates tend to perform in the translation paper and can be regarded as essential guide-lines as to what should be done whenever you embark on a translation, and, more importantly, when you sit down to tackle the translation on the day of the examination.

1. Read the French thoroughly several times. Even if you can understand it without difficulty, it is important to get the *feel* of the passage. Do not aim at understanding only the words. Read into the passage so that its logic, if it contains an argument or discussion, is clear to you. If it is narrative, description or dialogue, try to picture the situation and keep it in your mind. This will ensure that you translate not just words but ideas and that whenever you translate a word or phrase you relate it to its context.

2. Although, quite obviously, you should not attempt to translate the French word by word, you should make sure that you have taken account of *every word* of the original. Candidates regularly lose marks needlessly because words have been carelessly omitted. It is easily done; the translation may make perfectly good sense in spite of one or two missing adverbs or adjectives. It is therefore important to make a final check in order to compare what you have written, sentence by sentence, with the original passage.

3. When you read the French attentively in order to grasp its full meaning you will give careful thought to all *grammatical structures*. There are, however, certain aspects of grammar and syntax which

cause problems more frequently than others. An analysis of 250 scripts produced in past examinations shows that particular attention should be given to the following five areas:

(a) *Use of tenses* (easily the most frequent source of error). Candidates tend to misinterpret compound tenses (e.g. elle avait regressé; il se serait accru), particularly when they are uncertain of the meaning of the verb (a 'double' difficulty is likely to lead to at least one error). They also frequently overlook a change of tense (e.g. from past to present, from simple past to pluperfect) in the original.

(b) *Relative pronouns.* Qui, que, qu', ce qui, ce que, ce qu' are very frequently confused, usually with disastrous results for the rest of the sentence.

(c) *The articles.* Many candidates are careless in distinguishing between the definite and indefinite article and sometimes between the definite article and the possessive adjective or demonstrative adjective. To write "<u>a</u> typewriter" instead of "<u>the</u> typewriter", "<u>the</u> letter" instead of "<u>this</u> letter", "<u>his</u> umbrella" instead of "<u>an</u> umbrella" may not alter the sense very much but it may well make enough difference for marks to be lost. It is therefore important to check details of this nature.

(d) *Pronouns.* Many candidates interpret pronouns rather carelessly. Errors arise when candidates do not distinguish between direct object and indirect object pronouns (so that a sentence such as "je lui/leur présentai Jean" is translated incorrectly as "I introduced him/them to Jean") and when they relate the pronoun to its noun (with the result that <u>he</u> is written for <u>she</u>, <u>he</u> for <u>it</u> and so on).

(e) *Conjunctions.* A mistake involving a conjunction is very noticeable since it will affect the sense of the whole sentence. It is not possible to list here all the conjunctions which you should know but it can be said that the following have caused numerous problems in recent examinations: en outre, du reste, encore que, alors que, aussitôt que, à moins que. If you are uncertain of the meaning of any of these then you should certainly look up co-ordinating and subordinating conjunctions in your grammar-book and revise them. The conjunction is a keyword which will often unlock the meaning of an entire sentence.

These five "danger areas" (a-e) do not constitute an exhaustive check-list but examining experience shows that they are major causes of difficulty and therefore they should have a place in your personal check-list.

4. Remember that you are aiming at a precise translation of the French. A loose translation will lose marks when words are added unnecessarily or when the sentence is recast for no good reason. When this happens the candidate's intentions are usually good: the addition of words or the rearrangement of phrases and sentences is meant to make the translation read more like English. What often

happens however, is that the addition of words or recasting alters the meaning of the original. Ask yourself very carefully, therefore, whether you are adding details to the original. Be cautious about rearranging the order of sentences and phrases. Recasting a sentence should be carried out not for the sake of it but only if it is the best or only way of putting the meaning of the original into English. Wholesale recasting is seldom or never necessary. The sensible rule to follow is that if the straightforward translation conveys the meaning of the French and makes perfectly good English, do not alter it.

5.   Remember that it is often acceptable to translate a word of the original by the "same" word in English (e.g. refuser will be translated by "to refuse", "inspecter" by "to inspect") if it fits the context and makes good sense. This has to be pointed out because candidates sometimes distort the meaning of the original by trying, without justification, "to get away from the French". If a transliterated word fits perfectly well into the English sentence you may use it. If there is a more common or more natural English word which conveys the right meaning, then use that instead.

6.   When you come up against a word which you do not know then adopt the approach described on p. 143. Do not follow the example of those candidates who first leave a blank space, return to it later,.make an uninformed guess at the word and then alter the rest of the sentence to accommodate the wrong translation.

7.   When you have finished the translation read it through from beginning to end simply to check the English. If it does not make sense then something must be wrong and you should therefore consider the original once more.

EXAMINATION QUESTIONS

1.

Depuis plus d'une semaine que l'Américaine l'avait fait inviter par Borel, Gérard avait eu le temps de s'y préparer. Tout était réglé d'avance, sa conversation, ses répliques et même son attitude en paraissant devant Daisy. Il entrouvrirait légèrement la bouche et resterait une seconde immobile, le regard fixe, comme fasciné. Toute la difficulté résidait dans la mesure: ni trop comédien, ni trop gauche. Cette scène qu'il avait répétée vingt fois, devant son miroir, et jusque dans son lit, faillit cependant échouer. L'Américaine, lorsqu'il entra, s'amusait avec ses amis: on ne peut pas prendre une mine ténébreuse devant une femme qui pleure de rire. C'est pourtant ce qu'il fit; le rôle était appris, il ne fallait rien y changer. Il regarda Mlle Daisy Bell sans un mot, la lèvre peut-être un peu plus amère qu'il n'avait décidé, et s'inclina lentement. Une telle mélancolie attristait son visage que leur gaieté à tous en tomba. D'où sortait-il celui-là?

«M. Paul Gérard, dont vous connaissez le nom et le talent» présenta courtoisement un jeune homme.
(London, 1980. *Le Château des Brouillards* by Roland Dorgeles.
— Albin Michel)

2.

En Angleterre la guerre de 1914–1918 fut suivie d'une grave dépression industrielle. Pendant quelques années de bons observateurs attentifs se demandèrent si l'Angleterre n'était pas condamnée. L'avance qu'elle avait prise, au dix-neuvième siècle, sur ses rivales avait été perdue. Ses industries, moins bien équipées que celles de l'Allemagne et des Etats-Unis, étaient en outre paralysées par des salaires plus élevés que ceux du Continent, et auxquels les Syndicats ne permettaient pas que l'on touchât. Son commerce extérieur était atteint par la disparition des consommateurs dans un monde appauvri; sa flotte marchande demeurait sans emploi. Pour conserver son rôle de banquier du monde, elle essaya de maintenir la valeur de la livre sterling et cette politique monétaire accrut encore le chômage. Les mines, les chemins de fer, les industries textiles employaient moins d'ouvriers. En 1926 un effort pour abaisser les salaires des mineurs provoqua une grève générale. Les journaux ayant cessé de paraître, le gouvernement annexa temporairement la BBC. Maître de l'opinion publique, soutenu par de nombreux volontaires qui collaboraient avec la police et assuraient le ravitaillement des grandes villes, le gouvernement vainquit la grève.

(London, 1985. *Histoire d'Angleterre* by André Maurois Fayard)

3.

—Roberte, es-tu prête? tonnait la voix de son père.

—J'arrive!

La jeune fille se précipita vers la penderie, arracha une robe, hésita, la rejeta, en choisit une autre, la rejeta également, se décida enfin pour une troisième, qu'elle enfila d'une coup sec. Toujours courant, elle introduisit le pied de vive force dans son soulier droit, qui bâillait au milieu de la descente de lit et, clopinant, poursuivit l'autre. Enfin son pied gauche recontra par hasard son soulier gauche et, laissant toutes portes ouvertes, Roberte enfila le couloir, dévala l'escalier, déboucha en trombe dans la salle à manger.

—Allons, allons! bougonna son père en l'embrassant, tu n'es tout de même plus une gamine.

Berthe, la bonne, avait déjà servie: les bols encensaient la table. A côté de celui de M. Gérane, brillait la topaze claire d'un petit verre d'eau-de-vie de cidre. Le juge était un homme fort digne, du type pesant, à moustache rarement humide. Cependant, fils unique de feu le père Gérane, gros fermier de Tiercé, qui lui avait *fait donner de l'instruction*, il avait conservé l'habitude paysanne de boire sa goutte chaque matin avant son café au lait. Les jambes nues de sa fille attirèrent son attention.

—Tu n'as pas de bas, reprit-il. On ne va pas à la messe sans bas. Mets au moins des socquettes. Allez, file!

(Oxford and Cambridge, 1984. *La Tête Contre les Murs* by Hervé Bazin. Bernard Grasset)

4.

Dans la presqu'île de Quiberon: un beau terrain de camping, vraiment! La densité de population y est très forte en juillet et août. Et pourtant, beaucoup de ceux qui passent ici leurs vacances y viennent depuis de longues années, avec un plaisir qui ne semble pas s'émousser.

A bien les écouter, on comprend qu'ils trouvent là plus qu'un temps de loisir: une autre façon de vivre. Pour manger la soupe de poisson ou le poulet des grande soirs, ils sont jusqu'à cinquante ou soixante à aligner leurs tables les unes à la suite des autres. Les comportements expriment une volonté implicite de faire disparaître les barrières que le mode de vie actuel multiplie dans la vie courante. Tout le monde parle à tout le monde, y compris à l'inconnu qui vient d'arriver, tout est occasion d'entraide. Les enfants, en particulier, sont partout chez eux, non seulement acceptés, mais choyés comme rarement ailleurs.

L'étonnant est qu'il n'y ait pas saturation, au bout d'un moment, et que cette belle entente réussisse à tenir jusqu'au bout des vacances. (London, 1982. 'Mille Petites Républiques Paisibles', by M C Betbeder, *Le Monde* 10.8.80)

5.

– Je vais gagner le jardin botanique, annonça le conducteur. Je suppose que ce que vous avez à me dire est plutôt désagréable, non?
– Oui, acquiesça Kago en conservant une mine impassible. Très désagréable.
– De quoi s'agit-il, monsieur Kago? Des affaires ou d'autre chose?
– Voilà précisément ce qui doit être éclairci, émit d'un ton réservé son passager. Au cours de mon inspection quotidienne, ce matin, j'ai découvert un micro dans le bureau de M. Sevran.

Coplan tourna vers lui un visage incrédule.

– Déjà? s'étonna-t-il, quêtant de plus amples détails.

Kago approuva de la tête et dit, avec une ombre de sarcasme:

– Vous voyez que nos précautions ne sont pas inutiles. Hong Kong est un vaste nid de serpents, monsieur Coplan. Une île bien commode, à certains égards, mais truffée de dangers. Je vous signale que j'ai laissé le micro en place.

– Hein? Comment? fit Coplan tout en négociant un virage. Mais cela va nous paralyser!

– Sans doute. Pendant quelques jours au moins, que nous mettrons à profit pour élucider certaines questions. Nous ne pouvons rien bâtir de valable sur des bases incertaines: le but est trop important. (London, 1981. *Coplan Traque le Renard* by Paul Kenny. Fleuve Noir)

These past questions will give you an idea of the different types of French passage that may be set. Broadly, they are narrative/ descriptive, discursive/documentary and narrative/dialogue.

You should try your hand at translating them, or at thinking the translation through, bearing in mind the points which have been discussed earlier in the chapter.

Questions **4** and **5** are translated for you. Consider the following points before tackling the questions yourself.

Question 4

(a) This is an example of the kind of passage which tests the ability to express oneself in English as much as the ability to understand the French. The difficulty is to find expressions and construct sentences which read naturally. What will you do, for example, with those sentences which are rather elliptical in construction?

- Dans la presqu'île de Quiberon: un beau terrain de camping, vraiment!
- A bien les écouter, on comprend qu'ils trouvent là plus qu'un temps de loisir: une autre façon de vivre.

Here is may be necessary to remodel the sentence, perhaps by adding a verb, until it sounds like English. But do not lose sight of the original.

(b) There are probably certain words that you do not recognise, such as s'émousser, les comportements, entraide, choyés, entente. However, you should be able to infer their meaning when you have the context clear in your mind:

- S'émousser: there are a great many people on the campsite, people have been coming for years but their enjoyment never_____(?)
- choyés: children can feel at home everywhere, they are accepted, but *more* than that they are_____(?)

Remember to use all the clues provided by the sentence or surrounding sentences:

- Les comportements: Les comportements expriment une volonté implicite. "Implicite" (implicit, unspoken) will throw some light on "comportements". If a desire is not expressed in words, how is it likely to be expressed? By actions, attitudes, behaviour, sign-language? Obviously certain possibilities are more likely than others.

(c) Be careful of those phrases which are easy enough to understand – densité de population, un temps de loiser, la densité est... forte, au bout d'un moment, etc. – but which you will not be able to translate literally. "The density is... strong", "at the end of a moment", etc. would not, of course, be acceptable.

(d) It will be helpful to try to picture what is described: Pour manger la soupe de poisson ou le poulet des grands soirs, ils sont jusqu'à cinquante ou soixante à aligner leurs tables les unes à la suite des autres. If fifty or sixty people are eating together outside what are they likely to do with their tables?

(e) Look at the structure of the more complex sentences. Try reading them quickly and then more slowly. Find the object and subject of the verb "multiplie" in Les comportements expriment une volonté implicite de faire disparaître les barrières que le mode de vie actuel multiplie dans la vie courante. Make sure that you grasp the overall structure of L'étonnant est qu'il n'y ait pas saturation, au bout d'un moment, et que cette belle entente réuississe à tenir jusqu'au bout des vacances. The two subjunctives will help you to understand that both clauses are introduced by L'étonnant est qu'/que.

Question 5
(a) When translating dialogue it is again important to understand the situation, to be clear about who says what and to picture the scene so that you can ensure that each word and sentence is appropriate in its context.
(b) It is important to reproduce as far as possible the natural speech rhythms of English. "Does it sound natural?" "Would one say that?" are the questions that you must put to yourself as you translate.
(c) The question of register is important. It does not follow necessarily that the language is familiar simply because it is the language of a conversation. The speakers may be speaking formally and carefully. However, you are obviously more likely to meet familiar or even slang terms in a passage of dialogue. Be prepared therefore to produce a colloquial rendering, but only if the original justifies it.

Translation – Question 4
In the Quiberon peninsula there is indeed a beautiful campsite. The number of people there is very high in July and August. And yet those who spend their holidays here have been coming for many years with a pleasure which never seems to diminish.

If you really listen to them you can see that what they find there is something more than a period of leisure time: they find a different way of living. When they eat the fish soup or chicken which they have on special evenings, as many as fifty or sixty of them will arrange their tables next to each other in a long row. People's behaviour expresses an unspoken desire to do away with the barriers which the way we live today makes increasingly numerous in everyday life. Everyone speaks to everyone else, including the newcomer, everything provides an opportunity for people to help one another. The children in particular are welcome everywhere, not just accepted but made a fuss of as they rarely are elsewhere.

What is astonishing is that people do not soon feel they have had too much of it and that this splendid spirit of understanding can last until the end of the holidays.

Translation – Question 5
– I am just coming to the botanical gardens, announced the driver. I suppose that what you have to tell me is rather unpleasant, isn't it?
– Yes, agreed Kago, continuing to look impassive. Very unpleasant.
– What is it about, Mr Kago? Business or something else?
– That is precisely what has to be made clear, said his passenger, guardedly. While carrying out my daily inspection this morning, I found a microphone in Mr Sevran's office.

Coplan turned to look at him disbelievingly.

– Already? he said in astonishment, seeking fuller details.

Kago nodded and said with a touch of sarcasm:

– You can see that our precautions are not without use. Hong Kong is a huge snake-pit, Mr Coplan. A very convenient island from certain points of view, but riddled with dangers. Let me point out that I left the mike where it was.

– Eh? You did what? said Coplan, negotiating a bend. But that will stop us doing anything!

– I dare say. For a few days, at least, which we will put to good use in order to throw light on certain matters. We cannot build anything worthwhile on shaky foundations: the objective is too important.

FURTHER READING   P. Lyon (ed). Penguin Parallel Texts. French Short Stories. Penguin.

Chapter 13

Literature

Many examination syllabuses, particularly at A-level, give candidates the opportunity to study literature, and in some cases this is compulsory. If you are studying for your examination at a school or college, it is likely that your tutor will already have chosen your set texts for you, bearing in mind the overall needs of the class. If, however, you are preparing for the examination as a private candidate or if you need for some other reason to choose your own set texts, you should check carefully the printed syllabus of the appropriate Examination Board. Remember that the syllabus must bear the date *when you expect to take the examination* and not the date on which you start your course of study. Usually candidates are required to study about four texts chosen from quite a long list and covering different literary genres (plays, novels, short stories and poetry) and historical periods (usually the seventeenth century onwards). It is most important that your choice should meet the Board's requirements. If you are retaking your examination, you cannot assume automatically that the books you studied before are still on a list. You must check this carefully – a quick glance at the list is not enough. Remember that it is not unusual for set book lists to change very slightly from year to year and lists which may appear identical at first sight can in fact contain minor changes.

Unless you already have quite an extensive knowledge of French literature, you will need some help and advice when deciding on your set books. If most of your study will be undertaken privately, you will probably be wise to choose either twentieth-century prose works or texts for which you know that good annotated editions or helpful critical commentaries are available. Candidates preparing for the examination at a school or college often have their texts provided for them, but even so it is helpful to have your own personal copies if you can afford them. This will enable you to write notes on the text itself –

reminders of the meaning of difficult words, underlining of useful quotations and brief comments on particularly significant parts of the work being studied. One of the most efficient ways of revising is the careful rereading of texts which you have thoroughly annotated yourself. A word of warning, however, about notes which may have been made on a text by a previous user. As far as possible these should be ignored. They are unlikely to have the same significance for you as for the original writer. At best they may prove to be a distraction and at worst they may actually be wrong.

Since many of the texts which appear in set book lists are major works of literature, it is inevitable that a considerable number of them will exist in English translation. Attitudes towards the use of translations vary greatly, but all teachers would agree that they can *never* be a substitute for the original text. Ideally all works of literature should be studied directly in the original language; therefore, if you do decide to make use of a translation, it should only be because you feel that this will genuinely help you to understand and appreciate the French text. The following are the most likely reasons for which a translation may validly be used:

1. To obtain a rapid overview of a number of books, in order to select the one(s) which you would most like to study as a set text.
2. As a means of getting started on a text which you are finding difficult. Some candidates choose to read an entire work in translation before embarking on detailed study of the French text, but this can seriously impair your enjoyment and appreciation of the original which can no longer be read with spontaneity.
3. To check the meaning of individual words and phrases which you find obscure.

If, however, you can manage without a translation, you will be wise to do so. Certainly it should be no more than an initial aid and your main study, as well as all your revision, should be based on the original text only. The reasons for this are obvious. Firstly, examiners are very experienced at spotting candidates who are unfamiliar with their French texts. (It is not only those candidates who are unwise enough to quote in English in their examination answers who give themselves away!) More importantly, however, you will have missed many of the satisfactions of studying literature in a foreign language. The purposes of the literature section of the syllabus are twofold and interdependent – they are to enable you to extend your own knowledge of the foreign language by detailed study of works in which it is admirably used, and to use this extended knowledge to read ever more widely and appreciatively. You are missing a great deal – not only in examination terms – if you do not acquire a thorough knowledge of the original text. This may be a struggle at first, but it will be worth it.

ESSENTIAL PRINCIPLES

STUDYING FOR THE EXAMINATION

Early reading material

Earlier in this book you were advised that the best way to extend your French language skills was to use them as widely as possible and not simply to concentrate on the specific exercises required for your examination. Similar advice holds good for your work in literature. You will appreciate your set books more and will study them more satisfactorily if you have acquired good general reading skills. It is possible that you already have experience of reading fairly extensively in French and know the satisfaction and progress which comes with reading your first full-length book in a foreign language. However it is also possible that you are not yet at this stage and need help with getting started. You would do well to begin with fairly short items which are not too daunting – newspaper or magazine articles and short stories. These need not be "literary" in style, but be sure that you choose items which are well written, with good sentence structures and vocabulary which is free from jargon. From this you can progress to novels – again do not choose anything which appears forbidding to begin with. Choose a work which is not too long, in language which appears reasonably accessible at first glance. It does not matter if the content is "light", as long as the work is well written. Of course there are also established works of literature which are relatively simple in style and can be taken as your starting-point. Stories by Maupassant and novels such as *L'Etranger* by Camus or *Bonjour Tristesse* by Françoise Sagan can be appreciated even by a relatively inexperienced reader.

Approaching the set texts

The way in which you approach the study of the set texts themselves will naturally depend on the advice given by your tutor. Where possible it can be helpful to have read the *entire* work straight through before you begin studying it in detail in class, but there are some circumstances when this may not be appropriate. Some teachers find it advisable, particularly near the beginning of the course, to give their students special help with the opening sections of a book, especially if the structure of the work is in any way complicated – for instance if it includes a flashback or if the relationship between the characters is not immediately obvious.

If poetry is included among your texts or if you are studying a relatively early work, you are also likely to need help at first. In order to read French poetry or verse drama appreciatively and with ease, you must become familiar with the basic conventions of versification, since these differ considerably from the traditional forms you have probably already encountered in English. Of course, *metrical structure* is no more than the bare framework of poetry, but without some knowledge of it you will not be able to appreciate fully the qualities of a poem and the skills which have gone into its construction. At a more practical level, you will also find it harder to quote accurately in your examination if you do not understand the metre being used. Examiners frequently spot errors in quotations in the first instance because they are metrically incorrect. You need not become obsessed about the niceties of versification – examination questions do not require you to go into intricate detail or to be able to use complex terminology – but you do need to understand the basic principles.

Similarly, if you are to study one of the great seventeenth-century dramatists (the work of Corneille or Racine or some of the plays of Molière), you must understand the verse structures used – and in particular *the alexandrine or 12-syllable line* – if you are to hear the rhythm of the speeches correctly. Needless to say, you are expected to set these out as *verse* and not as prose when you quote them in your examination answers. You need not be daunted by the prospect of studying seventeenth-century authors provided that you have some initial help. The text can look forbidding at first sight, but the language of classical drama is much less difficult than you might suppose and can be easily grasped by the modern reader with a little practice. It is the experience of many examiners that seventeenth-century plays make stimulating examination texts and candidates not infrequently write well on them, sometimes producing their best answers. Nevertheless they are not to everyone's taste and the class tutor is probably the best person to decide on their suitability. Works written before the seventeenth century are much more difficult to study and considerable knowledge of French is required before they can be read with ease. Hence they only appear on some post A-level syllabuses.

Whether or not you have read the whole of a set work before beginning to study it in class or with your tutor, you should *always* prepare carefully for each lesson, going carefully through the appropriate parts of the text. "Passive learning", whereby you simply wait for your tutor to tell you what each part of the text means and do not tackle the difficulties yourself, will only slow down your progress. Obviously you will make notes in the course of your lessons and you may also be given some sets of notes by your tutor. Such sets of notes can be very helpful provided you use them sensibly. They may just be factual (giving details of the author's life or essential background information) or they may be more concerned with literary criticism (for example with matters such as style or characterisation). Notes of this latter kind can be useful if they serve to stimulate your own ideas, but you should be wary of learning them by rote. In an examination you should always express ideas which *you* have thought out for yourself and which you can substantiate. In the same way works of criticism and the introductions to annotated editions can be very helpful in suggesting lines of thought and ways of interpreting a text, but you should never simply "learn" another person's opinions. Think about them and take them seriously because reputable critics will know much more about your set authors than you do, but do not accept an argument with which you do not agree. And if you do not agree with something or, more importantly, if you do not understand it, do not learn it.

Making notes and references

When you have completed the detailed textual study of each set work and can read it with ease, you should set about making careful notes on it in preparation for your eventual revision. It may seem self-evident to say that you must know each text in its entirety, but in fact not all candidates allocate their study time with sufficient care, and it is the experience of examiners that quotations and references are often drawn from the early parts of set works, the later stages being much less well known. Be sure that this does not happen to you. It is a problem which can arise in connection with any book, but is most likely to occur if you are studying a collection of short stories or poems. Remember that you must allow time to study and revise them all. In your examination answers you cannot of course refer to every part of a set collection and you will need to be selective. If you are answering a general question on a collection of stories or poems (for instance on Maupassant's use of humour or the main characteristics of Verlaine's style), you must refer to several of them to illustrate your arguments. Be sure that you are adequately prepared so that you can make your choice wisely – if you try to deal with them all your answers will run the risk of becoming scrappy and superficial, but a very limited range of examples will restrict the scope of your discussion. So know each text thoroughly.

While making notes you would do well to compile a list of useful quotations, indicating briefly the reasons for your choice. Where applicable you may like to collect quotations under different headings (such as what they show about various characters or the author's style or ideas). Be discriminating in your selection and make sure the quotations are not too long, since you will need to learn them accurately by heart. It is possible that your tutor will indicate some of the key quotations to you, but add to these any which strike you personally as interesting – these are the quotations which you are most likely to remember and an examiner will find it refreshing not always to encounter "stock" examples.

In your notes you cannot hope to cover every aspect of your text which could possibly be the specific subject of an examination question, but you should attempt to deal with all the major features. These will vary from one text to another, but careful thought should reveal them to you. They are likely to include some or all of the following points:

1. The main themes of the work and the ways in which they are treated. These could include such topics as friendship, honour, hypocrisy, avarice and so on.
2. Characterisation. Think about each character in turn and consider which adjectives you could use to describe them and how these could be substantiated from the text. Be prepared to compare and contrast characters and to discuss the relationships between them and their influence on one another.
3. The role or function of each character. What do they contribute to the novel or play? Are they important in the plot, for shedding light on other characters, for expressing the author's ideas, for contributing humorous elements, and so on?

4. The motives and reactions of characters and the extent to which they are responsible for what takes place. The role of fate may be included here.

5. The title of the work. Does it have any special significance? Would any other title be appropriate?

6. The structure of the work. How is the plot handled? Does it contain flashbacks? Is it in diary form? How is tension created? If you are studying a play, how effective would it be on the stage?

7. The setting. Does the work have a regional, geographical or historical setting which enhances its effectiveness?

8. **The author's ideas. These may include social satire (as in the work of Beaumarchais or Voltaire for instance) or may be more philosophical (as in the work of Sartre or Camus). If your set author is also a philosopher you will need to have some understanding of his/her ideas and to be able to explain them clearly in your own words. Technical terminology can be useful if correctly used, but is not essential and should certainly never be used to mask lack of real comprehension.**

9. The author's style. This can include the quality of the description and the narrative method chosen, such as use of the first person and its effectiveness.

10. The major qualities of the work. What are its merits? Why is it an important work of literature?

Obviously the above list is not exhaustive nor does all of it apply to every work, but it should suggest ideas for the planning of your own notes. Do not learn these slavishly and insist on forcing every quotation into an examination answer or on making a set of pre-learned notes fit another topic. In the examination room you must *think* about each question and *select* the material which you can use.

In addition to studying the texts themselves, you may well want to read the opinions of critics as well as other works by your set authors. These will help to develop your judgement and critical awareness, but remember that in the examination room it is the prescribed texts themselves that you will be questioned on.

EXAMINATION QUESTIONS

These are usually of two main types:

1. Context questions in which an extract from the text is given, together with questions arising from it.
2. Questions requiring an answer in essay form.

1. CONTEXT QUESTIONS

The main purpose of these is to ensure that you have studied the text closely and with understanding, although it is unlikely that you will be asked to translate parts of the extract given. You should always read the questions which accompany the extract with great care in order that you may understand their implications fully. Usually you will be asked to do some or all of the following:

(a) Identify the point in the text where the extract occurs. This does not necessarily mean that you have to give the precise number of the scene or chapter. What is important is to be able to describe briefly and clearly, without undue narration of the plot, exactly where the given passage comes from. You should of course be able to say if the passage occurs at a crucial point in the structure of the work – for example if it is the opening or final scene of a particular act in a play.
(b) Explain the significance of specific sentences or phrases.
(c) Comment on certain aspects of the content of the extract, such as what is its importance in the plot, what it reveals about the characters involved, how it contributes to our understanding of the author's ideas, and so on.
(d) Comment on the content of the extract in relation to the work as a whole.

The following examples of context questions will help you to understand these points more clearly.

Example I

Beaumarchais: *Le Mariage de Figaro*

(For those who have not read this play, the situation is as follows: Suzanne, the Countess's maid, is to be married to Figaro, the Count's valet. However the Count, weary of the wife he once loved, has designs on Suzanne and the intrigue hinges on his being outwitted. The scene quoted below – Act II scene 24 – occurs after a series of farcical incidents in the Countess's apartment. The young page, Chérubin, was being dressed in Suzanne's clothes in order to take her place at a rendezvous with the Count, when the latter arrived unexpectedly on the strength of an anonymous note from Figaro falsely warning him that his wife had an admirer. After remaining in hiding during scenes of complicated activity, Chérubin managed to jump through the window, watched only by Suzanne, but his escape was almost discovered by the Count on the arrival of the gardener complaining of damage to his plants. Eventually all is well and Suzanne and the Countess remain alone.)

(i) Situate the following passage in its context, explaining the significance of the phrases and sentences underlined.
(ii) Show what the scene reveals of the relationship between Suzanne, la Comtesse and le Comte.

SUZANNE, LA COMTESSE.

LA COMTESSE, *dans sa bergère.* – Vous voyez, Suzanne, la jolie scène que votre étourdi m'a value avec son billet.
SUZANNE. – Ah! Madame, quand je suis rentrée du cabinet, <u>si vous aviez vu votre visage! il s'est terni tout à coup; mais ce n'a été qu'un nuage, et par degrés, vous êtes devenue rouge, rouge, rouge!</u>

LA COMTESSE. – Il a donc sauté par la fenêtre?

SUZANNE. – Sans hésiter, le charmant enfant! Léger... comme une abeille.

LA COMTESSE. – Ah! ce fatal jardinier! Tout cela m'a remuée au point... que je ne pouvais rassembler deux idées.

SUZANNE. – Ah! Madame, au contraire; et c'est là que j'ai vu combien l'usage du grand monde donne d'aisance aux dames comme il faut, pour mentir sans qu'il y paraisse.

LA COMTESSE. – Crois-tu que le Comte en soit la dupe? et s'il trouvait cet enfant au château!

SUZANNE. – Je vais recommander de le cacher si bien...

LA COMTESSE. – Il faut qu'il parte. Après ce qui vient d'arriver, vous croyez bien que je ne suis pas tentée de l'envoyer au jardin à votre place.

SUZANNE. – Il est certain que je n'irai pas non plus. Voilà donc mon mariage encore une fois...

LA COMTESSE *se lève*. – Attends... Au lieu d'un autre, ou de toi, si j'y allais moi-même?

SUZANNE. – Vous, Madame?

LA COMTESSE. – Il n'y aurait personne d'exposé... Le Comte alors ne pourrait nier... Avoir puni sa jalousie, et lui prouver son infidélité, cela serait... Allons: le bonheur d'un premier hasard m'enhardit à tenter le second. Fais-lui savoir promptement que tu te rendras au jardin. Mais, surtout, que personne...

SUZANNE. – Ah! Figaro.

LA COMTESSE. – Non, non. Il voudrait mettre ici du sien... Mon masque de velours et ma canne, que j'aille y rêver sur la terrasse. (*Suzanne entre dans le cabinet de toilette.*)

(JMB, 1985)

The questions on this passage require you to fulfil all the tasks listed under (a), (b) and (c) above. However you will also notice that you cannot adequately deal with the question which requires you to show what the scene reveals of the relationship between Suzanne, la Comtesse and le Comte *unless* you also know and can refer back to the relationship between these characters in the earlier part of the play. Hence the task listed under (d) is also partly required of you, even though it is not specifically expressed in the wording of the question. (Of course this does not mean that you are required to *narrate* what has happened earlier.) Notice also that the sections underlined are not linguistically complex, but it is necessary to understand the events and characters to which they refer if they are to have any real meaning.

Example II

Mauriac: *Thérèse Desqueyroux*

(For those who have not read this book, the passage occurs near the beginning of the novel when Thérèse, accompanied by her father, is travelling home from court after the case against her – that she tried to poison her husband – has been dismissed for lack of conclusive evidence.)

What is the situation at this point in the novel? In your opinion, how does Mauriac wish the reader to react to this description of Thérèse? Examine the methods used to obtain this reaction, and show how these are typical of Mauriac's methods in the novel as a whole.

Elle enlève son chapeau, appuie contre le cuir odorant sa petite tête blême et ballottée, livre son corps aux cahots. Elle avait vécu, jusqu'à ce soir, d'être traquée; maintenant que la voilà sauve, elle mesure son épuisement. Joues creuses, pommettes, lèvres aspirées, et ce large front, magnifique, composent une figure de condamnée – oui, bien que les hommes ne l'aient pas reconnue coupable – condamnée à la solitude éternelle. Son charme, que le monde naguère disait irrésistible, tous ces êtres le possèdent dont le visage trahirait un tourment secret, l'élancement d'une plaie intérieure, s'ils ne s'épuisaient à donner le change. Au fond de cette calèche cahotante, sur cette route frayée dans l'épaisseur obscure des pins, une jeune femme démasquée caresse doucement avec la main droite sa face de brûlée vive. (Cambridge, 1983. *Thérèse Desqueyroux* by Mauriac. Bernard Grasset)

The questions on this extract differ from those in example one in that although you are again asked to locate the passage in the text, no comment on specific words or phrases is asked for. However, very close examination of the text is necessary in order to deal with the reader's reaction to this description of Thérèse and the methods used to obtain it. Notice also that the final question is much more general in application than any of the questions in example I and will particularly require consideration of later parts of the novel.

Example III

Camus: *L'Etranger*

(This extract is easier to follow without previous knowledge of the text than are the two other examples. The work is written in the first person by a young French Algerian named Meursault. In the first part of the book, from which this extract comes, he describes events in his daily life which culminate in the shooting of an Arab. Part two of the book tells of his trial.)

(i) Relate the following passage to its context.
(ii) Show what it reveals of the relationship between Meursault and Marie.
(iii) To what extent does it help the reader to understand Meursault's character?
(iv) What significance do you attach to Meursault's comment on Paris at the end of the passage?

Le soir, Marie est venue me chercher et m'a demandé si je voulais me marier avec elle. J'ai dit que cela m'était égal et que nous pourrions le faire si elle le voulait. Elle a voulu savoir alors si je l'aimais. J'ai répondu comme je l'avais déjà fait une fois, que
5   cela ne signifiait rien mais que sans doute je ne l'aimais pas.
«Pourquoi m'épouser alors?» a-t-elle dit. Je lui ai expliqué que cela n'avait aucune importance et que si elle le désirait, nous pouvions nous marier. D'ailleurs, c'était elle qui le demandait et moi je me contentais de dire oui. Elle a observé alors que le

10   mariage était une chose grave. J'ai répondu: «Non.» Elle s'est tue
un moment et elle m'a regardé en silence. Puis elle a parlé. Elle
voulait simplement savoir si j'aurais accepté la même proposition
venant d'une autre femme, à qui je serais attaché de la même
façon. J'ai dit. «Naturellement.» Elle s'est demandé alors si elle

15   m'aimait et moi, je ne pouvais rien savoir sur ce point. Après un
autre moment de silence, elle a murmuré que j'étais bizarre,
qu'elle m'aimait sans doute à cause de cela mais que peut-être un
jour je la dégoûterais pour les mêmes raisons. Comme je me
taisais, n'ayant rien à ajouter, elle m'a pris le bras en souriant et

20   elle a déclaré qu'elle voulait se marier avec moi. J'ai répondu que
nous le ferions dès qu'elle le voudrait. Je lui ai parlé alors de la
proposition du patron et Marie m'a dit qu'elle aimerait connaître
Paris. Je lui ai appris que j'y avais vécu dans un temps et elle m'a
demandé comment c'était. Je lui ai dit: «C'est sale. Il y a des

25   pigeons et des cours noires. Les gens ont la peau blanche.»
            (JMB, 1985. *L'Etranger*, by Camus. Gallimard)

This set of questions is obviously different from the set in Example II, since you are not asked specifically about either the style or the book in general. Careful examination will reveal them to be quite close in type to those in Example I, even though their layout appears different at first sight. In considering questions (ii) and (iii) you will see that inferences about both relationships and character have to be drawn from the extract given, and sound general knowledge of the text is required for this to be done satisfactorily. This is particularly so in the case of the question on Meursault's character which implies wider knowledge of his personality on which this extract may shed some light. Although no phrases are underlined as they were in Example I, the final remark about Paris needs commentary (question iv). However, in this case, you are not asked so much to explain a reference to another incident in the text as to examine the implications of Meursault's comments about Paris. As in the Beaumarchais question, the words themselves are easy to understand. Here it is the *interpretation* of them which is testing.

2. QUESTIONS REQUIRING AN ANSWER IN ESSAY FORM

You have already been given advice in Chapter 2 on the writing of literature essays. You may find it helpful to go back over that advice before considering the following examples of examination questions. Remember that the length of examination answers is not in itself important and should never be regarded as a criterion of excellence. It is the quality of the content which counts. Essays should always be illustrated with precise references to the text and brief, apt quotations, whether or not this requirement is specifically stated in every question. In the following list questions have been based on those in some recent past A-level papers and are intended to illustrate some of the points on which it was suggested that you should make notes (see above, pp. 156–157).

1.

Prévert: *Paroles*. "A major theme of *Paroles* is compassion for the less privileged members of society." Discuss this statement.

2.

Corneille: *Le Cid*. Compare and contrast the characters of Rodrigue and don Diègue. To what extent do they have the same values?

3.

Pagnol: *Le Château de ma Mère*. What were the most important influences on Marcel's development during childhood?

4.

Anouilh: *Becket*. Choose three characters other than Becket and the King and discuss their function in the play.

5.

Racine: *Britannicus*. Examine the motives which underlie Néron's behaviour in this play.

6.

Camus: *L'Etranger*. Give an account of Meursault's reactions and emotions at his trial. To what extent can the reader sympathise with him at this point?

7.

Molière: *L'Ecole des Femmes*. To what extent do you think that Arnolphe brings about his own downfall?

8.

Gide: *La Symphonie Pastorale*. Examine the significance of the title of this book.

9.

Troyat: *Grandeur Nature*. Discuss the structure of this novel and comment on the way in which Troyat has introduced parallel characters and situations.

10.

Alain-Fournier: *Le Grand Meaulnes*. Examine the ways in which Alain-Fournier creates the atmosphere of mystery surrounding "la fête étrange".

11.

Beaumarchais: *Le Mariage de Figaro*. Discuss the importance of costume, props, settings and physical action in this play.

12.

Prévost: *Manon Lescaut*. What picture of eighteenth-century life is given in this novel?

13.

Sartre: *Les Mouches*. Show how this play exemplifies Sartre's existentialist view of life.

14.

Verlaine: *Romances sans Paroles*. Discuss the way in which Verlaine treats landscape in the poems in this collection.

15.

Maupassant: *Quinze Contes*. Without retelling the story, explain what you consider to be the chief merits of *En Famille*.

SAMPLE ANSWERS

Obviously it is impossible to give the one perfect answer to a question about literature, for much will depend on the personal style and approach of the writer and examiners often award high marks for very different essays on the same topic. In any case it is unwise to model your own style of writing on that of another person; you will do much better if you polish and improve a style which is natural to you. Nevertheless you will need to have some examples of what constitutes an acceptable standard. The following essays were written in examination conditions, with a time allocation of 45 minutes, by *students* who had just finished their A-level courses. They represent a standard which examiners would find very satisfactory and which should not be beyond the reach of most serious students.

Example I

Balzac: *Eugénie Grandet*

(Set in Saumur in the early nineteenth century, this novel tells of the restricted and impoverished life of Eugénie, the only child of a rich miser, and of her hopeless love for her irresponsible Parisian cousin Charles.)

Question: Do you agree that the main interest in this novel is the study of the way in which avarice destroys human relationships? Support your discussion with precise references to the text. (London, 1985)

In his novel *Eugénie Grandet* Balzac depicts two kinds of society, the provincial and the Parisian. In both money occupies the thoughts of nearly all the characters and it is their greed for it which leads to their frequent disregard for moral standards.

In Monsieur Grandet Balzac has created a miser whose obsessions are monstrous. He resides in the provinces, at Saumur, where he is the richest man in the area, and because money buys respect in provincial society, he is held in high esteem by the local people. Balzac writes of the lawyer, Monsieur Cruchot, and the banker, Monsieur des Grassins: "Ils témoignaient publiquement à Monsieur Grandet un si grand respect . . ." In fact these two families from the town of Saumur do their very best to gain favour with Grandet, in order to win for one of their members the hand in marriage of his daughter Eugénie. The Cruchots and the des Grassins are attracted to the idea of marrying Eugénie into their families solely because they would be marrying her wealth and all the respect and dominance it brings with it. Hence their outward friendliness towards Grandet is merely a superficial façade; any desire for friendship with him is based entirely upon gaining his money, and we are shown how a simple human quality such as friendship is destroyed and remoulded around greed.

Grandet, as the main embodiment of the avarice that is rife in the provinces, is presented by Balzac as being an extreme and not an exception in his lust for money which has become an obsession. He himself admits: "La vie est une affaire." Business deals come before everything else and he has lost all perspective on life. He is devious and cunning. "Financièrement parlant, Monsieur Grandet tenait du tigre et du boa." Money corrupts his relationships with fellow businessmen. He stutters when making a deal in order to cause confusion, and he gains pleasure in exploiting others. Grandet's lust for money has destroyed any possible sympathy he might have felt for other people, to the extent that his only use for others is as a means to gain money.

Grandet's family life is sad and almost unbelievably restricted. His care for Eugénie stems from the fact that she will be his heiress and therefore will be entrusted with his fortune. Hence, when she asks for his deathbed blessing, he can only say: "Aie bien soin de tout. Tu me rendras compte de ça là-bas." Previously Grandet's thoughts had stayed in the present and he would act upon his desire for money without thinking of the consequences. Balzac reminds us that all misers think this way: "Les avares ne croient point à une vie à venir, le présent est tout pour eux." Grandet cares little about the effects of his behaviour on his family. He cannot even show his daughter natural fatherly affection. The only time when he appears to do this, calling her "fifille", is when he has completed a successful business deal. When Charles weeps for the death of his ruined father – the miser's own brother – Grandet can only say: "Ce jeune homme n'est bon à rien, il s'occupe plus des morts que de l'argent." As his wife lies dying, Grandet refuses to call a doctor, whom he would have to pay. He changes his mind when he is informed that if his wife dies he will have to part with much more money because of Eugénie's inheritance rights. This is a sad reflection upon his attitude to life. He cannot show his daughter fatherly affection, he has no respect for his dead brother, and he holds his wife in such low esteem that his beloved money has become more important than love for her.

Balzac's interest in the theme of a desire for money destroying human relationships is evident also in the way in which he depicts Parisian society. Paris and the provinces are portrayed as different in matters of fashion and finesse, but a consuming desire to gain money is apparent in both. In Paris, as in the provinces, money has corrupted friendship. Balzac writes: "Là, pour voir juste, il faut peser chaque matin la bourse d'un ami." Friendship has become superficial because it is based on the money in a friend's pocket, rather than the feeling in his heart. Charles Grandet is the product of such a society. After his father's bankruptcy and suicide he knows only too well how his former friends would treat him. "Il connaissait assez la société de Paris pour savoir que dans sa position il n'y eût trouvé que des coeurs indifférents ou froids." He is sadly aware of the rebuff that would await him if he returned penniless to Paris: "Ni mon âme ni mon visage ne sont faits à supporter les affronts, la froideur, le dédain qui attendent l'homme ruiné." But although Charles is aware how he and his society have replaced love and true feeling with interest in one another's wealth, it is a situation which he accepts. In Paris we hear of "double corruption, mais corruption élégante et fine, de bon goût".

Charles is briefly awakened to the sincere and self-sacrificing love of Eugénie. She, along with her mother and their servant La Grande Nanon, is depicted by Balzac as being pure and innocent. She is "l'Ange de Pureté", untouched by the corrupting power of money. Thus her love for Charles is based on true human feeling; but Charles, though momentarily struck by the natural charm of such a relationship, stops returning Eugénie's love when he is once again drawn into the world of money. He joins the slave trade and leads a debauched life, devoid of morals, and his love for Eugénie is immediately abandoned.

Thus Balzac illustrates for us the corrupting influence of a desire for money. We have seen how Grandet mistrusts everyone and has no true feelings for his family; and Charles, a product of a society dominated by money, abandons his love for Eugénie to return to his corrupt world. Therefore, because Balzac shows us the power of money to destroy wherever the action of the novel takes place, it can be seen as the most prominent and persistent theme in the book.

Notice that this student has a clear essay plan, which the introduction does indeed *introduce*, and that the conclusion follows naturally from the content of the essay. The question has been answered in a direct way, with no padding, irrelevance or unnecessary narration, and the arguments are well illustrated with brief, apt quotations.

Example II

Colette: *Le Blé en Herbe.*
Flammarion

(Written in 1923, this book tells of the painful development of an adolescent relationship between two childhood friends, Phil and Vinca, who every year have spent the summer holidays in a villa shared by their families on the coast of Brittany.)

Question: Examine the picture of family life which Colette presents in this novel. Your answer should be supported with precise references to the text. (London, 1985)

One of the most striking features of *Le Blé en Herbe* is undoubtedly Colette's insight into the confused emotions and strained relationships of adolescence. The novel is written through the eyes of the adolescent characters Phil and Vinca, and in particular the action of the story stays in constant touch with Phil; therefore every event, character and detail of the environment is presented from the viewpoint of the adolescent. In *Le Blé en Herbe* family life has a very important role; it forms a secure, comforting presence at the edge of Phil and Vinca's perceptions, yet for the most part it is portrayed very hazily. This is because the children make a constant attempt to divorce themselves from the influence of their parents and from their childhood, represented by their parents' presence and even by the holiday villa itself.

While family life is centred in and around the villa, the domain of Phil and Vinca is to be found beyond such boundaries; they escape to the coast whenever possible and seem intimately connected with the natural environment. Their perception of other members of their family is very cloudy; the parents are referred to as "les pâles Ombres" and seem "à peine présentes". Phil and Vinca are very much wrapped up in their own emotions and in their feelings for one another, and it seems that, as adolescents, they are seeking to liberate themselves from the constraints and influences of family life: "Ils goûtèrent une solitude parfaite, entre des parents qu'ils frôlaient à toute heure et ne voyaient presque pas." However, they cannot entirely escape from the influence of the family, for their interests and aspirations have obviously been shaped by their parents. Vinca speaks of her mother's plans that she should take over the care of the household and of her younger sister Lisette in the future, while Phil describes the years ahead as "ces années où il faut avoir l'air, devant papa et maman, d'aimer une carrière pour ne pas les désoler".

There are continual reminders in the novel both of the childhood which Phil and Vinca have lost and of their aspirations to form a family themselves. Watching Vinca and Lisette on the picnic, Phil dreams of filling a paternal role in this scene and fantasises about forming a family with Vinca:

> Il fut en même temps un Phil très ancien et sauvage, dénué de tout, mais originairement comblé, puisqu'il possédait une femme…
> Un enfant… C'est juste, nous avons un enfant…

Clearly then, Phil has been influenced by the family life of which he is a part, even though he often feels misunderstood.

The parents appear in few chapters of the novel; they are seen mostly within the villa, at mealtimes and in the evening, and they are described as "les Ombres familières, devenues presque invisibles" who are treated by the adolescents with indifference or even with vague scorn. Yet the scenes which involve all the family are important in that they provide the secure background against which the relationship between Phil and Vinca develops. Colette describes two middle-class families with the same concerns for their children, the same interests and topics of gentle, everyday conversation. The relaxed relationships between the parents serve to emphasise the agonised, tormented love which Phil and Vinca often experience, and there are occasions when the adolescents seem to respect and admire their parents' maturity and calm attitudes:

> Ils envièrent… leur facilité au rire, leur foi dans un avenir paisible.

For the most part, however, Phil and Vinca feel a slight disdain for their parents, and seem to believe it impossible that these figures – these "parents-fantômes" – could ever have experienced the agony of adolescent passion. When, at a moment of secret distress, Phil sees his father approaching, he seems no more than "une apparence humaine agréable, un peu cotonneuse, à contours flous".

Both Phil and Vinca look forward eagerly and impatiently to

their own maturity, and their romantic idealism is in sharp contrast to their parents' straightforward realism – when Monsieur Ferret talks romantically of the moon, it seems incongruous within the adult conversation. In one sense family life exerts a restricting influence on Phil and Vinca and they seem unable to find adult identities in their parents' presence. For example Phil's father rebukes his son's silliness thus: "Ce n'est pas seize ans, c'est six ans qu'il a!" At the same time, however, the adults' peaceful, simple outlook on life, epitomised in Monsieur Audebert's description of his own pleasures – "Le pays, la maison. Et puis les Ferret... Tu verras comme c'est rare, des amis avec qui on passe l'été tous les ans, sans se faire de mal" – provides a comforting image, and suggests in a quiet and attractive way the future of the tormented adolescents in the novel.

Notice how in the opening paragraph this student has been careful to tie in general remarks about the book with the specific question asked. The main body of the essay is well constructed with ideas flowing on naturally from one another, and appreciation of Colette's writing is evident. The use of quotation is good and in particular provides a skilful conclusion.

Doubtless, having read this chapter, you will have a final question to ask: How will your literature answers be marked? Of course the precise methods used vary from one Examining Board to another, but the following basic principles hold good no matter which examination you are taking:

1. Does your essay answer the question set?
2. Has precise, relevant knowledge of the text been shown?

If the answer to both these questions is yes, you can rest assured that your work will be adequate.

FURTHER READING

J. Cruickshank (ed). *French Literature and its Background* vols 2–4. O.U.P.
A. Lagarde et L. Michard. *Les Grands Auteurs Français du Programme 17th, 18th, 19th, 20th Centuries*. Bordas.
The following series contain critical commentaries on many A-level set texts:

Studies in French Literature. Edward Arnold
Profil d'une Oeuvre. Hatier
Lire Aujourd'hui. Hachette
Théâtre et Mises en Scène. Hatier.

Chapter 14

Oral work

Oral examinations in modern languages are undergoing considerable change, mainly because it is recognised that ability to speak the foreign language in everyday situations is the skill which is most likely to be of practical use to the learner outside the classroom. The changes which are being made mean that more emphasis is placed on oral communication. A greater percentage of the marks may now be allotted to this section of the examination (up to 20% of the total for some A-level syllabuses and as much as 40% for certain A/S-level syllabuses) and oral examinations are generally becoming more broad-ranging and more life-related. They demand more of the candidate in the examination room and they require more specific preparation but they also give you the opportunity to follow up your own interests through the medium of the foreign language, to become more involved personally and to feel that communicating in French is a useful, 'real life' activity.

However, before getting involved you should find out precise details of what your oral examination will consist of. Syllabuses vary quite widely (for example, across the whole range of A-level and A/S-level syllabuses the weighting for the oral varies between 10½% and 40%), they may differ from one language to another and it is possible that changes have only recently been introduced. Use the syllabus regulations therefore to answer the following questions.

- How long does the oral examination take?
- What proportion of the total subject mark is allocated to it?
- Is the examination divided into parts with a separate mark for each?
- What exactly will you be required to do for each part of the examination?

- Is there specific preparation which should be completed before the day of the examination (e.g. prescribed reading, compilation of a dossier, preparation of a chosen topic, etc.).
- How much preparation time (if any) is allowed immediately before the oral?
- Will the oral be conducted by an external examiner or by your own teacher?
- Will the oral be recorded? (The tape-recorder puts some candidates off if they are not prepared for it.)

The oral, because it requires you to put on a performance in a live situation face-to-face with an examiner, can make the most confident candidate feel nervous. However, it will help you to overcome nerves and to concentrate on the task in hand if you know exactly what is going to happen and have had a few practice runs under examination conditions.

ESSENTIAL PRINCIPLES

WHAT IS THE EXAMINER LOOKING FOR?

Above all, the examiner will set out to judge your ability to communicate naturally in French. In order to do this he will consider a number of factors. One of them will certainly be the accuracy with which you use the spoken language but you should be reassured to know that this is not the only factor and that the examiner will not be concentrating exclusively on your mistakes and simply be waiting to pounce on the first wrong gender, wrong verb ending or mispronunciation. If you are engaging him in conversation and getting him interested in your ideas and opinions he is likely to ignore errors which do not seriously get in the way of understanding and indeed he is not likely to notice every slip that you make. Of course, he will reward accuracy but he will also consider your fluency, your ability to "keep going" and the range of vocabulary and structures that you can handle spontaneously. He will also be influenced by your willingness to talk and to take the initiative and your ability to follow up points and add comments in a natural way. It is as important to try to be lively and outgoing and to have something that you really want to say as it is to form grammatically correct sentences.

In most oral examinations the examiner will use a grid to help assess the candidate's ability to take part in a conversation or discussion. The grid shown at Table 14.1 is typical of those used in A-level and A/S-level orals.

Table 14.1 Typical examiner's grid: A-level and A/S-level orals

	Pronunciation and intonation	Fluency	Accuracy	Range
Very poor	Hardly comprehensible	Responds with only 2/3 words	So incorrect that communication is not possible.	Cannot produce full sentences; very anglicised.
Poor	Very anglicised (e.g. English "r", "l", English vowel sounds).	Poor comprehension. Halting. Understands basic questions.	Much basic error (e.g. in tenses and verb forms).	Only simple sentences; vocabulary limited.
Adequate	Nasals and most vowels correct but phrases disjointed, intonation un-French.	Can produce a sentence or two at a time but needs prompting.	Basic structures correct but attempts at complex language produce error.	Beginning to use more complex sentences. A little idiom.
Good	Intonation reasonably French. Phrasing better. Some mispronunciation.	Little hesitancy; keeps going over several sentences; can take the initiative.	Mostly accurate (e.g. genders, verb forms). Simple language very accurate.	Can vary structures. Wider vocabulary; uses subordinate clauses, range of tenses.
Very good	Sounds genuinely French but with occasional mistakes in pronunciation and intonation.	Almost no problems of comprehension; capable of continuous flow; ready to lead the conversation.	Very few errors even in quite complex language.	Knowledge of idiom; wider use of adjectives, adverbs; more complex sentences.

Of course, there is no point in trying to have such a grid in mind when you are talking to the examiner but it is useful to refer to it when you are trying to find ways of improving your oral performance. It will show you that if you are to create a good impression in the exam you must provide evidence of your ability to speak. You should not limit yourself to brief, simple answers and then wait in silence for the next question. You should endeavour to put several sentences together at a time in order to elaborate on a statement, to add an alternative point or a personal opinion. You should show that you can "think out loud" and move on to an associated idea as one does in a more natural conversation. Give the examiner something for which he can reward you. He must have something to go on; even if he knew that you were a native speaker he could not give high marks if you were generally uncommunicative, no matter how authentically you shrugged your shoulders and told him "Bof! Je n'sais pas, moi".

APPLIED PRINCIPLES

Whether you are aiming to improve pronunciation, intonation, fluency, accuracy or range of language you should spend a good deal of time listening to spoken French. The advice given in Chapter 11 will help you to improve your ability to listen and will give you some ideas about what you should listen to. Listening to interviews, discussions, talks, radio "phone-in" programmes and (preferably unscripted) recorded dialogues will provide you with models of natural speech which you will consciously and even unconsciously imitate. By listening to French spoken spontaneously in a wide variety of everyday situations you will not only become familiar with the stress, rhythms and intonation of native French speakers you will also learn to identify and reproduce those phrases which serve as a support or framework to practically any conversation or discussion. For example, those space-filling phrases which do not mean very much but give the speaker time to think and organise what he is going to say: Alors . . .; Bon alors . . .; Moi, ce que je pense, c'est que . . .; Attendez voir . . .; Euh, c'est-à-dire que . . .; De toutes façons, il n'était pas là tout à l'heure, vous savez. You will learn how to pause, hesitate, correct yourself or ask to have something repeated or clarified while still keeping the conversation going.

PRONUNCIATION

You will probably have mastered the basic sounds and patterns of stress and intonation if you are embarking on an advanced course, but it is unlikely that your pronunciation, your French accent has no further room for improvement. It is as well to put it to the test well before the day of the exam. You should enlist the help of the French "assistant" or some other native speaker to help you identify persistent errors and particularly those which stand in the way of communication. The correction of just one or two recurring errors (e.g. interference of English "r" or "l", failure to stress the final syllable of a word or word group, failure to nasalise nasal vowels) can raise the level of performance quite considerably.

Many students have improved the Frenchness of their accents when they have been made aware of some of the general characteristics of French pronunciation. For example, that the production of French vowel sounds requires a certain muscular tension in the speech-organs and that the rounding of the lips plays a much greater part than in the pronunciation of English. Some students improve their delivery by "thinking towards the lips" when they are speaking French or even by keeping in mind the way in which a French speaker forms his words when he is speaking English with a French accent.

When you have diagnosed your pronunciation errors the use of a course in French pronunciation (such as French Pronunciation by Martineau and McGivney) will provide exercises and explanations which will help you to put them right. If you have access to a language laboratory with a tape library it is likely that various types of pronunciation exercises will be available on tape. Alternatively, it is useful to make use of material which has been recorded for Listening Comprehension. A recorded text is "exploded", that is it is re-recorded with blank intervals on the tape so that the student can listen and then imitate and record manageable sections of the text. The exercise is best done in a language lab but can also be simulated with a cassette recorder which has a pause button. If, after listening and repeating, you read and record the entire passage you will help to prepare for the reading aloud which forms part of a number of advanced oral examinations.

FLUENCY

You will show the oral examiner that you have fluency if you are able to sustain the flow of the conversation, responding where necessary with continuous stretches of speech. The candidate who can "keep the momentum going" clearly performs much better than someone who can "manage only a word or phrase in response to prompting". Succeeding in this area comes partly from motivating yourself to communicate, from being determined to say something and partly from your ability to produce continuous French, to string sentences together.

The best way of improving performance is by performing, by putting yourself into situations where you have to make the effort to produce spoken French in order to communicate. If you have no opportunity to converse with a native speaker then practise with a friend or use a cassette recorder to record your own ad-lib accounts of everyday situations, events and routines. The important thing is to develop strategies for finding your way round difficulties, such as resorting to simpler constructions and paraphrasing. It is also useful to record yourself ad-libbing on a given subject, allowing your thoughts to be directed by the French phrases and vocabulary which come to mind, simply for the practice of putting sentences together to produce continuous discourse.

There are useful exercises which can be practised in the language lab (or with a cassette recorder) which will improve fluency:

- Listen to a dialogue or recorded inverview which is short enough to be memorised. Record the dialogue further on on the tape but with one of the voices erased. The exercise is to fill in the missing side of the dialogue. The dialogues in *Guide Pratique de la Communication* (see Further reading) are excellent for this purpose.
- Use a cassette player with a pause button. Listen and re-listen to a passage of recorded French until you understand it clearly then, using the pause button replay it in short sections. Replay a group of words and repeat them; replay the following group of words and then repeat from memory the first group followed by the second group; replay a third group and repeat groups 1, 2 and 3, and so on. It is possible to repeat quite lengthy stretches of speech in this way. You will improve your aural memory and your fluency.
- If you have access to a language lab with a tape library listen to a story, anecdote or news bulletin. Make brief notes and then attempt to reproduce and record the story or account using only your notes.
- In the language lab listen to a spoken text then rewind and speak and record the text on the student track as you listen to the master track, using it to "cue" yourself.

You should also make use of the exercises in your course-book to help you build sentences. The structural exercises in *Faisons le Point* (see Further reading), for example, which are in semi-dialogue form, are ideal for such practice, particularly if you can work with a partner. Pattern practice such as the following will help you to build sentences and improve fluency:

Exemple: C'était le manteau du professeur qui était accroché là?
Réponse: Je ne sais pas si c'était le manteau du professeur, mais c'était bien un manteau d'homme.

There then follow cue sentences to which you supply the response, e.g.

Q. C'était le bruit de l'avion de Londres qui vous a réveillé?
A. Je ne sais pas si c'était l'avion de Londres, mais c'était bien un avion.

or

Exemple: Vous avez accepté de faire cette course?
Réponse: Oui, non que je la fasse volontiers.

Q. Elle a accepté de faire le ménage?
A. Oui, non qu'elle le fasse volontiers.
Q. Il a accepté de remplir les fiches?
A. Oui, non qu'il les remplisse volontiers.

You can record the cues on a cassette recorder and practise the exercises orally or you can practise them as mini-dialogues with a partner. The format of "cue plus response" provides good practice for the oral.

ACCURACY

It is important in the oral to produce spoken French which is grammatically and syntactically accurate as the examiner will base his assessment partly on your competence in this area but accuracy does not have the same importance in the oral as it does in the essay in French or in the prose. The reasons for this are that the examiner does not (and cannot) concentrate on grammatical accuracy alone as he is testing your overall ability to communicate, and secondly, the grammar of the spoken language is different because many of the grammatical changes which operate in the written language are not apparent in speech. This should help you to feel less inhibited when you are speaking French.

Examiners' comments show that errors most frequently involve: tenses and verb forms (e.g. the candidate gives all verbs the same ending or simply uses the infinitive), adjective agreements which cause a sound change (particularly adjectives such as important/importante, intelligent/intelligente, intéressant/intéressante, etc.), genders, prepositions and the agreement and order of pronouns. It is wise to make sure that you are accurate in these areas but it is also important to find out what your own weaknesses are. It is, of course, the recurring errors, those which are going to help create an overall impression, which should be given priority treatment. Isolated mistakes, unless they interfere with comprehension are more likely to pass unnoticed or be forgotten.

There is, however, the problem of finding out where your weaknesses are when you never see your mistakes underlined in red.

Some teachers tackle the problem by running a tape-recorder during a conversation class. The recording is then transferred to the language lab and recorded on the master-track but with blank spaces provided so that students can record a corrected or improved version of faulty or clumsy sentences. The exercise is useful because it identifies errors and makes learners aware of the gap between what they want to say and what they can say. You can, of course, record yourself ad-libbing on a chosen topic, giving an account of the day's events, describing a sequence of pictures, producing an oral version of an essay which has been set, and then replay it and correct yourself.

When you have discovered what your repeated errors are you can work on selected language-lab drills to put them right. If you do not have access to a language-lab tape library you can find material for practice in a workbook such as *French Revision Drills* (see Further reading) which contains drills for individual practice to be used with or without a tape-recorder.

RANGE

When the examiner marks your oral performance for range he will be looking for variety of expression, evidence that your linguistic knowledge does not restrict you to one or two simple sentence patterns, and for depth of vocabulary. If you display linguistic range you will show that you have the terms to make comparisons and contrasts, judgements, suppositions, and hypotheses. You will be able to add conditions, restrictions or examples to statements that you make and express personal opinion. You will have knowledge of idiomatic expressions. You will show that you are able to communicate at a more advanced level because you can develop your thoughts, elaborate on points and get more deeply into the subject. The candidate who scores a low mark under the heading of "range" will produce only simple sentences, perhaps nothing more than half sentences or phrases. Vocabulary will be limited and possibly repetitive.

In a recent oral examination different candidates made the following replies to the question: Est-ce qu'il est important que les enfants lisent beacoup?

(a) Je crois que oui, enfin, j'en suis convaincue. Les enfants aiment bien les livres, c'est-à-dire les histoires. A mon avis la lecture est un moyen de développer l'intelligence d'un enfant. Son imagination aussi, ses sentiments. C'est pourquoi les parents doivent faire lire les enfants. Pas seulement l'école, les professeurs, mais les parents.

(b) Oui, très, très important. C'est important pour les enfants dans l'école primaire. Les enfants apprennent. Ils apprennent beaucoup de choses. Il peut . . . ils apprennent la vie. Des choses nouvelles. Ils aiment lire des livres.

Candidate (a) had a greater range. She had more freedom to develop her thoughts and express an opinion. Candidate (b) did not have the confidence to chose other sentence patterns and therefore, although he communicated quite adequately, what he had to say was more limited and less interesting.

All your other language activities, listening comprehension, intensive and extensive reading, essay-writing, will improve your linguistic range but it is also a question of confidence, practice and being able to involve yourself fully in a conversation so that you feel that you really have something that you want to communicate.

Most oral examinations are structured to contain more than just general conversation although part of the time is nearly always devoted to this. Other elements are likely to be:

(a) Reading aloud

The candidate reads a short, unprepared passage or part of one which has been studied beforehand. The aim is twofold. It is a fairly mechanical exercise which helps the candidate to settle and it is a test of intonation, phrasing and pronunciation. If it is part of your examination remember that it is worth practising. The reading takes place first and is therefore your opportunity to create a favourable first impression. Lack of practice shows. Candidates are unable to "get their tongues round" certain sounds (e.g. nasal vowels, the French "r"; the sound [u] in "pour", "cours" etc.; the sound [y] in "rue", "concurrence") – they read in a monotone and do not phrase the words in groups in order to make the meaning clear.

(b) Discussion based on a stimulus

One stage in the oral is likely to be discussion based on the passage read aloud, on work prescribed for other areas of the exam (e.g. set texts or background topics), on a topic or dossier prepared by the candidate specially for the oral or on visual material such as maps, graphs, diagrams, statistics or photographs provided by the examiner. It is important to know beforehand what the procedure will be and to have practised with similar material. If you have prepared a selected topic the examiner will assume that you have chosen it because you have a particular interest in the subject and that you have spent time on it. Do not disappoint him by being unresponsive and uninformed.

(c) Role-play

Recent A-level and A/S-level and other oral examinations include a role-play. A task (which usually involves giving or eliciting information) is set within a given situation involving two participants which is described to the candidate beforehand. The candidate enacts one role, the examiner the other. Typical examples are:

(a) You have accompanied a school sports team to France to act as interpreter. The leader of the French team (played by the examiner) has organised a list of activities which the French are very keen to take part in. You and your team are not interested in some of them and have certain other suggestions (you are given a list). It is your task to discuss the arrangements with the French leader and to come to an agreement.

(b) You have obtained a summer job on the reception desk of the Diners' Club. The Managing Director of a French Company has heard about the Diners' Club and phones you to find out more about it. You read a text (in English) which gives you information about the Diners' Club so that you are prepared for answering the questions the Managing Director will put to you.

(c) You work for a London publishing house. You receive a visit from your opposite number in a French company who wants you to handle one of their books. In the course of the discussion you are required to find out certain information (notes in English tell you what to find out).

In the oral, whether it is in a role-play or in a discussion or in general conversation you will find it necessary to carry out a number of language functions which arise out of an "interview situation". For example, you may find it necessary to

- defend a point of view
- introduce yourself
- express agreement/disagreement
- express a personal opinion
- make a judgement
- engage someone in conversation
- terminate a conversation
- ask for/give information·
- make requests

It is therefore worthwhile listening to recorded interviews as part of your listening comprehension programme in order to note the way in which French speakers carry out these functions (both the phrases which they use and the intonation and pronunciation of the phrases). *Guide Pratique de la Communication* has a repertoire of conversational phrases and vocabulary organised according to function under headings such as Remercier/répondre aux remerciments; Demander des informations pratiques; Exprimer une opinion/demander son avis à quelqu'un etc. which can be very usefully studied as part of your preparation for the oral.

IN THE EXAMINATION ROOM

1. Make sure that you know exactly what you are expected to do. Where do you wait? What preparation is there immediately before the interview? Will you be allowed to use a dictionary to do it? Will you be allowed to take any notes into the interview room?

2. Make good use of the preparation time. Keep calm and work steadily even if the tasks seem difficult at first. If you have to prepare a reading passage, read it out loud to yourself. If note-taking is allowed, make only brief, useful notes.

3. Be prepared for exam nerves. Few candidates are really unaffected by them, even when the examiner is their own teacher. However, the examiner will do his best to put you at your ease.

4. Remember that the interview is intended to be natural conversation or discussion and therefore one would expect the "accidents" of normal communication. If you do not understand something ask for further explanation; if you feel that you have expressed yourself badly then try again, using simpler terms. It is not a question of "make or break" every time you open your mouth.

5. Look the examiner in the face and speak clearly. Do not mistake speed for fluency, take your time. Be confident but don't overdo it (like the candidate who on being shown a picture of a bird, leaned back with his hands in his pockets and said "C'est un oswo, obvieusement!"). Remember that although you may communicate in a natural and relaxed manner, the situation is quite a formal one. It would therefore be out of place to use slang or familiar expressions.

6. Do not be content with monosyllabic answers to the examiner's questions. Try to take the initiative and develop the conversation. The examiner will be ready to prompt you but he will also be quite pleased if you do not make him work too hard. On the other hand it is not a good idea to respond over-enthusiastically to the introduction of a topic that you know little about; you will not be able to answer the supplementary questions. Instead, take the initiative and try to turn to a different subject.

A STEP FURTHER

An important step further which most students are keen to take is to go and try out their French on French people. Going on holiday to France is one possibility but it *can* be a limited linguistic experience, particularly if you go as a member of an English-speaking group. It is more useful to take part in some purposeful activity which will bring you into contact with French people and possibly enable you to earn some money. It will require a certain amount of resourcefulness to find vacation employment in France but there are two books published by the Central Bureau (for educational visits and exchanges) which are helpful and obtainable from most bookshops. In *Home from Home* and *Working Holidays* you will find details of visits which can be made to France and ideas for working holidays, together with addresses and useful advice. If you are interested in working as an "animateur" or "animatrice" in a "colonie de vacances" (helping to look after French children between the ages of 6 and 16 – you choose your age-group – and organising activities for them), further information can be obtained from the Cultural Attaché at the French Embassy in London.

Home from Home, Central Bureau
Working Holidays, Central Bureau.

Addresses
Central Bureau
Seymour Mews House
Seymour Mews
London W1H 9PE

The French Embassy
58 Knightsbridge
London SW1X 7JT

FURTHER READING

R. Martineau and J. M. McGivney. *French Pronunciation*. O.U.P.
Alan Chamberlain and Ross Steel. *Guide Pratique de la Communication*. Didier.
Eric Astington. *Faisons le Point – A Course in Advanced French*. Heinemann
J. J. Walling. *French Revision Drills*. Interlang Ltd.

LISTENING

(See also Ch. 11 "Listening Comprehension".)

BBC Schools Radio, "Horizons de France" (contains authentic interviews).

Index